Barbel

Barbel

Barbel Catchers and Friends

The Crowood Press

First published in 1988 by
The Crowood Press
Ramsbury, Marlborough
Wiltshire SN8 2HE

British Library in Publication Data

Barbel: barbel catchers and friends
1. Barbel fishing
I. Title
799.1'752   SH691.B3

ISBN 1 85223 077 0

Typeset by Quorum Technical Services,
Cheltenham, Glos.
Printed in Great Britain at The Bath Press

Contents

Introduction

In December 1984, John Dennis telephoned me to discuss a possible author for a pike book the Crowood Press wanted to publish. I knew the angler in question; he is a man who has caught fine fish. But, the more I thought about his experience, the more I saw his limitations. What was his experience on reservoirs, on big, fast flowing rivers? How well did he know Ireland? Had he fished shallow lakes a great deal and could he even be described as an expert on Broadland?

I realised that in fact there was no single man who could write with absolute authority on every water type in the British Isles. And so between us, Martyn Page and I assembled over twenty pikers, all leaders in their field, and *Pike – The Predator Becomes the Prey* was born. The result was pronounced a success and *Carp – Quest for the Queen* quickly followed to further applause. Even when Crowood produced *Roach – The Gentle Giants*, I still did not feel properly qualified to talk about my favourite species everywhere and so called in a fresh team.

It was at this point that I was asked to edit this work on barbel, put together by members of the Barbel Catchers Club. I took the job willingly from the start, but, as the book unfolded, I became more and more involved – and fascinated. It very soon became apparent that never had my hunch over the multi-contributor book been better vindicated. Article by article, I realised that never has so exact a picture of a British species of freshwater fish been put together. The wealth of detail in this book is mindblowing. Every river, every method and every bait is covered here, and always by a man who is expert on his water.

The manuscript landed on my desk in the last days of May, just a couple of weeks before the start of the new season. I had planned to start off with tench – I had been baiting a swim for a long while already. But this book made me change my mind. There was so much I wanted to try that the first days of the season found me barbelling on the River Wensum.

I had one fish the second or the third evening. Not huge, it was nonetheless beautiful, and so wildly fit and strong that my heart beat as frantically as the rod bucked. There just simply isn't a better fish that swims and there is no doubt in my mind that, because of these Barbel Catcher guys, we will all see many more of them on the bank in the future.

John Bailey

Tactics

PETE MCMURRAY

Q. How do you spot barbel?
Half the battle in catching barbel is locating fish, and this is so much easier when you can see them. Water clarity is the key on the chalk-based rivers such as the Hampshire Avon, the Berkshire Kennet and the Wensum in Norfolk. Here it is possible to spot barbel in relatively deep water. Spotting trips are best undertaken in perfect conditions; sunny still weather at midday when the sun is at its highest offers the best light penetration, and wind which causes ripples on the water will not be a problem. Polaroid sun-glasses are essential even on dull days as they counteract the reflected glare from the surface of the water. Spotting barbel is a bit of a knack and it takes practice. Very often the first thing you see is the pinkish pectoral fins, and suddenly a barbel materialises into view. It pays to look good and hard into any potential swim, especially around weedbeds. Many times you will notice a barbel as the weed moves in the current – perhaps not the whole fish but just a fin or a tail.

Q. How do you find them when you cannot see them?
When you cannot actually see the barbel because the river is too deep or the water just too coloured, you have to rely on watercraft to note potential swims. It would take a chapter on its own to describe every type of barbel swim, but I will try to cover a few of the most popular: weirpools; the point where a deep run starts to shallow up; sharp bends where the main current is diverted across from one side of the river to the other; narrow points where the current runs faster; and, perhaps my favourite, a deepish run under the bank which is undercut. There are many others but these are the classic ones to look for. Cover is very important to barbel. That is why they are great lovers of weed of all kinds – streamer, cabbages and bulrushes.

On rivers like the lower Severn and some of the Yorkshire rivers where there is little weed, the barbel will use anything which affords them cover. Bear this in mind when looking for swims. Chapter 8 covers swims of this type in more detail.

Q. Is a swimfeeder always effective?
The swimfeeder is a brilliant method of fishing particle baits such as maggots, casters, hemp and sweetcorn, because it gets loose feed down accurately into the swim with the hookbait. The standard approach when using, say, maggots would be a medium-sized feeder with normal-sized holes. Recasting about

every fifteen minutes is about par for the course. Many times this is good enough to get a few barbel feeding and you should get a bite or two. But if you cannot get a bite, or if the swim dies after the capture of a couple of fish, try a variation. Step up the rate of feed by changing to a larger feeder which has been cut and slotted so that it empties within five minutes. Also introduce two or three dropperfuls of maggots. With this extra bait going into the swim and recasting every five minutes, I would expect some action within an hour or so. It is almost as if the barbel can resist a trickle of bait but once a certain point is reached they are stimulated into feeding.

Occasionally the reverse will work, so cut back on the feed flow. This is done by taping over most of the holes in the feeder. The point is not to sit there hour after hour. If you are not getting bites, then experiment. Because feeders are so effective with barbel they get used a lot and on hard fished stretches of rivers the fish can wise up. Although still attracted by the feed, they are cautious and often hold back downstream of the feeder, picking off bait that the current trundles down. The hookbait attached to the line just

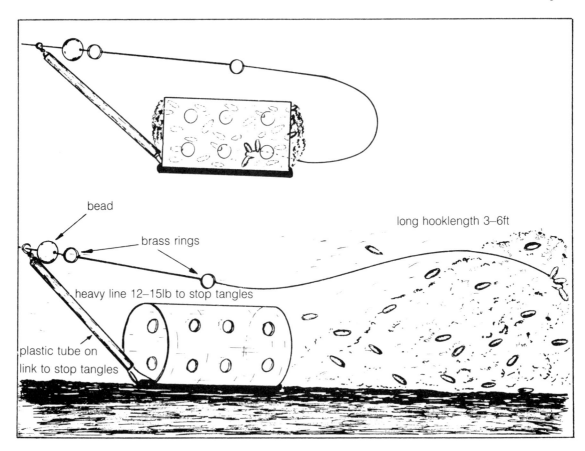

bead

brass rings

long hooklength 3–6ft

heavy line 12–15lb to stop tangles

plastic tube on link to stop tangles

The exploding feeder. The hooklength tucks into the feeder with the feed and very dry groundbait.

sits there not moving and so is ignored.

One way of overcoming this is to use an open-ended feeder and tuck the baited hook and hooklength in with the feed. When the feeder settles, the groundbait starts to break up, releasing the feed and the baited hook as well. The bait then has a chance to behave like the rest of the feed moving down in the current. Obviously this movement is governed by the length of the hooklength, so a longish one is best, say from four to six feet. I have found it beneficial to make sure that the hook comes out of the feeder in an explosion of bait, so mix the groundbait as dry as possible. I use coarse brown bread crumb.

Q. Whenever I see anglers fishing for barbel, they are always legering. Can you catch them with float tackle?
Yes, you certainly can. In fact, a float is the best way of presenting a moving bait through a swim. By holding back hard, it is possible to work a bait inch by inch down a swim. This is absolutely deadly. The problem is that, like most anglers, I can float-fish a rod-length or so out, but two or three lengths out and I am struggling. Now I am far from being a good float angler, but compared with a lot of specimen-hunter types I am brilliant. There are many swims where trotting a float is out of the question, but the truth is that many barbel fishermen ignore it completely and leger all the time. This is a great shame, because it is a super method.

The float can also be used with a static bait 'laying on', where the shot and bait are lying along the bottom. It is a pleasant way to fish and watching a float rather than the rod top makes a pleasant change. Laying on is limited to

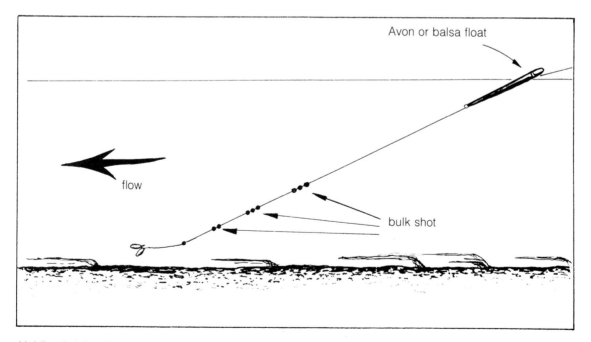

Holding back to inch a bait through the swim.

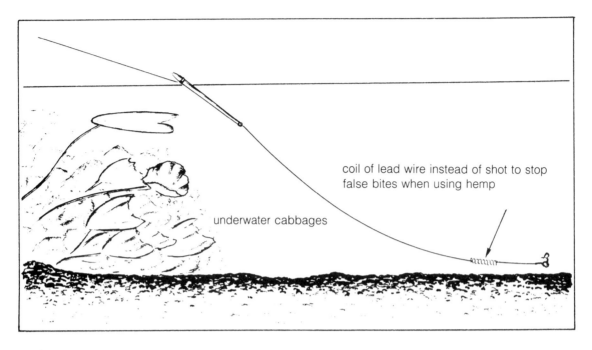

coil of lead wire instead of shot to stop false bites when using hemp

underwater cabbages

Laying on.

swims close to the bank and is used extensively on the upper Thames, where many of the barbel swims are right in close under your feet. The disadvantage is that a higher proportion of barbel appear to get foul-hooked with this method. This is probably because the line rises from the shot to the float almost vertically, with the likelihood of a barbel brushing against it and giving a false bite which could lead to a foul-hooked fish.

Q. *When would you freeline?*
Freelining, as the name implies, is fishing without any lead on the line. It is very useful where a moving bait is called for. Very often it is the only way to get a bait into the right position. For example, by freelining down the current it is possible to work a bait right under a weedbed. That is freelining in

its purest sense, but on many occasions just enough lead is used to hold the bait close to bottom, but not so much as to anchor it. This is what I call trundling and it is a brilliant way of searching out feeding barbel. This is a mobile approach and many likely swims can be searched in a day. Finding the right amount of weight to suit the flow of different swims is really a matter of trial and error. By holding the rod you should be able to feel the weight bouncing and rolling along the bottom. It is not as difficult as it sounds and soon comes with a bit of practice. There is certainly more to legering than just anchoring a bait hard on to the river bed.

Q. *Do barbel always feed on the bottom?*
One look at their underslung mouths shows that barbel are designed as

bottom feeders, and I am sure that 95 per cent of all barbel are caught on bait fished on or close to the river bed. But there are exceptions. A match angler recently told me of an 8lb barbel he caught on the lower Severn whilst trotting for roach. He said that his bait was at least five feet above the bottom. I have seen barbel in the Parlour on the Royalty Fishery come to the surface to take pieces of floating bread in the close season, and in fact they have been caught on the surface. But I feel that these are unusual examples. Barbel in the main feed on or close to the bottom.

Q. *What about fishing in weedy or snaggy swims?*
Such swims can be very rewarding because barbel love cover around them, whether it is weed or snags or both. The most important rule is 'land the fish', so tackle must be strong enough to do that – it is no good hooking a barbel of a lifetime only to lose it.

First, weed. When a barbel has taken refuge and bolted under a weedbed, the first thing I do is try and get downstream of it, and pull in the direction of the current. If you can now get the line as straight as possible to the fish most of the weed is flowing in the same direction and should not be too much of a hindrance. The problem is more difficult when it is impossible to get downstream of the weeded fish. In these situations the tackle and particularly the line must be strong enough to pull through the weed and keep pressure on the hooked fish. The idea is to make the barbel keep moving. It will eventually tire and can then be worked either back upstream or downstream, depending on which way it ran after being hooked. Once the line is more or less straight to the fish it is plain sailing. As a rough guide, where there is plenty of room to get downstream of the swim I would use lines of from 5 to 7lb BS but where a swim is tight for space – for example, between two trees – then use lines from 8 to 10lb.

Snag fishing is a bit different in that, once the barbel has reached the snag, in

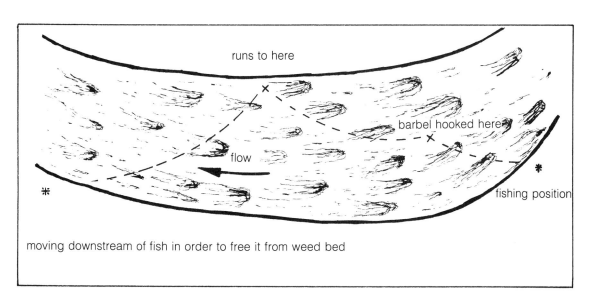

moving downstream of fish in order to free it from weed bed

most cases that is it and you cannot get it out again. We are not talking about nice, soft, bendy weed but large rocks, trailing masses of tough willow roots, fallen branches and even whole trees. In swims where there is just one snag with plenty of open water around it quite light tackle can be used, and the fish 'conned' away from the danger area by using very light pressure. I have landed barbel to over 9lb on 4lb line and a size 14 hook from swims like this, and lost very few fish. (The actual technique is described in the Lower Severn and Tributaries chapter.) Where the swim is littered with snags and there is no open water to play with, the tactic is to 'hit and hold' trying not to give the barbel an inch of line. The tackle must be extra strong: rods of 2 – 2 ½lb test curve, line of 12 – 15lb BS, and hook sizes 4 – 6. With these tactics many big barbel have been landed from terrible swims, particularly on the Yorkshire Swale. The technique is described more fully in the Yorkshire Rivers chapter.

Q. What about end rigs for barbel?
End rigs for barbel fishing are largely very straightforward. The vast majority of captures are made on simple running legers, but there are occasions when something else is required. The hair rig is a brilliant innovation which has helped in the capture of many big barbel recently. Its main advantage is that it allows the angler to use heavy tackle but still gives the bait a reasonably natural presentation. There is some controversy over using what could be called an unbaited hook, and some anglers will not use it as they feel that there is a great danger of foul-hooking fish. Obviously, it is for every angler to make up his own mind over the ethics. Personally I have caught over a hundred barbel using the hair and have never had any problem with foul-hooking. The actual length of the hair can vary, depending on the size of hook and type of bait. I use hairs between ½ and 1½ inches. The latter is my absolute maximum – any longer would be asking for trouble.

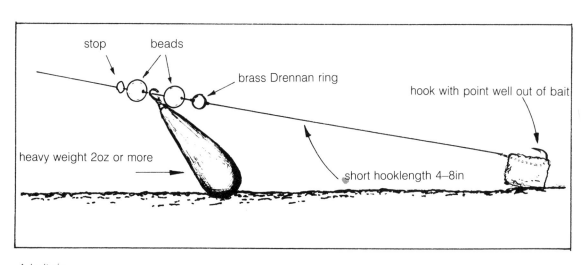

A bolt rig.

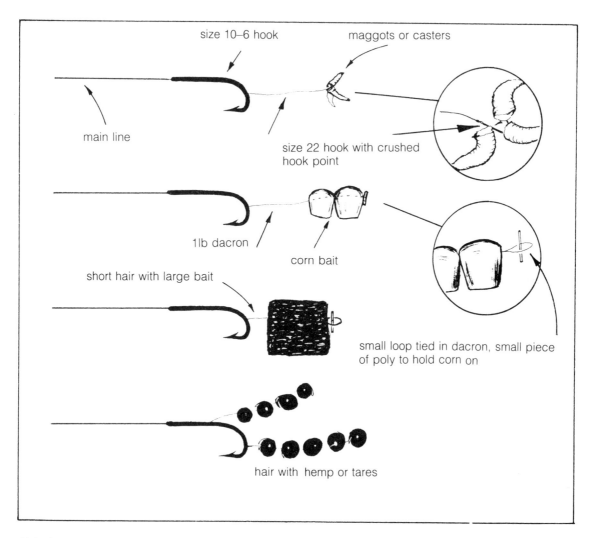

size 10–6 hook

maggots or casters

main line

size 22 hook with crushed hook point

1lb dacron

corn bait

short hair with large bait

small loop tied in dacron, small piece of poly to hold corn on

hair with hemp or tares

Hair rigs.

The bolt rig is an idea borrowed from the carp fishermen. The principle is to use an extra-heavy weight close to the hook. When the barbel picks up the bait, the heavy weight causes the hook to prick the fish's lip. It then panics and bolts off. Barbel have tendency to do this anyway, so this type of approach works well in provoking a very positive reaction. I will not call it a bite because the fish is already hooked. I find its uses limited to times when barbel are picking up baits and spitting them out again quickly before a strike can be made.

Q. *What is the best time of the year for barbel fishing?*
Barbel are noted as a summer and autumn fish – a generalisation which is wrong. They can be caught during any month of the season. In fact the winter

months have a habit of turning up some of the biggest specimens. Andy Orme's 13lb 7oz Hampshire Avon fish came in February, Dave Plummer's 13lb 6oz specimen from the Wensum in March, and there have been many more. Although barbel have been caught in very cold conditions, undoubtedly a period of mild weather is best and in the winter this inevitably means rain, so the river will be high and coloured. These are the conditions much favoured by the barbel specialists on lowland rivers such as the Hampshire Avon, the Dorset Stour, the Berkshire Kennet and the Wensum, but on rivers like the Severn and the Yorkshire rivers, which are fed high up in the hills and mountains, this rain can mean that the water rises ten or fifteen feet, making them unfishable for long periods throughout the winter. So much depends on the type of river you are fishing. My own choice on the Severn would be late autumn, but perhaps on the Hampshire Avon a mild spell towards the end of the season would give you an excellent chance.

Q. *How do you catch the biggest fish in a swim?*

This is the beauty of fishing in clear water for barbel. It is possible to pick out the biggest fish and catch it. Let us picture a fairly typical situation. You have spotted two barbel lying under a weedbed close to the bank, and have introduced with a bait dropper a pint or so of hemp and corn on a patch of gravel above the weedbed. Soon both fish move up and start to feed – hesitantly at first, but after five minutes both are merrily hoovering up hemp and corn. You get a good look at them and estimate that both weigh about 5lb.

Two other fish now make an appearance. One looks a fair bit bigger – 8lb, perhaps even 9. It is noticeable that the bigger fish is a little more cautious, holding back from the feeding group. Carefully we introduce some more bait six feet further upstream and the three smaller fish, which are well and truly feeding, move up after it.

Now this gives us the chance at the big fellow on his own. First try at him with a size 8 hook and three grains of corn is ignored, although he has taken the loose grains. He has obviously seen hooks and corn before. We need a rethink. The tackle has to be fairly strong as there is a lot of weed and it is impossible to get below any hooked fish. Line of 8lb is just about the safest minimum. This is a tailor-made case for the hair rig. A shortish hair of 1 inch tied to the bend of a size 8 hook and two grains of corn should give us the best chance. Some more bait is dropped in to keep the three smaller fish happy whilst we concentrate on the big fellow, which has again dropped to the back of the swim. A dozen or so grains of corn settle on the gravel around the hookbait.

Shortly he moves up and starts sucking up grains one at a time. As he approaches the bait he dips down. The gills move. A split second later he turns his head, and as we strike he goes wild, charging off into the nearest weedbed. But with 8lb line and the strong hook there is only going to be one winner. A few minutes later we are removing the hook from the top lip. The scales prove we were not far out with our estimate – 8lb 9oz of bronze, fighting barbel! A nice little story with a happy ending, but one that has been played out many times in the clear waters of the Avon, Wensum, Kennet and other barbel rivers like them.

To sum up, as with most fishing it pays to have an open mind and a flexible approach. Avoid being too dogmatic – for example, do not persist with the feeder regardless of conditions. Try to think about your tactics and the barbel's reaction to them, and you will be successful.

The Royalty

RAY WALTON

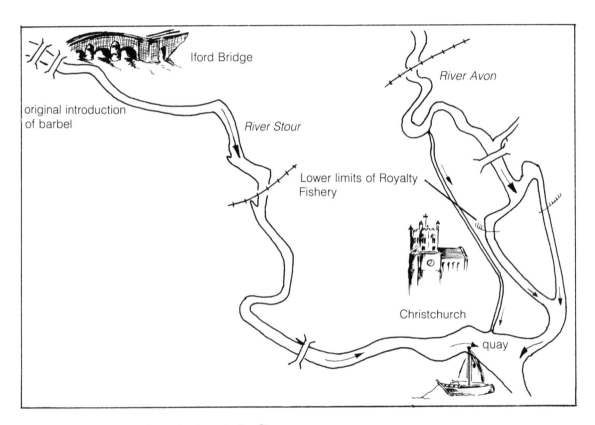

The migration of barbel from the Avon to the Stour.

The Royalty starts at the alder bush at the lower end of the Winkton beat and boasts some of the most productive barbel haunts on the Hampshire Avon. It is a fishery full of legends, tales, joys and heartbreaks. Its swims have character and charm, and most have true or tall stories to tell, both past and present.

The Glories of the Past

In the late 1890s one hundred barbel were taken from the River Thames at Staines, transported to Christchurch and released into the River Stour at Iford Bridge. The more intelligent

16

Edward Upton caught this tremendous 13lb 2oz barbel in October 1970.

amongst these bronze princes and princesses deserted the main group, travelling upstream and then pedalling backwards, and eventually found their way into the then glorious Avon through the joint estuary at Christchurch. From here they travelled upstream and found the perfect habitat: clear water running over golden gravel, lush weed growth, and abundant natural food. On the Royalty they multiplied and grew into a legend. In the early years there were times when only four or six anglers were permitted to fish on any one day and you could expect to have a length of the fishery all to yourself to pursue the Nottingham style, tight corking, or the clayball technique. The most successful fisherman of the day was undoubtedly F. W. K. Wallis, who skilfully applied his Trent talents to the lush waters of the Royalty with devastating results. On one notable occasion in September 1933 Wallis landed no less than ten doubles, including specimens of 14lb 4oz and 13lb 8oz, two of 11lb 8oz, three of 11lb, and three of 10lb. In 1937 he landed a barbel of 14lb 6oz, which equalled the British record previously held by another Royalty fish caught some three years earlier by H. D. Tryon, and by Mr T. Wheeler's Thames barbel caught at Molesey in 1888. Some noted Royalty barbel are given in the table overleaf.

17

Noted Royalty Barbel, 1929–1981

lb	oz	Captor	Month	Year
14	6	H. D. Tryon	September	1934
14	6	F. W. K. Wallis	September	1937
14	4	F. W. K. Wallis	September	1933
14	4	M. W. Haytor	—	1929
14	3	G. Keeber	—	1934
14	2	A. Jessop	—	1968
14	0	G. Keeber	—	1934
13	14	C. A. Taylor	September	1937
13	12	J. B. Parkinson	—	1947
13	12	J. Day	October	1962
13	10	S. A. Warth	—	1947
13	9	S. A. Warth	—	1946
13	8	F. W. K. Wallis	October	1934
13	8	F. W. K. Wallis	September	1933
13	7	J. Harrigan	November	1964
13	5	F. W. K. Wallis	October	1934
13	4	F. W. K. Wallis	October	1934
13	4	S. Saunders	October	1958
13	4	W. Warren	—	1959
13	4	W. Warren	February	1961
13	4	E. Thorne	October	1975
13	4	J. B. Parkinson	—	1948
13	4	F. W. K. Wallis	—	1931
13	3	F. W. K. Wallis	—	1935
13	3	D. Baptist	—	1981
13	3	B. A. Knightsbridge	November	1934
13	2½	J. B. Parkinson	March	1950
13	2	J. Lander	November	1948
13	2	E. Magderburge	—	1953
13	2	J. Lander	—	1952
13	2	S. Dixon	August	1957
13	2	R. Hoare	October	1965
13	2	J. Harrigan	November	1965
13	2	E. Upton	October	1970
13	1	K. W. Clower	September	1959
13	0	J. Follet	September	1966
13	0	B. Blackman	October	1966
13	0	C. Flint	July	1970
13	0	E. Gray	October	1930
13	0	S. Freeland	September	1929

Some of the heaviest barbel foul-hooked and documented from the Royalty include a 16lb 8oz monster in April 1931, by Roy Beddington jun. while salmon fishing. A fish of 15lb 12oz fell to the Manager of the fishery, Mr Haytor, in March 1943. Barbel of between 15lb and 18lb have been reported captured or found dead by anglers from the 1920s onwards. The mystery of why those huge barbel, estimated at between 17 and 20lb, were never caught continues to intrigue and boggle the mind.

Royalty Barbel

Deformed Fish

Deformed barbel on the Royalty fall into two types – 'S' and 'L'. S-shaped fish are twisted along the back from side to side. They are usually in very healthy-looking condition, despite the handicap. L-shaped fish have the signs of a broken back and are usually out of condition. These unfortunates are generally dark in colour, have large, bulging eyes, and appear to be on their last legs. Both types tend to be caught where flow is not at its greatest, but seemingly live and feed normally. When hooked they fight with dignity, but their shape prevents them from being dynamic fighters.

Having caught these barbel over the years I now treat them with that little bit of extra care and attention. The problem is that on occasions with low summer levels these fish tend to lie up in certain well attended areas and are caught more often than not by unsuspecting anglers who have not had barbel of this kind before. On a popular fishery such as this, they can be caught day after day; they become exhausted very easily when hooked as they cannot keep their balance as normal and tend to kite, twist and have great difficulty in trying to stabilise themselves. I must stress that the quicker they are returned to the water the better the chance of a full recovery.

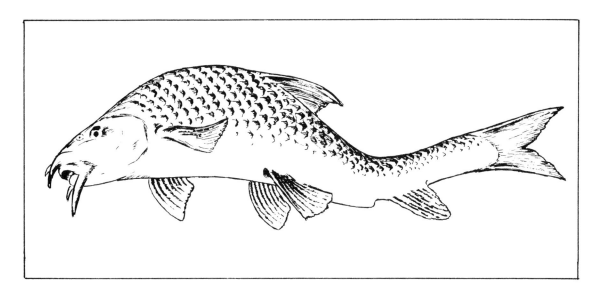

A deformed barbel.

If I spot a deformed fish in summer, when the water is gin-clear, I leave it well alone.

Fortunately, over the years the numbers caught are minimal; usually about four fish are captured repeatedly throughout the fishery. The cause of the deformity is said to be a virus which attacks the spine, or a very active spawning session in which the back is broken. However, I suspect that the L-shaped deformity may be a result of old age.

Blind Fish

I have come across two types of eye deformity – a glazed white film over the eye and a cracked eyeball effect. Like the deformed individuals, these fish are few and far between. Only one eye is ever affected. The glazed eye appears on old, out-of-condition barbel and the cracked eye on normally healthy fish. Both types can be caught anywhere on the fishery as they are of the wandering type – probably because they can't see where they're going. I have never ever caught a barbel with both eyes affected. Hook marks appear on the same side of the mouth as the bad eye. Could the cause of the glazed eye have something to do with flash effect from cameras?

Old Fish

In recent years my catches on the Royalty have started to include barbel which appear to be old and out of condition. They vary in weight and measurements but all seem to have similar characteristics – dark colour, eroded tails, occasional glazed eyes or pop-eyes, below-average weight for size measurements, and generally no strength or energy.

These fish clearly follow the same path through the fishery. Individuals which I caught in fair numbers in June and July on the lower water were recaptured at intervals throughout

19

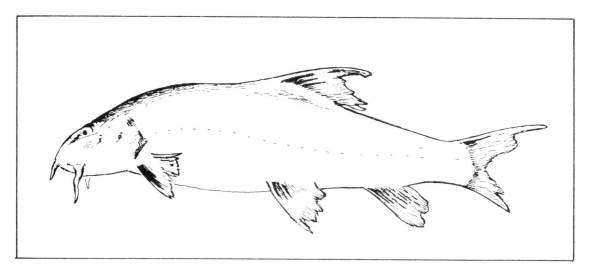

An ageing barbel.

August, September and October as I moved upstream, finally reaching the vicinity of the Great Weir. I have experienced this three years running, but not on such a scale as this year (1986–7). I can only conclude that these barbel make their way upstream to the weir to die, as old fish identified one season do not reappear the following year. However, I have never found a dead Royalty barbel. Another interesting phenomenon is the high proportion of old fish I caught in June 1986. Obviously, after a very cold winter a late spawning was on the cards. When I started the season in June, it was very hard going; barbel were just not in their usual haunts. I caught more chub in five days using my normal barbel tactics than in the previous three years put together. And, of the six barbel I did catch, four were old fish. Had the healthy barbel gone off to the spawning grounds and left behind the old fish which no longer take part in the spawning ritual?

Fluctuations in Weight

I log hundreds of barbel each year and it has become increasingly apparent that most fluctuate in weight and measurements throughout the season. It is very difficult to keep track of and recognise the majority of barbel captured, but a great number have certain marks or characteristics that make the job a little bit easier. One outstanding example of fluctuation of weight, length and girth measurements was first encountered on 9 August 1986. I was fishing with John Medlow in the Great Weir when he hooked and landed a very big barbel which weighed 9lb 13oz and measured 30 × 15½ inches – a very long fish for its weight, and quite skinny. Stretch marks showed on the stomach and the fish was generally not in top condition. We agreed that it had probably just finished spawning, late as it was. Compare the weight of this fish with that of others I have caught of similar length: 10lb 4oz, 29 × 16½ inches and 10lb 11oz, 29¼ × 17 inches. Clearly John's fish had the potential to become a good double once back in top condition. It had three other distinctive features – split pectorals, one hard scale, and two warts on the back end.

As the autumn approached we paid particular attention to the weirpool and put a lot of time and effort into trying to locate this barbel – but, alas, to no avail. On 1 November, again with John as companion, I rolled a bait through a shallow run below the Parlour. A fish gave the slightest touch to the bait, and I was in. As I drew the barbel over the net I saw the scale on its side and knew it was John's fish. On the bank the fish looked overall bigger and in fine condition. The stretch marks had disappeared and the stomach had filled out. We measured the fish very precisely; it went 30¼ × 16 inches and weighed 10lb 11oz.

One other example – this time in reverse. On 14 September 1985 I caught a fine barbel of 10lb 11oz from the Telegraphs, again a very distinguishable fish. Recaptured on June 16 1986, the first day of the season, the same fish weighed 9lb 14oz. Clearly anglers recapture certain fish at different weights throughout the season without realising it, which may create a false impression.

Movements

Some Royalty barbel wander the fishery from top to bottom, whilst others stay put and move through localised patrol routes only.

On the lower water, small pockets of barbel (from two to five fish) can sometimes be encountered moving upstream from the bypass through to the Housepool at particular times of the season.

Lucky is the angler who locates a larger pocket – it is a rare event. The pockets of barbel seem to come together and intermingle only at spawning and in times of heavy flood. There seem to be no major shoals permanently together from Fiddler's downstream to Johnson's. Normal average catch rates range from 0 to 3 fish for a summer's day (13-hour daylight session), but usually the captures, if any, come within the space of a very short spell at any time during that period. However, as there are fewer barbel present below the Housepool, the average size has proved to be far greater than above. The full range of barbel from 0+ to 10+lb is present.

Tide and Barbel Escape Routes

As the Avon meanders through the last of the Royalty bends on its course to the sea, it meets its final obstruction – the tide. The effect can be great or small, according to the daily tidal range. The way the tide controls the Royalty can be fully understood only by long-term study and at the time of writing I really don't know half of it. As the tide ebbs and flows, its effect can be felt right up to the Great Weir. The farther you travel downstream nearer to the sea, the greater the effect of the rise and fall in level. For example, in summer when the river is at a normal, constant and seemingly safe, slow running level, the powerful flow of a spring tide can often cause the river to rise swiftly and burst its banks without warning. This is a common feature below the bypass and sometimes up as far as the Telegraphs. When rainfall raises the level of the river, the normal tidal flow can cause the upper reaches of the Royalty to burst its banks, also. As the tide ebbs, the river drops back into its normal channels. Tidal effects often cause flood conditions all through the fishery. At the Great Weir, with flood conditions and a powerful spring tide, the water levels both upstream of the sluice gates and in the weirpool itself are virtually equal. When all sluice gates are open fully on each side of the salmon ladder, there is a blowback effect which causes a complete reversal of flow upstream through the ladder. At this point the combined equal levels and reduced water velocity provide a perfect exit for the barbel (and other species) to leave the Royalty to journey and explore upstream without too much of a problem. I can only prove that salmon go all the way through, but when experimenting in these conditions in winter I have caught a barbel in and halfway up the salmon ladder. An even easier escape route is up through the west side of the Parlour pumphouse, which is one of the usual routes taken by salmon coming upstream to spawn. They have a virtually straight run through. Daylight can be seen from below through to the Cinder Path. In higher levels there is no step and the Barbel have only the water velocity to contend with. The water passing through the pumps is controlled, as is the flow out of the Parlour.

Now we drop down to the rapids on the lower water. In normal low summer levels, the rocks and boulders on the head of the falls become visible and a step from the lower level to the upper becomes more apparent. Quite rightly, you would not expect any fish to come over the falls at this sort of height without making themselves very conspicuous. However, when the tide comes in, the level over the falls rises so that the stones and boulders become submerged. The rapids become smooth and the step disappears. Barbel, chub, salmon, mullet and flounders are five species I have seen coming over the falls without difficulty at this particular time in clear conditions.

Going back a few years, to 1896, it is clearly documented that barbel were introduced into the Stour at Iford Bridge, and the theory is that they travelled downstream as well as up. If going downstream, the barbel would pass through brackish water to reach the mouth of the Avon in the joint estuary. I have caught barbel from the lower boundaries of the Royalty and there seems to be no reason why even today Stour barbel don't enter the Avon through the joint estuary.

An Experiment in the Waterloo Area

Having taken time out from fishing the upper reaches to pay particular attention to the Waterloo stream area, which is highly affected by the tide, I found some very interesting facts. Anglers are rare here – only youngsters fishing for dace and chub and the odd local fishing for sea trout and chub at the boundary. Over the years I have found only one angler who knows of a barbel being caught – a fish of 2lb. However, while searching the area in thirteen sessions over three months from September to November I located 13 barbel, including recaptures. The majority had healed hook marks, two had a blind eye, others had split pectorals and dorsal damage and three were in top condition. Yet to my knowledge no one had hammered the fish down here so as to cause this sort of damage: some of these barbel had obviously come down here from elsewhere to recuperate. Two were recognised as Pipes fish and one as a Roadbridge regular. Could the brackish water of the lower reaches have a beneficial effect in helping the barbel recover from their wounds and mishaps? As we know, salt in the right doses is commonly used to cure infections in aquarium fish.

Another interesting fact came to light in the Waterloo area. The water temperature is always approximately 2°F higher than anywhere upstream. I discovered that the fluctuation was caused by the effluent flowing from the sewer outlet situated at the first bend at the

T-junction, where a pipe enters the river. The effluent is dark Oxo brown in colour and looks disgusting. Testing indicates that the discharge is not a danger to fish life, even though readings are far higher than anywhere else on the fishery. The pH is normal. The strange thing is that the ducks, mullet and small fry love it.

Surface Feeding

11.30 a.m., 14 July 1986. Water temp 64°F. Air temp 87°F. Overcast. Hot and muggy. I noticed the surface weed move for no apparent reason. Then it began. Fish were moving under the surface weed, making sucking and slurping noises, definitely eating something. Knowing that mirrors and

A surface-feeding barbel.

common carp are quite numerous and increasing in quantity and size all through the Royalty, I assumed that these were surface-feeding carp. At no time could I glimpse the fish as the weed was so dense. A sense of challenge and excitement came over me as the fish moved around, pushing up the weed and leaving trails behind them. I had no barbel to my credit that morning, so I decided to put a bait on top of the weedbed and try to catch the carp.

I waited and waited for the fish to reappear in the area, then cast a large lump of luncheon meat in the vicinity of the moving weed. The only reasonable way I can describe the actions of the invisible fish is of Jaws going for a victim. It was amazing. At first nothing really happened. The fish would push up the weed, swim along under the surface and then disappear, without trace. Obviously they could not see the meat, and, hoping that the fish would pick up the aroma, I adjusted the rig so that the weight would pull and sink the bait further into the weed. A fish rose again and my heart began to thump as the monster beneath moved closer to the victim. Then it turned away, taking a completely different route, still pushing up the weed with its back. After a while frustration set in. I was getting nowhere.

Intercepting trundled bait.

After recasting and repositioning bait where the fish had previously disappeared, I waited patiently. He rose again six or eight feet away. This time, as the carp moved, I started quivering the rod, causing the meat on the surface weed to vibrate and shake. Within a split second the carp changed direction towards the meat. It stopped directly underneath and started poking at it. The vibration had done the trick and now the fish had picked up the aroma. But then another problem presented itself. The carp couldn't break through the surface weed to get the meat. Every time he poked at it from underneath, it bounced up and down. He would then go away and reapproach from a different angle. Then a definite change took place. He seemed very frustrated, as though he wanted this piece of meat badly. He started rising about three feet from the bait, lunging forward quite viciously, chomping and slurping at the weed as he swam closer and closer to the prize. Then with a heavy surge, he tried to dislodge the meat. A heart attack was on the cards for me at this time as I knew I had nearly cracked it. Gerry, my companion of the day, was already on his back in deep shock. 'This is it!' I cried. I pulled the meat across, so that it toppled into half an inch of surface water on top of the weed. With the meat on top and still 80 per cent visible, the carp began another of his vicious attempts. This time we knew he had to get it. Slurp, munch, closer, closer – a final almighty lunge and the meat disappeared. The line began to whiz down the hole through the weed. Gerry and I looked at each other, startled. I didn't strike. Regaining my senses, I tightened up. The carp was on

and the problem now was to get the fish back to the hole from where he had taken the meat. I always use heavy tackle, which made the job easier. Finally, both of us totally flipped. I netted the carp, but – surprise surprise – it wasn't a carp at all. It was a barbel – 4lb 8oz!

Feeling very pleased with myself at having experienced something very special I couldn't believe my eyes when the weed started moving again. At first I thought I must be seeing things. It must be the fish I had returned moments earlier. But then the weed moved again on the left and then on the right. There were another two in different patches, pushing up the weed again. Anyway, I landed another barbel weighing 6lb 2oz and lost two others which slipped the hook in the dense weed. I must tell you that although I could see the gravel bottom at the edge of the weedbeds, at no time did a single fish attempt to take a piece of meat from the bed of the river. This area was approximately four to five feet in depth.

Finally, as I was thinking to myself that this was one-off day, the same thing happened again, this time in a different area. I saw the weed bulge and move and, applying the same rather unusual tactics as before, I eventually landed a superb barbel of 5lb 3oz, again in broad daylight on an August afternoon.

Winter Fishing

Winter fishing for barbel is often misunderstood and wrongly explained. Many anglers fish for barbel when the weather breaks after a nasty cold spell. However, the three important factors on determining whether you will catch

The Great Weir Pool in flood in winter.

A great achievement! Ray Walton caught this 8lb 2oz barbel at a water temperature of 35°F and an air temperature of less than 25°F.

on the day are water temperature, water level and water colouring.

When the air temperature starts dropping off during autumn, so the water temperature decreases accordingly. As the water temperature drops, so does the body temperature of the barbel and the metabolism winds down. At this time of the year there is a transition period when the barbel's feeding habits change. They eat less; the fishing becomes harder. However, as the winter months continue the barbel tend to acclimatise to the colder conditions. So, while a water temperature of, say, 44°F can produce disastrous sessions in October or November, in January or February the same temperature can often produce superb fishing. Although I have caught barbel at water temperatures between 35° and 40°F, these occasions are quite rare and barbel feeding in earnest at these temperatures are uncommon.

The water level on the Royalty is governed by at least five factors at different times of the year: the natural rainfall, tidal effects, the opening and closing of the Great Weir, the Little Weir, and others further upstream, and weed growth. In summer, it really doesn't matter what the level is because of the head of barbel present. Barbel will feed all through the fishery at unpredictable times during the day and locating them is not difficult as they are well distributed. In autumn and winter the level becomes more important as the water temperature drops. If a drop in temperature coincides with a drop in level barbel will be hard to catch, more so if the water is clear. If the level is high when the water temperature drops, chances are better, although still limited. Generally, the higher the level in autumn and winter the better the prospects.

Colour is not that important in summer, as gin-clear water can be advantageous to the angler – it is possible to watch and stalk barbel, and observe feeding habits and patrol routes. Although the barbel can be shy, they are not uncatchable and can be encouraged to show themselves. In summer weed cover is more important to the barbel than colour.

In winter, colour becomes the most important factor, even more so than water temperature and level. A small influx of colour in low levels and temperatures, which are otherwise dire, can often stimulate barbel to lose their inhibitions. If a bait is well presented *close* to a stimulated barbel in these conditions, then it can be enticed to take. If the water is both high and coloured in winter, believe me, these are favourable conditions. If the colour fades and the river remains high catch rates will diminish rapidly, but odd fish will still be caught. If the colour fades, coinciding with a drop in level, catch rates will diminish the lower it gets.

These conditions combined with high and lower water temperatures can make a difference at times. Generally the rule is the higher the water temperature in winter the better the chances, although on some occasions I have experienced the complete opposite and the temperature has had to drop before I began catching.

Extra Barbules

In September 1986 while unhooking a barbel from the Waterloo area I noticed something unusual and very strange.

After examining the mouth of the barbel for hookmarks, I found that one of the rear barbules had growths protruding from the back of it. At first, I didn't really think much more about it and explained it away as just a one-off. Over the four previous years, I had caught only a few barbel with barbule problems and they were minimal. Some fish had only three whilst one other had the normal four but with one front barbule divided into three at the tip, like tiny fingers. I put this deformity down to damage caused by unhooking.

While fishing the Housepool on 6 December 1986 I caught a barbel of 7lb 5oz and – lo and behold – there was a fifth anterior barbule, although not so completely developed as the main four. The following day I had another 7lb fish, again with the extra barbule. On 13 December I caught another barbel, 9lb 1oz, which again had an extra anterior barbule. This one was more developed than the previous two, and gave me my first opportunity to photograph the feature. All these three fish were caught in the Housepool. On 14 December, whilst fishing Trammels, I caught a fish of 4lb. This barbel had the beginnings of two extra growths appearing from the posterior barbules. Up until then all the extra barbules were still quite small and were not as fully developed in size as the others. On Christmas Day, I caught another barbel of 4lb 11oz from Greenbanks. This one was different. The extra barbule on this fish had started growing off a main anterior, and was the longest and most developed yet. I continued the observa-

Extra anterior barbule.

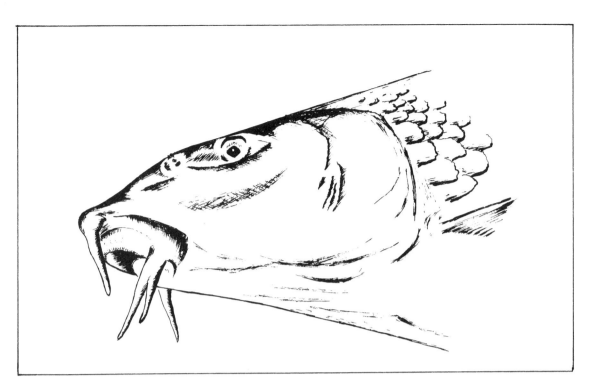

Extra posterior barbule.

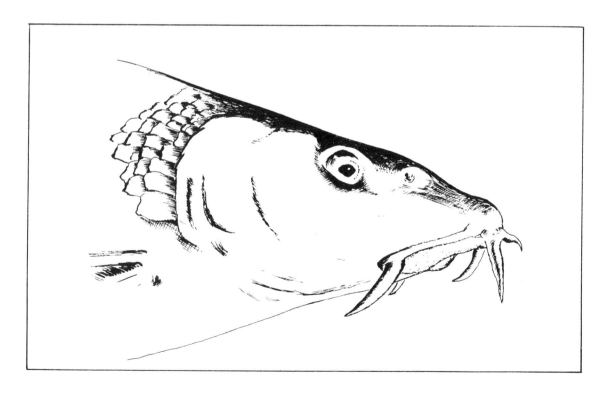

Extra anterior barbule.

29

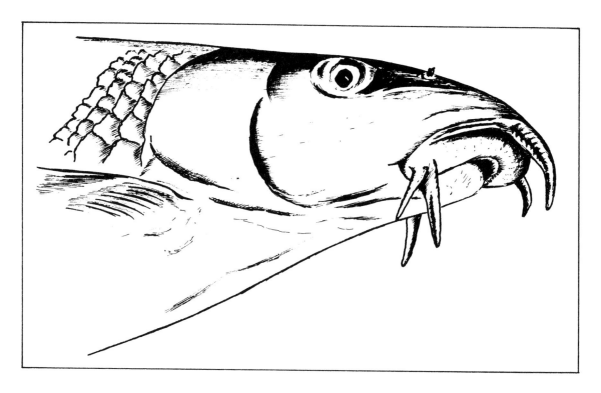

Extra posterior barbule.

tions and between 6 December 1986 and March 1987 I caught 72 barbel of which 20 had extra growths. One notable fact was that the growths increased in length and overall size as the month of February passed. All varied in length. Some were anterior others were posterior. Some were completely separate from the main four, while others branched off these. On 28 February an 8lb 5oz specimen was captured with a full-length extra posterior barbule.

The Swims

The Great Weir

Day tickets are available only for the east bank of the Great Weir. The compound on the west bank has to be booked. The Weir fishes quite well throughout the summer and autumn when water levels and conditions are favourable. Barbel run to an average size, with doubles making the odd appearance. In the summer months catches can vary from day to day, with anglers taking some nice fish from Jack's Corner and the Sill. The tail of the main flow is another productive spot. Good catches are often taken from the compound when a shoal is located, and recaptures are common, with fish being caught sometimes more than twice in a session. Meat, worms, and maggots all produce and groundbaiting can be advantageous when conditions allow. A fair number of barbel, usually found in the upper Trammels, move into the Weir at unpredictable times, travelling up through Haytor's or Edward's, and good sport can be had if they are located. Catches tend to decrease as the season progresses into late autumn and winter, mainly when the level rises and fishing becomes difficult due to the fast flow, weed, and debris. November also marks a decrease in catches due to pike fishing. Barbel weighing up to 11lb were captured in 1984–5 as were a number of lower doubles. Legends and recent rumours of very big fish moving into the Weir make this an area well worth investigating.

Edward's

Edward's is the gravel run-off from the Weir with clumps of weed distributed throughout its shallow area. In summer fishing is usually hard, although barbel can sometimes be seen. Trotting can

take the odd fish during the day, but dusk proves to be a better time; barbel move up from the Trammels and drop down from the Weir and so chances of a good catch improve from either end. High water levels make this run fast and practically unfishable. In winter it becomes barren and featureless and proves very difficult for most. Best left for the salmon angler and me!

The Trammels

The Trammels is arguably the most productive and consistent area on the fishery today. Throughout summer and autumn large shoals of barbel inhabit the weedy shallows and in normal and low summer levels and clear conditions they can be spotted moving up and down the gravel runs. Amazingly, they are not easily spooked and will frequently come close in throughout

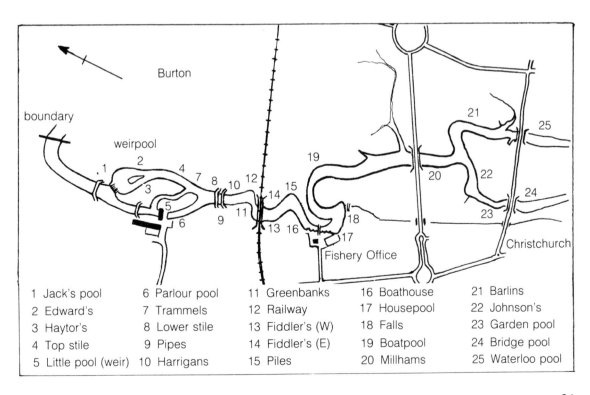

1 Jack's pool	6 Parlour pool	11 Greenbanks	16 Boathouse	21 Barlins
2 Edward's	7 Trammels	12 Railway	17 Housepool	22 Johnson's
3 Haytor's	8 Lower stile	13 Fiddler's (W)	18 Falls	23 Garden pool
4 Top stile	9 Pipes	14 Fiddler's (E)	19 Boatpool	24 Bridge pool
5 Little pool (weir)	10 Harrigans	15 Piles	20 Millhams	25 Waterloo pool

the day. Their feeding habits and movements make compulsive watching. In some swims visibility is excellent; and you can actually eye the bait, not the rod, and priceless information can be noted and memorised as fish move in to investigate the offerings.

From the end of Haytor's downstream, good catches are commonplace in summer, with five or more fish being taken in a single session. Average sizes are between 4 and 7lb; fish of 8–10lb usually come as one-offs. Recaptures are common. All usual methods catch, but feeder and rolling tactics together with loose feed get the barbel moving and bites come more quickly. Best baits are maggots and meat, although, as the season progresses and after fish have been hooked a few times, a change to bread or sweetcorn is very effective on occasions. When chub are present, catapult floating casters into the swim. This will bring them to the surface and the activity attracts barbel. Rolling meat through the swim at this time can bring good results. An 11lb 6oz barbel and a 6lb 2oz chub were reported taken in the 1983–4 season and several low doubles in 1984–5. Barbel of 10lb 4oz and 10lb 10oz came out in 1985–6, and one of 10lb 2oz in 1986–7. Strong tackle is advisable as many breaks occur when anglers try to retrieve fish from the dense weedbeds on the far bank and mid-stream. Winter fishing can be good, when water levels are high and coloured.

The Little Weir

The run-off from the Little Weir is sometimes good, but often a slow area in summer. During the day it seems to be a 'passing through' swim for barbel moving up the Trammels. Again, they can be spotted in clear water and odd fish can be taken, but it doesn't seem to be a classic feeding place in daylight. Although very large fish are sighted, they never seem to be interested in feeding and move on upstream. Chub can usually be spotted in the shallows and again loose-feeding with maggots and casters can bring them to a frenzy. Barbel are stimulated and tend to move in on the action from time to time. Freelining or trotting with small baits is worth trying, while meat at dusk is a must. Winter fishing becomes very hard work, with bites being hard to come by. Higher water levels form slacks a little downstream and fish move close in to the bank. Again, dusk is a better time to fish but occasional blanks must be expected.

Watersmeet

The point where the Parlour pool joins the main river is known as the Watersmeet. Fishing from the east bank in summer and autumn is consistently productive, but this is a very sought after area, with anglers trying day after day to get in amongst some very obliging barbel which lie in the weedy shallows under the tree and along the sandbar in mid-stream. Shoals can often be encountered and fish of 4–7lb are usually featured in catches, with larger specimens being taken on the odd occasion. From early morning right through to late afternoon you can expect to have spasmodic sport, but the evenings sometimes prove a little disappointing. Link-legering and block-end are the usual daytime methods here, but meat, stationary or rolling, can on occasions be the better choice. The chub and barbel in this area have a distinctive habit of picking up the feeder and shaking it to release the feed inside, so false bites are very common. Trotting downstream through the weedbeds can often pick up a good number of fish in the hot sunshine of the summer and wading can be an advantage in low water conditions. Higher water levels can make this area very difficult to fish, but close in a small slack is formed which can be a very good mark in these conditions. Winter fishing can be very hard, as the barbel tend to move down and across to the west side and generally stay there, leaving anglers chalking up a few blanks before they realise what the situation is.

Engineers

Engineers can be fished in all types of conditions usually with good results. Situated downstream of the Parlour, Engineers is a popular trotting area with its shallow weedy channels holding some good barbel and carp. Chest-wading in summer is a favourite move here when fishing the trees of the garden and downstream around the bend. Sometimes very big catches are taken and large barbel and carp often turn up. Landing these fish can be a problem when wading, unless the angler is experienced.

The Rushes

The Rushes are between Engineers and the Top Pipe. They are shallow with dense weedbeds, and strong tackle should be used. In summer it is sometimes difficult to fish due to the weed and low water levels; although fish are caught, this swim doesn't really come

into its own until November and December. Good catches are common, with fish in the 4–7lb range. Specimens are taken in amongst these and the best fish reported in 1984–5 weighed 11lb 2oz and 10lb 8oz. In winter and high water conditions, the Rushes are a must, with fish of 10lb 9oz and 10lb 4oz in 1985–6, and 10lb 11oz in 1986–7. A superb glide is formed where the Parlour flow hits the main river course and reasonably comfortable fishing is possible. Shoals usually located in the Pipes, Greenbanks, Trammels and the Parlour take turns in frequenting this area throughout high water levels in winter.

The Pipes

There are now two water pipes spanning the top of Greenbanks and the Pipe swims are well noted barbel haunts on the Royalty. Barbel can be spotted easily if you look down from either pipe when the water is clear in summer. Note their positions and patrol routes and you can have some great fun in trying to outwit the crafty ones. Trotting through the Pipes is a practised method here and at times some big fish can be located moving up through the area. Large catches are often reported. Again, all methods produce. A deep hole between the pipes is usually a hotspot at various times during the season and the slack close in is quite consistent, especially in high water conditions. Specimens to 11lb 5oz and lower doubles were taken in the 1983–4 season and some enormous fish have been sighted. A little downstream from the Pipes on the east bank is where Jack Harrigan landed his 13lb+ barbel, and the swim is named after him. It used to be deep here but it has now silted up and is completely changed. The west bank is a very productive patch where catches of up to fourteen fish in a session were recorded on the opening days of 1986–7.

Greenbanks

Greenbanks is a very productive area in the summer months, with barbel in the 3–6lb bracket being common in most catches. A shoal inhabits the area and they travel up and downstream at times. Sometimes it can be rather difficult to track them down and roving tactics can often pay dividends. Trotting or rolling through can generally sort out where they lie and good catches can be taken if they are encountered and drawn into feeding. Maggot can be deadly on these occasions. If a large shoal is not found, then small pockets of barbel should be located in various parts of the area. I have found that they tend to feed at uncertain times, probably due to the effect of the tide. Larger specimens are sometimes taken by the cattle drink near the railway, but from the lower Greenbanks on the west side water levels make the whole area very difficult to fish, let alone catch from. Running-off times can be very good, however. Cold conditions make the

The famed Railway Pool.

fishing hard, although if the water is coloured it is worth persevering.

The Railway Pool

This pool is well known for big barbel past and present. Its swims have a hypnotic effect that can put you in a mood of anticipation and keep you on the edge of your seat throughout a session. It is basically a sit-and-wait game here, and those anglers with the greatest patience and determination will reap the rewards. Hook a fish and they can hear your heart pound from the next swim! Your mind is seized with thoughts of record-breaking doubles. It's a strange feeling that will keep you coming back for more and get you totally hooked on barbel.

When the river is clear in summer and autumn, barbel can be spotted swimming about in the weedbeds midstream and close in. Again, observations can be made and different tactics can be put into operation. During the day, try dropping some bait into the edge; a single barbel sometimes comes close in to investigate, although nine times out of ten it has no intention of feeding at that particular moment. These fish seem to be scouts for a shoal and often return in the late afternoon or dusk and clean up. Good catches are often taken. If you think about it, a great many anglers empty their unwanted bait in to the edge when packing up. It's common sense what happens next! Trotting, link leger, block-end, rolling and stationary tactics can all take fish when used in the right conditions, but persistence is normally required. Meat and maggot take the majority caught, with bread, worms and sweetcorn being somewhat slower.

Groundbaiting and using pieces as a hookbait can sometimes bring results when other methods fail. The barbel most commonly caught weigh between 6 and 9lb, with lower doubles being taken more frequently than on other parts of the fishery. Deformed fish are also present, and are residents.

In 1943 M. W. Haytor, a previous manager of the fishery, foul-hooked a massive barbel weighing 15lb 12oz from this pool, and sightings of possible 20lb monsters were made by many experienced and respected anglers in past years. Joe Day's record barbel of 13lb 12oz was taken from the Railway in 1962, and even today large barbel, although rare, are sometimes spotted when conditions permit. In some cases it's quite easy to overestimate the size and weights of barbel when in the water, though I have often found that it is equally possible to underestimate.

Fiddler's

In summer and autumn Fiddler's is very shallow and weedy, and holds a fair head of barbel. Trotting all the way through the area is very rewarding when fishing in the early morning. Barbel can sometimes be seen moving in and out of the weedbeds and when this occurs freelining or the float can often take them. During the day stationary baits are often ignored and create slow fishing. Barbel of 3–6lb are the most common in catches, with larger specimens tending to show at dusk. Meat and maggot seem to be best. Top Fiddler's was one of the late Jack Harrigan's favourite autumn haunts giving him nice catches when trotting, and some big fish.

Mugs' 'Ole

This swim is usually fished close in and, although it produces occasionally, it is slow and groundbaiting is often required (note the name). In 1986–7 the bank collapsed into the water and changed the swim close in.

Joe's 'Ole

Joe's 'Ole, on the other hand, is a very productive swim, with barbel, chub, dace, roach, bream and pike obliging. Loose feeding with maggots and casters every now and then gets them interested, and trotting through with light tackle will take dace and chub in quantity throughout the summer. However, barbel often move in on the action and, while some are caught, breaks are common with unsuspecting anglers. It becomes a very good barbel haunt at dusk, with nice fish taken on stationary or rolling baits. It can be fished in winter and high water levels with some confidence of catching, although tactics have to be changed to suit.

The Piles

In 1984 the Piles had to be rebuilt due to the collapse of the east bank, which divided the end of Fiddler's as far as the falls. Vast quantities of gravel were removed and now the river bed has changed accordingly. The Piles looks similar to the Railway in many respects, but alas does not produce as frequently. Anglers who fish this area usually find it very slow going, with barbel not coming to the net in numbers. It is another place where patience and determination must be used for any chance of success. Trotting along the Piles used to be a good method, with bait-dropping helping to bring the fish on, but nowadays anglers tend to use stationary methods. It is worth trying some of the tactics mentioned in the Railway swim. The late Bill Warren, current holder of the British chub record, and with some terrific barbel to his credit, used to fish this area. Beware. It is very deep.

The Boathouse

The Boathouse area has a small number of very attractive swims. Although it is another slow area, it holds some exceptional fish in its deep holes and glides. They sometimes drift downstream below the Boathouse and can occasionally be seen lying in the deep water. Not many barbel are caught but it is a very interesting part of the fishery.

Dick's 'Ole

This spot above the Boathouse is usually a sit-and-wait swim, and it's not unusual to doze off here. However, it does produce out of the blue, with fish of 11 and 12lb being taken in past years. Four barbel over 10lb were taken in 1984–5.

The Footbridge

When arriving at the car park, your first view of the fishery is a beautiful sight. The deep smooth glide running from the Footbridge into the main House-pool is a barbel catcher's dream. When I was first introduced to the Royalty, I was placed on the car park wall and felt very excited and confident at having such a perfect-looking swim. Of course I did not realise why no one was fishing here, even though the rest of the fishery was chock-a-block. It was the late Jimmy James, who was unfortunately

The Boathouse Pool – scene of many epic captures.

disabled and restricted to fishing this area, who put me on the right track. He explained to me the dos and don'ts of barbel fishing and I caught my first barbel from here; it weighed 6lb 4oz.

Captures are frequently made from the car park wall and opposite at dusk as barbel move upstream from the Housepool and along both banks. I have taken fish of 10lb 4oz and 10lb 6oz from here, together with others of higher than average size.

The Housepool

This is another very popular area in summer and autumn – not that it has a big head of fish, but somehow it looks so inviting and relaxing. However, it does hold some very nice barbel and chub. In summer it tends to get over-fished, with different anglers using all sorts of baits and methods. The occasional fish is caught but catches of six or more in a session are infrequent. Stationary methods seem to produce the barbel, and the best times are early morning and dusk. Although meat and maggot account for most barbel, experimenting with other baits can often pay off. The area seems to come on at certain times during the season; sometimes you just cannot catch for ages, then suddenly it's alive. In winter, high water conditions make this a very worthwhile area to fish. Although the slacks prove to be slow, wandering about and trying different swims and tactics can often produce a fish or two. Six doubles were caught in these conditions in the winter of 1984, with some catches of five barbel being taken in a session. In the winter of 1985 I caught barbel here in water temperatures as low as 35°F and air temperatures below 25°F.

The Falls

The Falls are worth trying at the beginning of the season. It is a fact that some barbel and chub lie here for a short period after spawning (this has proved to be true on some openings but not on others, depending on early or late spawning cycles). If the fish are found to be here, float, link and rolling tactics – with meat, maggot, or worm – will take them in daylight hours, while at dusk stationary baits are effective. In this area the state of the tide has a noticeable effect on when the fish feed. The tail end of the swim can often turn up big barbel throughout the season.

The stretch below the rapids can be a better proposition if the fish cannot be located in the shallows. Deep holes and slacks can be found around the bend, while the main flow runs on the east bank. These swims can provide some good sport on occasions but it can be slow. Odd fish are taken during the day, but late afternoon and dusk are the more productive times. All baits are worth trying and groundbaiting can encourage the fish to feed. The slower water and slacks often turn up something very good at high water levels and in winter.

The Telegraph Slack

The Slack is another legendary swim which still produces the big 'uns now and again. A barbel of 12lb 11oz was caught by a fisherwoman not so long ago and another of 11lb 8½oz was also

reported. Dusk is usually the productive time and in summer sunbathing is more appropriate for the holidaying angler, but odd fish do come out of the blue during the day. Flood conditions are good for the big-fish angler. A fish of 12lb was reported in 1983–4, one of 10lb 11oz in 1985–6, and one of 10lb 6oz in 1986–7.

The Boatpool

The Boatpool is a swift flowing area, with good productive swims on both banks, but patience is often required to get results here. These swims often get fair attention in summer and autumn, with some good fish being taken on feeder and legered luncheon meat. Fish of 13lb have been caught from here in the past and more recently (1982–3) barbel to 11lb 9oz have been caught.

The Roadbridge

Before the bypass was built a rowing boat was moored in Barlins Creek for the convenience of fishermen wishing to cross the cut. This wide piece of water is interesting. I try to apply to it the knowledge I've acquired from fishing in the Railway Pool. There's no doubt that very big barbel lurk about in the dense weedbeds in midstream. It's very unusual to catch a lot of barbel but this is compensated by the higher than average weight – 6–8lb. Trotting down to the Bridge in the main drag can often turn up trumps, as can legering well into the weed. Fishing underneath the road bridge often turns up fish unexpectedly, especially when it's hard work elsewhere. Barbel can often be seen in the channels from the vantage-point of the bridge itself. The wind down here is often a nuisance and can become uncomfortable. Chris Wild took a barbel of 12lb 3oz in 1983–4 and other low doubles were reported.

Millhams

The river in this area is very shallow and weedy. Good catches are sometimes reported from the Armchair swim, but less frequently than in earlier years. Barbel in the 3–8lb range usually fall to roving tactics, and this method often pays dividends on this stretch. Some very large barbel are present in the area, but are very elusive and well covered. Most of my captures have come from around the road bridge and the last twenty yards of the straight. The effect of the tide plays a very important part in the barbel's habits in this area, as in Johnson's, where the flow is greatest. Feeding times and patterns are hard to predict and vary considerably. This is an open stretch of water where the fishing can be very slow and frustrating at times. Persistence is required.

Johnson's

This area, the right fork of the river, is well worth trying whenever fishing below the bypass. The main run is on the far bank, flowing under the overhanging trees, whilst slackish water is found close in. Trotting with maggots can be very productive on hot summer days, with static meat baits best at dusk. High water levels and colouring, especially in winter, make this corner of the fishery very attractive and I have had some good days here, taking barbel in water temperatures as low as 41°F and when other areas haven't produced. In days past, doubles from Johnson's were reported, as well as chub to 6lb.

Nowadays you can expect to catch barbel to 8lb, with meat, maggot and casters being well received. Doubles are rare. Generally a very good area, and one well worth investigation.

The Parlour Pool

This is the famous pool where barbel can sometimes be seen feeding above the sanctuary chain. It is amazing. The size of some of them makes your eyes pop out. Legend has it that the daddy of them all lives here, but I'm sure it must be the mummy, as male barbel rarely exceed six or seven pounds. Not so long ago Jack Harrigan hooked into a monster while using light tackle to fox the fish. He estimated this barbel to be well over the present record after he nearly had it in the net, but, alas, it ran under the pumphouse grills and smashed him. Very large fish and catches are nearly always taken in summer and autumn, and the Parlour has to be booked well in advance. It is very expensive but the permit covers salmon and sea trout up until October and November respectively. Excessive amounts of water are extracted from the river at this point to supply the needs of the petrochemical plant at Fawley, Southampton – sometimes as much as 10 million gallons per day. Another 12 million gallons is pumped out to 265 square miles of the area surrounding Christchurch.

Waterloo

This, the left fork of the river, is another hard area where I have been experimenting. Although barbel are present, they are hard to find. They are probably lying further downstream past the boundary and tend to be caught only at the rise of the tide or at dusk.

The Middle Avon

PETE TILLOTSON

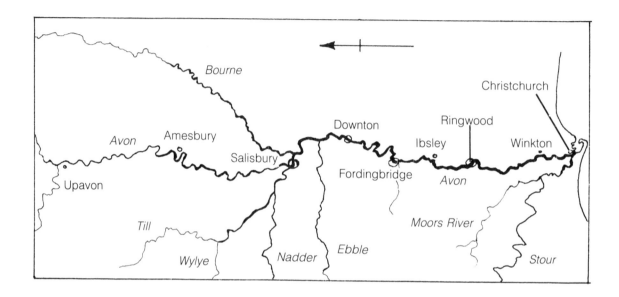

Winkton

This picturesque stretch of the Avon lies a mile or two above Christchurch. Day tickets are available from either the Fisherman's Haunt (a hotel by the bridge at Winkton) or Davis's Tackle Shop at Christchurch. It is an interesting part of the Avon with many varied swims, holding barbel in excess of 10lb, although I would say the average size of fish from here is around the 7lb mark. Apart from the main river there is a fast flowing sidestream which holds quite a few barbel. I do feel, though, that the bigger barbel are to be caught in the steadier and deeper water immediately above the top weir.

Bisterne

Another day-ticket water, albeit for only two months (September and October) of the year, is at Bisterne. Barbel go to about 11lb here, but location can be a problem. Large areas of the river are barren of barbel and it would pay to spend some time fish spotting rather than fishing blind. The top end of the fishery is very popular and is reputed to hold the better fish.

Ringwood

There is a wealth of water here and ample opportunities for day-ticket fishing. The famed Severals Fisheries lies here and for a reasonable price the chances of catching barbel are quite good. Christchurch Angling Club has a ticket stretch just below the new weir at Ringwood and 12lb fish are caught from this area every year, usually in the autumn. The stretch above the new weir is reputed to hold some very big barbel. Ringwood Tackle is the place for tickets and information.

Ibsley

Going upstream from Ringwood, the next port of call is Ibsley, another day-ticket stretch, although the number of rods allowed on the water is limited. This is another varied stretch, and includes a very interesting weirpool. A 16lb 1oz barbel was caught here many years ago, but I doubt if they go to that size here now. Ellingham and Bicton are other stretches nearby but they are members-only waters. Anybody considering fishing the Avon on a permanent basis should definitely consider getting a Ringwood or Christchurch permit – or both! These would cover most of the Avon and much of the Dorset Stour.

Fordingbridge – Burgate

One of the prime areas of the Avon, with barbel over 12lb caught every season. Opportunities for day tickets are good. You can fish the park at Fordingbridge (a rather shallow,

weedy, stretch), a small part of the town stretch, the restaurant stretch, the caravan stretch and the Salisbury AC stretch up to Burgate. In this whole length of generally fast flowing river there are quite a few barbel with a high average size.

Above Burgate

Downton, Charford and Breamore are all other ticket waters which hold barbel, but they are not fished seriously by specialist anglers and location could be a major problem. Higher up at Britford is the Trafalgar Water, which does hold some big barbel, but unfortunately it is not a ticket water.

To sum up, barbel are to be found in the Avon from Salisbury (and maybe above) right through to Christchurch. Day tickets are available on a lot of the river.

John Bailey Interviews ANDY ORME

In 1978 I read a most alluring article in *Coarse Fisherman* magazine. It was entitled 'A Journey to Paradise' and was written by a certain A. Orme. The subject, the Eden described, was the middle Avon, and ever since I have wanted to meet Andy to learn more about this fabulous river. When, in the summer of 1987, the opportunity arose it was all the experience I had hoped for.

One of the delights of angling is to hear an expert talk about a water he knows and loves. Swanton on the Avon, Wentworth on the Stour, Mac-Donald on Yately or Cassien, Amies on the Thurne system – it does not matter what the species or what the venue, the pleasure is the same. Certainly Andy reinforced the glamour and the romance I had always known the middle Avon possessed.

We talked big fish. That Ibsley giant of 16lb did exist. Andy has talked to the man who weighed it and he has no doubts at all that proper procedures were used. Equally, though it is now fashionable to discount Richard Walker's tales of 20lb fish in the middle Avon during the fifties, who can really be sure? Perhaps they are still there – tucked away in pockets of one or two along stretches that are little if ever fished.

A beautiful 10lb 10oz barbel caught by Simon Lush. This fish was caught four times in a two-week period!

Very possibly, the biggest fish – huge barbel indeed – lead life styles different from the 'ordinary' fish of up to eleven or twelve pounds. Perhaps their food requirements are different – do they feed exclusively on fish as they age and grow? Perhaps they inhabit different types of swim and live and move in a splendid isolation quite apart and untouchable.

Some will find this romantic and believe it unlikely that such fish can exist, but it is wise to take note of the case of what is in all probability the biggest ever Wensum barbel. To my knowledge this fish has never been caught. Many of the doubles and lesser fish have each been landed on innumerable occasions, yet this fish – possibly three or four pounds larger – has continued to escape. Luck? I think not. There must be a more rational explanation – one based much more on the true nature of these exceptional barbel.

However, back to the middle Avon and to reality. Andy's first point is that the barbel is not a widespread species along many miles of the river here. Generally there are few fish and those that do exist are exceptionally difficult to locate in a river carpeted with streamer weed for much of the year. This need not be a deterrent. In fact the opposite is very nearly true and Andy has adopted an approach that dovetails exactly to such a situation. He fishes the middle Avon as an opportunist, waiting for ideal conditions and only fishing when he knows the chances are at their best.

His periods on the river coincide with environmental extremes – flood conditions most especially, when he knows that the barbel will seek shelter in much more easily readable swims. Here, in slacks and eddies, they will be concentrated and will be feeding hard as the flood stirs up the food and induces an orgy of gluttony. These are the times when Andy is out, generally well into the evening and long after dark, adopting a roving approach, dropping chunks of meat into swim after swim till barbel are contacted.

It is for this very reason that Andy favours the winter as the best barbel season. Then the river becomes more predictable, more easily read. He avoids the very cold high pressure snaps when the river runs low and clear and when the barbel lie doggo on the bed. Once the mild westerlies start to push in the rain from the Atlantic, however, the river changes drastically. The water temperature can rise dramatically about ten degrees to a startling 52°F or so. Levels rise quickly and, once the middle Avon really begins to tank down, Andy knows the type of swim the barbel will be headed towards.

One of the best winter baits, he finds, is bread – especially in those areas that see a lot introduced by the roach men. Wessex roach anglers groundbait heavily and the surplus accumulates in the slacks, where the barbel gorge on it. The roach are there too, and Andy will go as fine as a 4lb hooklength of Drennan Double Strength to take possible advantage of both species.

His other major bait is Tesco's Chopped Ham and Pork. He uses huge bits on a size 4 Lion d'Or (with the barb flattened) with a range of semi-hammered leads in the 1½–2½oz range. When after the barbel pure and simple, he will use 8lb Maxima straight

Tony Hart with an 11lb 6oz barbel.

through to the Berkeley swivel and hooklength. His only sophistication would be the almost constant use of the PVA stringer made up to hold about eight lumps of bait. I did not get the impression for a second that high-tech tackle is the name of Andy's game. It is being there that counts, on a river he is intimate with, after a species he knows as well as anyone today.

In this same vein, he likes to touch leger, to be in constant contact with his tackle and bait. He always holds the rod and quite often legers upstream. He finds as a result that he never gets the rod-buckling bites that a self-hooked, scared barbel gives the less constantly aware angler. Touch legering enhances Andy's intimacy with the river and the species. He is so in tune with the Avon in these intensive spells of fishing that he can feel the bomb on the gravels and even sense how an interested fish is behaving. He is never taken by surprise by a barbel, unlike the sleeping long-stay bivvy merchants.

And how exciting a bite is as it develops along the line to those sensitive fingers! The Maxima comes alive; there is a tingling; there is an increase in pressure; he feels the leger moving and he strikes into another wild winter barbel.

One very important feature of Andy's flood barbeling is that success is no way confined to a falling river. In fact, the biggest fish have often come at the height of the flood in diabolical conditions when few anglers would think of being out. It is no wonder that throughout the winter months his rods are always made up, ready at home or lying in the car so that he can take immediate advantage of heavy rains to get down the Avon valley.

Andy's 13lb 7oz middle Avon fish was one of those captures – perfect in every way. It was in the most superb condition and it fell to his methods in the winter at a time of high flood. This magnificent barbel is the reinforcement of everything Andy has been doing and reporting over the years.

The other extreme of Andy's repertoire is trotting for barbel, especially in the earlier months of the season. He looks for a swim from three to five feet deep and flanked by weeds. These are a must – for, as he says, no weed, no barbel. If the swim is comparatively lightly weeded he will go to 3lb line but in more normal conditions this will be stepped up a pound. The float will be an Avon type, with wire stem, set over depth with no 4s near to the hook and AAs as bulk shot. The hooklength itself will once more be 4lb Drennan Double Strength.

The key to Andy's trotting is feeding heavily enough to draw the barbel into the swim and out of the surrounding jungles of weed. Then, bites can be amazing and the fight will test his 13-foot carbon all the way. The actual fight is an important feature of landing these summer barbel. He uses a Mitchell Match rather than a centre-pin to cope with those rocketing runs when the barbel comes towards him and a build-up of slack line could spell disaster.

He aims to get below his fish – it is quite impossible to pull fish upstream through weed like this. He puts all the pressure he can on a weeded fish and holds it there, quite constant and unyielding, till he feels the fish kick itself free. The wait can be as much as half an hour, but the downstream pressure will free a fish eventually and get it on the move once more. A soft rod is essential for this work and in Andy's eyes fast-taper affairs have no place on the middle Avon. The all-through action exerts colossal pressure but with a stretch and elasticity that always stands between him and a breakage.

The Dorset Stour

PETE READING

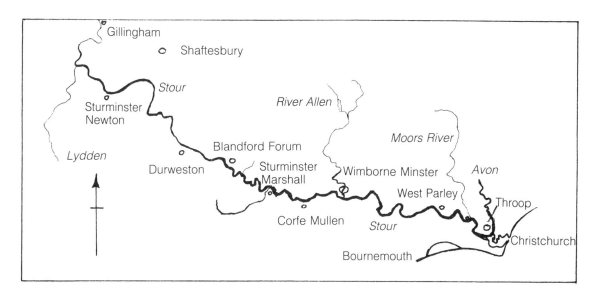

There are at least five rivers called Stour in England, but to barbel fishermen there is one only, the famous Dorset Stour, which originates around Dorchester in the heart of Hardy country, meanders through the Blackmore Vale, skirts north of the conurbations of Poole and Bournemouth and eventually joins forces with the Hampshire Avon just above Christchurch Harbour.

The word 'Stour' is thought to be of Celtic origin, and roughly translates as 'strong, powerful and fast-flowing'. Such a description still befits the Dorset Stour at times of high water, but land drainage and flood alleviation schemes have largely emasculated the river.

Fifteen years ago the middle reaches ran with a clear surging power that rivalled that of the Hampshire Avon. Today, the river limps rather lamely to the sea, its bed levelled, its bends straightened, and its flow interrupted by crude rough-stone weirs designed to maintain a reasonable summer low-water profile.

Despite these 'improvements', the barbel of the Stour have managed to survive, and apparently thrive. They are presently on the increase in terms of numbers and average size, and continue to attract keen barbel anglers from all over the country.

It would be true to say that virtually

all the barbel in the Stour are restricted to a length of river that is quite short compared with its total. Barbel fishing on the river is only really worthwhile between Longham Bridge, north of Bournemouth, and Old Iford Bridge, at Christchurch. The river below Iford is tidal, and the barbel population seems to be limited to one or two small shoals and the occasional adventurous individual. The fish that holds the record for the bravest Stour barbel was taken in 1985 from the Clay Pool, where the Stour and Avon meet, by Selwyn Mould, then Chairman of Christchurch Angling Club. At a little over 7lb, this fish took a fly meant for sea trout, and was undoubtedly rubbing shoulders with mullet, flounder and bass. Barbel are a rare capture from the lower Stour, but they do exist, and may be worth seeking out.

At the upper extent of the barbel zone, Longham waterworks forms the boundary. Barbel suddenly become very few and far between above this point, despite certain illegal stockings, and populations are low and highly localised. Shoals have been sighted at Blandford and as high upriver as Sturminster Newton and Fiddleford. Such fish would demand very intensive searching and almost total specialisation – a task for a dedicated resident rather than a visiting angler. To the visiting barbel enthusiast, then, the river between Longham and Iford is the target area, and indeed this is where all of my barbel fishing has been centred.

A lightning tour through this length of river may be of use to anglers not familiar with the Stour, and perhaps contemplating a visit in the near future.

The Fisheries

The **Longham Waterworks** fishing is controlled by the Bournemouth and District Water Company. When I applied for a permit, I was advised that it was a dead man's shoes job – which I suppose is Dorset parlance for a long wait! Some good fish in the weirs, though, and they do venture downstream in some years to the **Longham Free Stretch**. This short stretch below Longham Bridge and Longham Weir is not pretty or peaceful – you fish with the corporation rubbish tip behind you and a busy pub car park opposite. There are barbel, though, and you can fish at night, which is strictly taboo on club-controlled stretches.

Both banks downstream of Longham Weir are controlled by Christchurch Angling Club, and this stretch, down to the New Road Bridge, offers some of the best barbel swims on the middle Stour. The right-hand bank below New Road Bridge downstream to Throop's top boundary is free fishing, and, although the barbel are localised and difficult to find, they are well worth fishing for. Night fishing is possible here, and local tackle shops will advise on access.

The opposite bank from **Parley Church** to the Throop top boundary is controlled by the Ringwood and District Angling Association. It should be stressed that night fishing and close-season access to Christchurch Angling Club and Ringwood Angling Association waters is strictly banned and there are also a few short lengths of bank dotted along the river that are not accessible for fishing at all.

Peter Reading with an 11lb 5oz barbel.

We now reach the top boundaries of **Throop Fisheries**. Throop Fisheries is the jewel in the crown as far as the Dorset Stour's barbel fishing is concerned. The stretch between Throop Weir and Blackwater must contain more barbel than the whole of the rest of the Stour, and is a length of river steeped in barbel-fishing history. Many a young angler, myself included, started their barbel-fishing career at Throop and, although I rarely fish Throop nowadays, I am grateful for having the experience of learning much about barbel and how to catch them from such a special bit of river.

I started to fish Throop in 1969, and caught my first barbel, a seven-pounder, on a lump of cheese moulded round a size 2 Sealey Octopus, from Barbel Bend, which was just below the Bungalows, just below the Pig Chute, down from Pig Island! Every hundred yards of Throop has a name, some generally accepted, some personal to particular Throop regulars. One man's Nettlebeds is another man's Highbanks – what really matters is that Throop is a superb barbel fishery, and warrants attention from novice and expert alike.

The barbel peter out in terms of numbers above the New Weir and below the outfall of the Holdenhurst sewage works at the lower end of the fishery, but anywhere between these two points an angler stands a chance of exceptional barbel fishing. Bags of a dozen or more fish in the 4–8lb range are not uncommon, and double-figure fish are there to be sought out. The 13 and 14lb fish that were taken in the sixties are long gone, I fear, but nothing is really certain in fishing. Barbel have a habit of 'cruising' at a fixed weight for years, then suddenly packing on a few pounds for no apparent reason. Throop could produce a record yet, particularly from the deeper, duller, little-fished areas where fish can't be easily spotted, and a few bigger fish may be waxing fat in isolation, unmolested by holiday anglers with no time to risk going fishless for the chance of a really big specimen.

The boundary of Throop butts on to what is technically known as the lower Stour. All the available fishing from here to the sea is controlled by Christ-church Angling Club, and day tickets can be purchased for much of the river below Iford Bridge. Barbel were fairly common around Iford before the drastic pollution from the sheepwash storm-water drain in the early seventies. Nowadays, the barbel population is low, yet more fish are reported each year, and perhaps a new facet to the Stour's barbel fishing is developing.

Unfortunately, the Wessex Water Authority is intending to dredge much of the river bed between Throop and Christchurch Harbour in the winter of 1987–88 and the effect of yet another flood alleviation scheme is very

Trefor West returns a fine 8lb 4oz Throop barbel.

uncertain. Current plans will mean a lowering of summer levels below Iford Bridge of 350 mm, and a slight increase in mean velocity is forecast. If the barbel don't like it, Throop and the lower Royalty could benefit from an increased stock of disgruntled barbel, migrating to water more to their liking.

The tidal reaches mean the end of this condensed tour of the Stour's barbel zone, and, rather than continue in a general vein, I thought it might be more interesting to go into methods and tactics by recounting experiences in various swims over the years. Picking through my diary I have selected what I hope will be informative and interesting accounts.

June 1983 – Parley

Early season barbel fishing can be a very hit-and-miss affair. Sport is almost invariably slow and patchy, and a river in apparently ideal condition can seem to be devoid of barbel. The days after spawning are a difficult time for fish, and barbel are no exception. As soon as temperatures and water levels are suit-able, the barbel on this stretch congre-gate on the fast shallows, and this year in particular I had been studying them for some weeks. The spring was early and warm, and I had been fortunate enough to watch barbel spawning in late April, and at very close quarters. In the fast water under the bank, and at the tail of the weir, I had seen several big females, each flanked by two or three small, dark males, go through incred-ible routines, ranging from furious chasing around the weirpool to the strange ecstatic shuddering that accompanies the actual shedding of spawn.

Cooler weather in the week before the opening of the season had seen the fish slowly migrating back to their summer residences, and this scattering, and obviously slow regrouping, must account for the usual unreliable start to the Stour barbel season. An early spawning meant that there was a chance of a better start to the season, and the morning of 16 June saw me fishing with high expectations in a swim that had been well prebaited with corn and hemp. The Stour in June is usually tinged with algae and diatoms, and as a rule weedbeds are in no way established at that time. This year, the river was clear enough to spot fish on the shallows,

and a good deal of streamer weed was showing on the surface. Spawning activity on the downstream shallows had all but ceased – there just had to be barbel in the swim.

The morning mists had been burnt away by the sun before a barbel was to accept a hookbait, however, and that first barbel bite of the season was one that left no room for doubt. The rod knocked once, and walloped over as a fish of just under 9lb hooked itself. The Tree swim was awkward to fish, and awkward to play fish in, and that fish made things really difficult by going downstream, where I couldn't follow. After being teased back upstream again, it proceeded to bury itself first in the streamer in the middle of the river and then in the reedbed at my feet. Finally, it made the net, and as it lay gasping in the morning sunshine – admired by me, sweating and covered in mud, twigs and nettle stings – I realised how lucky I was to contact such a fish, and so early in the season.

As with most difficult swims, a rou-tine for playing and landing fish developed, and over the next few visits the Tree swim produced some more good fish, a few eights and big sevens, all falling to corn, fished with hemp in a small block-end feeder. Eight-pound line and a size 6 Lion d'Or proved adequate to keep fish out of the very dense bulrush beds that surrounded the feeding area, a narrow channel directly beneath the spotting tree that gave the swim its name. As June progressed, the river got clearer and I was able to spot the fish, which became ever more fin-icky. The weed got thicker too, and there were a few losses as fish burrowed under the bulrush root system.

49

I never saw a fish bigger than the nine-pounder, but the fishing was the typical close-range, intimate barbel fishing that you can never really tire of, with the Stour at its rare early-season best.

August 1976 – Throop Weir

The drought of 1976 coincided with the dredging and straightening of the Stour above Throop. There was no water running over the two side-sills of the weir at all and in places the margins of the river were so choked with duck-weed that it was impossible to fish. In places, the Stour stood still, and the barbel fishing was generally poor. Bar-bel hotspots were those short stretches where the river retained some flow over clean gravel, and one such hotspot was Throop weir itself.

For some reason, a considerable number of fish had holed up in the central concrete-walled box through which all the Stour's flow was now channelled. It was possible to see these fish, lined up side by side like sardines, from the walkway across the weir, and it was strange, initially, to realise that they were all facing downstream. As with most weirs, the sill was deeply undercut, with the flow turning back on itself in a great vertical eddy. It wasn't long before people worked out a way of catching these fish, and an unu-sual and specialised bit of barbel fishing it turned out to be. Few of the barbel in that weir box went over 7lb, but for a short while they provided good sport for those prepared to go to the trouble of presenting a bait in the right place. The right place was directly under the weir sill, and such fishing demanded wading out to the edge of the weirpool and casting directly up the weir box. We used medium-sized block-feeders, and plenty of maggots. Bites were positive, and fights from hooked barbel really weird. Fish would take an unbelievable amount of line as they swam into what was a considerably undercut 'cave' beneath the weir struc-ture. As they tired, we had to pump

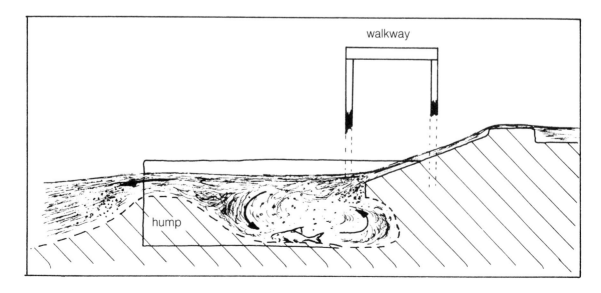

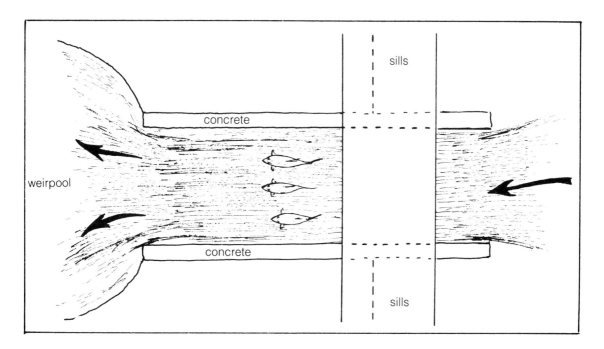

them almost to the surface to get them over the hump which was responsible for diverting the flow back on itself. Once out into the weirpool proper, playing and landing was straightforward.

I am not a great fan of weirs and weirpools for barbel. They are inconsistent and overrated, snaggy, noisy and not very relaxing places to fish. However, in certain weirs, at certain times, you can catch fish as long as you know exactly where to cast. The other weirs on the middle Stour are cobbled or gabion weirs; no more really than piles of boulders, they help to keep up water levels. There are now seven such weirs between Longham and the sea. They hold no great attraction for barbel, or for me, but they do allow the Stour to retain some dignity.

July 1982 – Longham

A summer flood is as welcome as high water in winter to the barbel fisherman. A flush of cool, coloured water can breathe new life into a low, stale river, and the Stour's barbel can get really turned on by such a change in conditions.

The initial rush of water is usually unproductive, and fishing is well nigh impossible anyway, with a river full of rubbish and weed – particularly silkweed, which lifts off the bottom in great mats. The slowly falling river after a flood is the prime time, when an otherwise fickle and finicky barbel can decide to have a good grub around.

A warm settled evening found me in one of my favourite swims, and, despite having taken only a couple of chub since the afternoon, I was feeling content and confident. The river had lost

51

much of its colour from the recent flood, and drifting weed was no longer a problem. The rod bumped and nodded almost continually as chub nuzzled the feeder, eager to hoover up the fresh hemp that it contained. Even hair-rigged corn will not fool chub very often, though, and I had caught most of the chub from this swim in the last few evenings. I don't really know whether chub are any brighter than barbel, but they certainly do not hook themselves as easily, certainly on corn. I think this is just as well, because they are enough of a nuisance as it is, when fishing corn over hemp.

The first stars had started to appear when the chub disappeared. For nearly half an hour the rod tip merely flexed gently in the current, and there was a wonderful calm stillness as dusk spread quietly over the valley. I leaned back in my chair and stretched backwards, watching as a few more stars twinkled into existence, and hoping for a last-minute barbel. There was a dull, metallic clunk that sounded like a tin being knocked over. I looked down to my right and it had been. I looked to my rod tip and it wasn't where it should have been; instead it was pointing downriver, and the reel was backwinding furiously. I was soon in rather nervous contact with a very powerful fish.

Playing a big barbel is absolutely terrifying. They have such power and stamina, rarely moving fast, but with such authority and determination that only a fool or a novice will try and dictate the fight. This fish just cruised off downstream, turned and stopped, not snagged, just stopped and sulking. A piece of drifting weed snaked across the line, and the fish moved inexorably upstream, gave a powerful lunge, and this time it did snag, horribly. By now I was standing knee-deep, with wet boots and cold feet, on a gravel bar just downstream from a snagged barbel. I felt the first wave of that intense despair that only fishermen who lose a big fish can experience.

I raised the rod and gently tightened on the fish, and for no real reason it came free, and a few bits of bulrush stalk came floating to the surface. As it came to the net, the fish did not appear to be that big, but as I hauled it up the bank and laid it on the grass it seemed to expand and grow into a great, golden beast of a barbel. It weighed 11lb 12oz and, despite a damaged tail, was a beautiful fish, and my biggest to date from the Stour.

September 1980 – Throop

Barbel and block-fed maggots go together like, well, chub and cheese, or carp and boilies. To my mind, there is no better bait in general for consistently catching barbel, particularly on hard-fished waters. When barbel are really 'going' on maggots, it is almost difficult not to catch them. This has led to some criticism of the method of block-feeding with maggots, invariably from people who have never really succeeded with them. Although they are generally effective, it is very possible to fish maggots badly, and fail, and also there is a risk of using maggots at the wrong time, or in the wrong swim. I love using maggots, when I can afford it, and the Stour has produced for me some memorable bags and big fish, using what some call the 'plastic pig'.

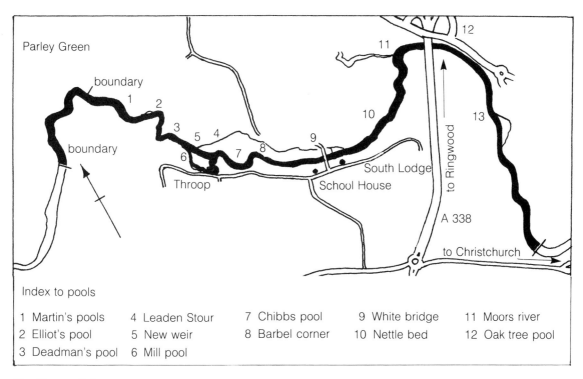

Index to pools

1 Martin's pools	4 Leaden Stour	7 Chibbs pool	9 White bridge	11 Moors river
2 Elliot's pool	5 New weir	8 Barbel corner	10 Nettle bed	12 Oak tree pool
3 Deadman's pool	6 Mill pool			

The Throop Fishery.

Stour barbel are no exception when it comes to liking maggots – they love them in the right circumstances. There are two situations in which maggots can be really effective – first, when you are faced with a swim which has a high barbel population, and you are in the mood to go for a good bag of fish; and, second, if you are fishing for a couple of big fish and you know that they are going to be suspicious of 'lump' baits, or sweetcorn, which can soon become a barbel deterrent.

On this occasion, I had found a swim that was literally packed with barbel, and had caught some bags of up to six or seven fish, first on meat and then on corn. These baits have a limited life, even when fished over a hemp attractor. Maggots can give a swim a new

lease of life, and so it proved in the case of the Suicide swim. When I first started fishing this swim it was like a barbel-fishing paradise – the stretch was syndicated, with only a few members, and it was rare to see another angler. The barbel were plentiful and had not been caught very often, unlike their brethren further upstream on the Throop Fisheries, which later gained control of the stretch.

The Suicide swim was one of those swims that looked very difficult to get fish out of, yet it was very straightforward once you'd tried it. It was an excellent maggot swim, with a weed-bed geography that channelled fish towards the centre of attraction – a big block-feeder. Very open swims are not easy to use maggots in – the whole crux

53

of maggot fishing is to produce a con-centrated narrow trail of feed, and a narrow channel in weed will do the job for you. In open swims, it is best to fish as close in as possible and use the bank as one side of your feeding channel.

There was no need in the Suicide swim – it channelled fish from a large holding area to a tight feeding area just under the rod tip, and once sufficient feed had been introduced the fish just queued up behind the block, almost waiting to be caught. Fourteen fish fell for the block that afternoon, and, if I remember correctly, they took bunches of maggots on size 12 Goldstrikes and 8lb Sylcast.

I have no time for the modern 'improved' block-feeders, by the way. They are flimsy and inefficient, and seem to be designed for a high turnover at the tackle shop. There has been no improvement on the standard cylindri-cal feeder, with soft polythene push-on ends. The argument that a flat feeder holds bottom better is ludicrous, as the shape of a feeder has very little to do with how well it holds. A similar argu-ment has been applied to ordinary leger leads, and this is even more nonsensical when you consider the size of an Arlesey bomb. A lead or a feeder is pulled out of position by the force of the current on the line, it is not pushed along the bottom by simple water fric-tion. Its shape is of no importance, and the best way to hold bottom is to use a heavier lead and/or thinner line.

Anyway, I digress, and holding bot-tom on the Stour is never a problem in summer nowadays. Catching Stour barbel can be a problem when the river is low, warm and clear, but choose the right swim, and feed it properly, and maggots can be a saviour, particularly when block-fed.

November 1985
Free Stretch, Muscliffe

Autumn on the Stour means that the barbel fishing is either superb or terrible – it all depends on the weather. A good flush of warm rain will clear out the weed and rubbish that has accumulated over the summer, and leave a nice, coloured river, fining down and full of barbel, which will have been stimulated into a final good feed before the winter. Most baits will work now, yet meat and cheese can prove very effective under such conditions. However, a dry September – October with a warm settled spell will leave the river low, clear and choked with weed, some of which will have begun to rot after the first few frosts. Silkweed, in particular, will be covering much of the gravel in a slimy green-grey layer. Barbel will tend to feed only sporadically, and spend a lot of time drifting aimlessly about. An area of clean gravel can be a pointer to a concentration of fish, and also fish that have been doing some feeding.

Particles are the key to dealing with barbel that are none too peckish, and either casters or maggots over hemp, fished sparingly and carefully, can prod-uce the goods when all around you are failing. This autumn had been a warm, dry and pleasant one, and the river was proving difficult, yet I had found a swim that was occupied by some good fish that were showing interest.

The swim was a dining-table-sized patch of clear gravel, which glowed like a golden beacon in a sea of dull green weed. This patch was on the far side of the river, and demanded accurate casting and careful feeding. It is possible to overfeed barbel when they are in a sullen mood, and so all feed, whether hemp or maggots, was introduced in the feeder, dispensing with baitdropper altogether. When plopping feeders into holes in weed, it is always best to overcast, draw the feeder back and then let it drop into place – not only is this more accurate, it doesn't scare the fish away for so long.

As is often the case on the Stour, chub were a nuisance, and I had just introduced a pint of maggots in a fairly short space of time in order to try to choke them off, as well as to stir up a couple of biggish barbel that were hanging around at the end of the swim.

The golden gravel patch was continually being criss-crossed by dark shapes – some obviously chub, and some, the longer, more slowly moving shadows, were barbel. Occasionally a fish would up-end and a tail would be clearly seen waving cheerfully, as a snout nuzzled the gravel or worried the feeder.

The barbel were cagey, and not really hungry. All afternoon I had been watching for them and for only a few minutes in any hour would they move up behind the feeder, and grub around in an unenthusiastic sort of way, before languidly turning round and scooting off downstream to disappear into the weedbeds.

A really long tail was needed to fox those barbel, and that is what they fell for in the end. They were by no means languid once they felt the hook, and both of the big ones fought furiously,

burrowing into the silkweed and dislodging clouds of silt. One weighed a fraction over 10lb, the other a few ounces under, and they were fine Stour barbel, fat and fin-perfect.

February 1980 – Throop

It is never too cold to catch a barbel from the Stour, but I must admit that my thoughts turn to other species when the first few heavy frosts have suddenly brought the curtain down on barbel fishing.

Only when conditions have been consistently warm, wet and windy for a few days do I consider winter barbel fishing, and under such conditions one can do worse than to rove around with luncheon meat, and pick up a few barbel from their winter swims. Such swims are difficult to find but as a general rule include any 'flat' water without undue boiliness, and rather deeper water is a good bet. Barbel do not move into slacks in either high water or winter conditions, although I do know people who pick up a few fish from swims that look slack. Invariably, such swims have an undertow and respectable current that does not show on the surface.

I am no expert on winter barbel fishing, although I know that it can be worth doing if you stick at it, and it demands a lot of dedication and accumulated knowledge in order to catch fish in a broad spectrum of winter conditions, rather than just in the mild spells.

One experience really brought home to me how differently barbel behave in winter compared with other times of the year. I was fishing for barbel on a sudden impulse and, armed only with a tin of luncheon meat for bait, I tramped down to a swim that had produced winter barbel for me before. The river was very high and coloured, the weather incredibly warm with a good south-westerly breeze. I collapsed in the swim (a smoker in those days!) and chucked in a few free offerings, followed by a rather large lump of meat on a size 4. Hardly had the lead settled when the rod tip began to tremble gently, occasionally giving the tiniest of pulls. I diagnosed eels immediately, but was intrigued to see these little bites gradually die away. Thinking that the wrigglers had nibbled the meat off the hook, I reeled in to find the bait untouched. I recast with a fresh piece of meat, only to find the same sequence of events recurring – a series of trembles and twiddles gradually dying away, with the culprit – whatever it was – losing interest.

Within half an hour I'd fined down my hooklength to 4lb, and was fishing with a lighter lead and small pieces of meat side-hooked on a size 8, and still no positive bite and no joy on striking – just those mysterious twiddles that died away after a while.

I think a long, soft quivertip would have been the answer, but in the end I contacted two of the fish that were giving those bites, by taking a foot or so of loose line between my fingers and giving a bit of slack when a better pull developed. They were barbel, and, although the two I caught were only five-pounders, I saw much better fish taken the following weekend by an angler using heavy bobbins as butt indicators. He complained that a lot of the fish that fell to his method were deep-hooked!

Since then I've seen barbel caught from a few feet of fast, boily water on days when the cat-ice in the margins hasn't melted all day – and I've had a couple in snowstorms myself – but my favourite fishing on the Stour is in the summer and autumn, when fish can be seen and stalked, lured into swims, fed and almost ambushed. Watching the fish is much of the attraction of Stour barbel fishing, and, often, walking the banks and looking for fish can be as enjoyable as the fishing itself.

The Stour is a beautiful and very special river, with very special barbel. Let us hope that the river and its barbel continue to survive and prosper.

The Upper Thames

STUART HAMILTON

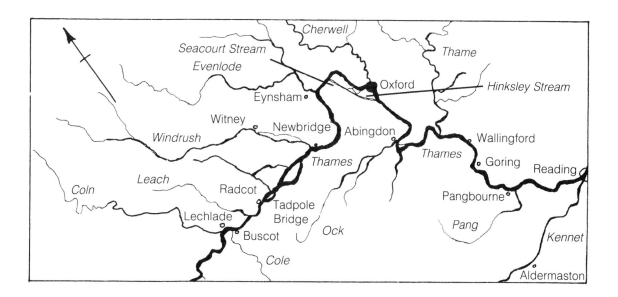

The Fisheries

There are barbel in the Thames as far upriver as Cricklade. The river is navigable as far as this, but just above the Coln confluence near Lechlade it is an infant river. Here it is in a natural condition, twisting and turning over a gravel bed with plenty of ranunculus and other plants. There are shallows just a few inches deep, with deeper pockets here and there.

Just downstream of Cricklade the River Ray merges with the Thames. The Ray carries a lot of treated effluent from Swindon and has caused heavy

mortalities in the past. However, there have been no more deaths in recent years to my knowledge. During the season the water from the Ray adds just enough colour to make the spotting of barbel difficult.

Lots of barbel spawn on the gravel shallows just downstream of Hannington Bridge – I've seen barbel to around 9lb in this area. This stretch to Lechlade is capable of growing barbel to a large size. The next tributary to merge into the Thames is Gloucestershire's chalk stream, the Coln. This river is controlled by trout interests, though the bottom half-mile or so held some barbel up to a few years ago until a chemical leakage killed every living thing in it. No doubt some barbel will return to it from the Thames in time.

The character of the river does not vary very much in size or character between Lechlade and Oxford. Near Lechlade two little rivers enter – the Leach (barbel-less), via St John's weir; and the Cole, via a manmade cut from the opposite side. There are some barbel in the mile-long stretch to the next lock and weir, at Buscot. Buscot weir and surrounds are National Trust property. However, this did not stop Thames Water building another weir, which now carries most of the flow. The river flows on over a mainly gravel bed for about three or four miles until it reaches Grafton weir. This marks the beginning of the Radcot stretch, for which day tickets are available from the Swan Hotel by the road bridge at Radcot.

Three miles downstream is the next weir and lock, Radcot. This is not a very attractive weir – there is no weir-pool as such; the flow simply rejoins the main river. In this stretch, the Canfield stretch, the river has a change of character. It is generally deeper (nine feet or so), its course is quite twisty, there is very little cabbage weed. Nevertheless, barbel seem to be around in reasonable numbers.

Rushey weir marks the upper point of the Tadpole Bridge stretch, which is an interesting area. There is a great variety of swims, and some nice patches of cabbage weed and onions. Day tickets are available from the Trout Inn at Tadpole Bridge. There is a side-stream here, the Great Brook, which holds a small number of barbel. This

little stream re-enters the main river just downstream of Shifford weir.

The next weir, Duxford weir, marks the start of a long, horseshoe-shaped backwater, which – before the Shifford Cut was dug to aid navigation – formed the course of the river proper. The backwater contains a fair amount of ranunculus. It follows a twisting course as far as the ford at the mid-point of the loop, whereafter it flows straight until it rejoins the Cut at Shifford weir. The Oxford and District Angling Association rent the next stretch, and the Angling Society the next whole stretch down to Northmoor weir provides good barbel fishing. Day tickets are available at the Maybush and Rose Revived pubs adjacent to the road bridge at the Windrush confluence. There are barbel in the Windrush up as far as Witney.

I have no first-hand knowledge of the water below Northmoor weir, but it could well be some of the best of the

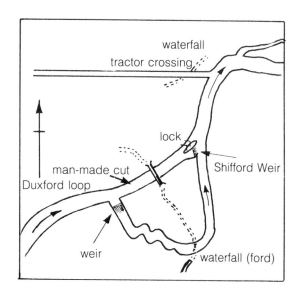

The Duxford Loop.

Simon Lush and John Knowles with barbel caught on luncheon meat from the Upper Thames.

upper Thames. Bablock Hythe, Eynsham and Oxford and its surroundings are all noted areas. In recent years the river around Oxford has produced quite a few barbel over 10lb, as it did from the mid-1960s to the early 1970s, when fish to over 13lb were caught.

Boats

The water quality of the upper Thames is good but the volume of the boat traffic in the summer stirs up the silt and chops the cabbage weed about severely. Unless you can fish in the evenings, you may well find that this boat traffic is too much to cope with between mid-July and mid-September. I don't think that it is the boats themselves that make the regular capture of barbel so difficult at this time of the year; the silt they leave suspended in the water upsets the fish. I don't recommend fishing the main river during this period.

Locating and Catching Barbel

In the early season some fish will be found around the spawning sites – areas of fast flowing gravel shallows. I would not be in favour of subjecting spawned-out barbel to further stress, even though – unlike roach and chub – they don't appear to be too knocked about by spawning. Some barbel do like the weirs and stay in and around them most of the time. These fish are best fished for with the feeder as a straight leger with the usual baits.

On the main river, on a stretch that I was unfamiliar with, I would first walk the bank when the river was at normal summer level. What I would be looking for is cabbage weed in the margins (there are some cabbages across the river, but these are not usually visible). Barbel like cover and in the Thames this is usually provided by cabbages. Barbel may also be present where the depth shallows up quite steeply – coming out of a bend, for example – though this is a less reliable guide. If I can find a good patch of weed or two, I put the tackle down well back from the water's

Simon Lush was rewarded with this magnificent 10lb 3oz fish after a two-year campaign.

Martin Brown with a rare Thames double.

edge and set up the rod, a carbon or glass-fibre one of twelve or thirteen feet with a nice, steady, through action. I use a Rapidex centrepin and 4lb or 5lb Maxima line. The float is an Avon type taking from 3 BB to 2 swan in weight. If the flow is too strong for this, it's best to use the feeder. I use the excellent high carbon steel hooks, spade end and size 14. I put a swan shot on the hook as a plummet and drop it around the edges of the cabbages to find the depth and where the cabbage is under water. I fix the weight about a foot from the hook. I then decide where I want to put the bait and, using a bait dropper, feed the swim with about a pint of hemp and half a pint of casters or maggots.

Barbel often indicate their presence by sending up little bubbles as they hoover up the bait, especially in a silted swim. It is quite common to foul-hook barbel in this situation. If there are a number of fish feeding in the swim, the chances are that one or two will swim against the line, making the float sink quite positively like a 'normal' bite. Unless hooked in a fin, foul-hooked barbel usually fall off. The tackle that I have recommended is, I would say, the lightest you can safely use. If you can get bites by using heavier line and bigger hooks then it is common sense to use them.

I find the float to be the most useful indicator. One has more time to react and with a light current and the fish against the bank it is without doubt the most obvious way to fish. However, some successful barbel anglers invariably use a quivertip for Thames barbel, and to be successful one has to be able to use all the techniques as river conditions dictate.

All the usual baits – maggots, casters, hemp, tares, sweetcorn, lobworms and luncheon meat – will be accepted by upper Thames barbel. For a day's fishing you will need about four pints of hemp and four pints of casters or maggots. It's always handy to have a few lobworms and a tin of luncheon meat in your bag. You can use sweetcorn both as feed and as hookbait, but I feel that barbel sometimes fail to recognise it as food and I do not have complete confidence in sweetcorn in every area I fish. I'm sure barbel regard maggots, hemp and casters as part of their natural diet, as so much is thrown in by matchmen and other anglers.

You will catch lots of other species whilst fishing for upper Thames barbel. This is part of the game. Usually, though, if you are blessed with some feeding barbel in the swim other species will not be a pest. Generally the best

time of day is from about 11 a.m. onwards. Sometimes the fish do not feed during the day, becoming more active around dusk, so it is always worth fishing until after it is dark.

A good time for barbel is the first few weeks of the season before the boat traffic is too heavy. Later on, fishing is largely restricted to evening sessions. Probably the best time for the barbel angler to put some fish on the bank is from mid-September on, until the water becomes too cold. Mild, settled weather is best, with the river almost still. Once the flow picks up the barbel become more active and free swimming, and in these conditions they will move away from the shelter of the cabbages. Obviously such conditions are no good for laying on with float tackle, so use the feeder when the flow is fast.

The Thames is a lovely river to fish for barbel. Usually the fish are under your feet, the average size is good and, although there will be blank days, the good days should become more regular as the angler gets to know the river and locates some reliable holding areas.

The Lower Thames and its Tributaries

BILL RUSHMER

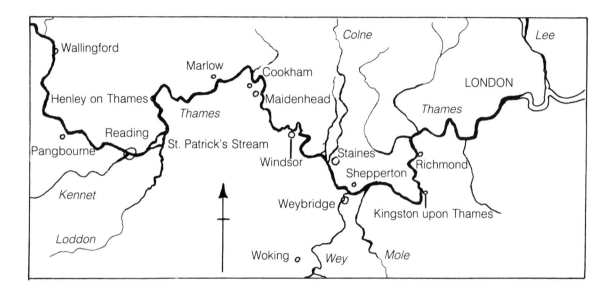

The Thames

At the age of 13 years I started serious fishing on the local stretch of the River Thames at Twickenham. This reach is tidal and in 1958 was dominated by huge roach shoals mixed with a good head of bream. Although I was initially more successful legering with bread flake, I was determined to master the use of the centrepin as my grandfather always appeared so much more successful than any angler legering. He would trot the swim with his old wide-drummed Allcocks Ariel centrepin to take many large bags of good-sized roach and bream. Locally he was acknowledged as a master in the use of the 'pin and he influenced my style of fishing more than any other angler. When he started to teach me his skills he always insisted that the 'pin gave him an edge over other anglers by allowing for superior bait presentation for all species. He was convinced that a bait properly trotted through and fished over depth by holding back was deadly for bottom-feeding species like barbel.

63

Over the next three years my grand-father taught me the art of centrepin fishing so that for my age I was developing into a very proficient float angler. He was so pleased with my determination and improving skill that he bought me a 4½-inch wide-drum Allcocks Ariel for my sixteenth birthday. This reel was to become the main tool in catching Thames barbel in the years that followed. I still regularly use this reel, which my grandfather had double-spoked for me – the reel is precision drilled to take a second dummy set of stainless steel spokes about ⅜ inch from the rim. The sole purpose of these spokes is to hold line without interfering with the balance of the reel – the original spokes are far too close to the middle for trotting. This modification gives superior line recovery without the need for masses of backing line. Other advantages are reduced line bedding and superior line drying. This modified reel with its wide drum is in my opinion far superior to the more modern Match Ariel, which I believe has too narrow a spool for good trotting.

In 1961 I bought a fishing punt that was moored in the tidal Thames at Twickenham and proceeded to catch some very large bags of roach and bream. My best catch at this time was a little over 54lb of roach with individual fish pushing 2lb. Naturally, I ventured into the weir at Teddington in search of barbel but met with limited success as barbel appeared to be very rare in the tidal section. In nearly thirty years' experience I have never known barbel to be prolific in the tidal reaches but they do have the habit of producing the odd good fish. I suspect that there are just a few roving shoals, as identifiable individuals often show up at different locations. I am convinced that many of the breakages and lost large fish involve carp rather than barbel, since experience shows that in the tideway at least twenty carp are captured for every barbel.

In the summer my friends and I would often take a punt upstream into the non-tidal river. As we had no engines we had to rely on the old-fashioned punt poles and paddles for propulsion, which restricted us to the sections below Penton Hook. However, Penton Hook was a good weir at that time and regarded by many as the Royalty of the Thames. But we found barbel in most weirs and likely-looking spots from Kingston upstream to as far as we could sensibly travel. It became obvious that if we wanted more barbel we would have to concentrate our efforts on the river above Kingston.

In the following years I teamed up with my old friends Dave Stroud and Adrian Ellis to fish for Thames barbel. We were lucky in that a friend of my father's had access to a Thames backwater at Sunbury. This water had a reputation for barbel, and indeed it was a barbel angler's dream. It had fast, shallow water flowing over a twisting gravel bed, with deep holes containing many natural obstructions such as fallen trees.

We started one early July morning to leger sausage meat in all the likely swims but became plagued with chub up to about 3lb. I then noticed a youngster walk past me to fish a swim below mine. He was legering whilst feeding heavily with hempseed and was quickly into a good fish, which smashed him up

64

in nearby tree roots. I walked downstream to see what he was doing and found that he was legering two grains of hempseed on a size 10 hook. He explained that he had read in the angling press how barbel were being caught by this technique on the Throop Fishery of the Dorset Stour. Then he had another bite, which he hit to find a powerful fish that was hugging the bottom. Obviously it was a barbel, which he lost in the same snag. I was impressed and remembered that I had hempseed with me, so I returned to float-fish hemp in my own swim. Unlike the swims below, my swim was turbulent and held large boulders that made float fishing nearly impossible as every time my bait left the bottom I caught a dace. I then decided to leger two grains of hempseed behind the turbulence created by a large boulder in the swim. Almost immediately I felt a shivering sensation on the line followed by a violent pull. I struck to feel the solid boring of the barbel. I played the fish carefully and soon netted a 4¾lb barbel.

Dave and Adrian then joined me as I fed in more hemp to continue legering.

'This is silly. We've legered these swims with sausage and cheese and only caught chub. Now we find barbel feeding on hemp in the heat of the day,' said Adrian.

'Could be just a fluke fish,' Dave replied.

'Yes, it must be. Oh, no, I'm into another one,' was my interrupted reply.

This fish was slightly larger than the first, weighing 5lb 4oz. A few minutes later it was followed by another barbel which proved that the first was no fluke. Both Dave and Adrian returned to their swims to follow suit, and were rewarded with instant success. We continued to catch barbel until we ran out of hemp with over fifteen barbel to our credit.

We returned many times to that venue during the summer to catch many individual bags of up to twelve barbel. As it turned colder we noticed that hemp became less effective, and after November we caught no more barbel on hemp.

During the following years we concentrated our efforts on developing methods for catching barbel. We found that hemp appeared to work best in hot conditions when the water was stale, needing rain to bring it back to good condition. Our results also showed that hemp worked best in the heat of the day, whilst the larger, more traditional, baits such as meat were more successful at other times. We also started to modify bait droppers in order to feed more accurately, and we would replace the weight on the dropper with about 3oz of lead, to take it straight to the bottom of the swim. These large bait droppers were also painted black to avoid scaring fish with the flash when they opened on the bottom. These modifications improved results.

As results increased, we carried out even more experimentation and started to float-leger with 12- or 13-foot rods and centrepin reels. These were used with light porcupine quills which had had their sharp tops removed to give a smooth dome top with the line between the float and leger weight lightly shotted to provide stability. Sometimes we found that the barbel felt the resistance of the rod top and ejected the bait. To

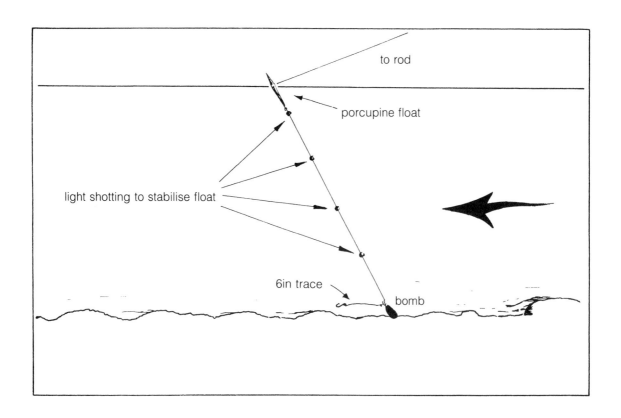

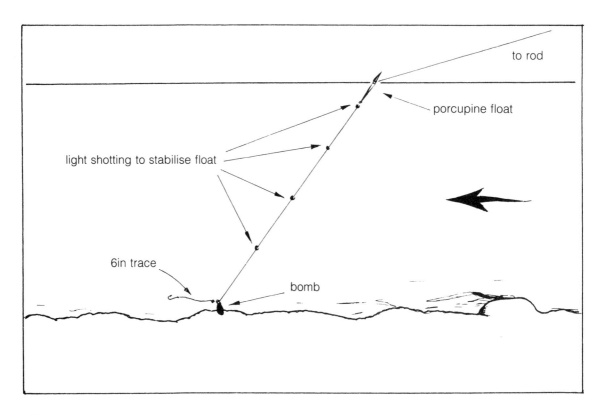

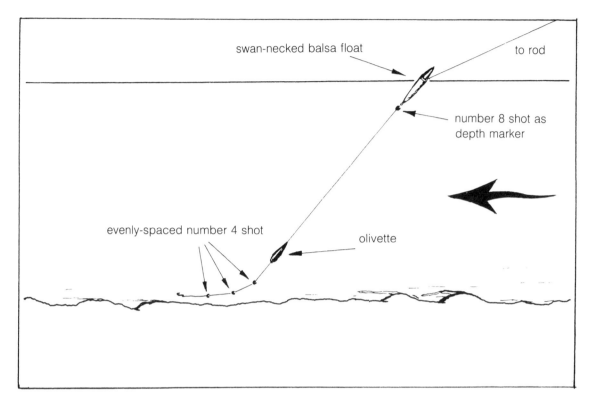

swan-necked balsa float

to rod

number 8 shot as
depth marker

evenly-spaced number 4 shot

olivette

beat this problem we would let the float settle to a position downstream of the leger. With this rig the barbel had a fair amount of free line before running into the resistance of the rod top without any loss of sensitivity in bite detection.

This method, coupled with the use of hempseed, gave some excellent catches – particularly in the Desborough Cut at Walton. We were also – like many top Southern matchmen, such as Ray Mumford – experimenting with roach poles converted into rods to hold the bait further out to achieve even higher returns.

We then decided to join forces with other friends to form the Optimas Specimen Group which was to concentrate much of its efforts on Thames barbel. The group had the advantage of having many well-known match anglers in its membership, including Ray Mumford and Ken Collins, together with a hard-core nucleus that still fished Thames matches. Naturally, we were able to pool information to build up a very detailed picture of barbel swims in the match-fished sections. This was a great asset, as the lower Thames can be a very difficult section to read, with most barbel-holding features well hidden from the bank.

The match sections suffered from heavy boat traffic as well as excessive daytime fishing, which forced a change of tactics to night fishing in order to obtain good results. We therefore gave up using hemp as hookbait to concentrate on night-legering tactics. We would still use hemp in the feeder and in the groundbait but use casters or maggots as hookbait. These tactics soon proved very successful, with the majority of members averaging about seventy Thames barbel per season.

Paul Lancaster was doing particularly well from the Desborough Cut and from behind Staines gasworks. He was normally float legering with hemp and casters and then switching to swimfeeder tactics in the dark.

Our greatest success came from the Galleries swim below Hampton Court Bridge. We knew that the section held some of the biggest lower Thames barbel, but they were difficult to locate. However, they were shoaled up off the Galleries and appeared in many match nets. We immediately switched our efforts to this area in the hope of catching one of the larger specimens known

to be in the section.

Although we met with instant success, it was not until September that catches were at their best. Dave Stroud, Paul Lancaster and I planned to fish the swim in mid-September. Dave was to fish on the Friday night whilst Paul and I were to take over to fish the Saturday night. Dave started his session with a very heavy bombardment with a bucketful of groundbait laced with crushed hemp, hempseed, casters and maggots. He proceeded to use a swimfeeder with maggots on a size 12 hook as bait to catch a total of twelve barbel to 7lb 8oz, averaging 5lb; six bream to 4lb, and ten roach to over a pound. The total bag must have been in the region of 90lb. Paul and I thought that Dave must have

A typical Thames barbel of 7lb 5oz taken long trotting with a centrepin reel by Bill Rushmer at Hampton Court.

fished the swim out but we followed using the same tactics, to catch a smaller mixed bag of barbel, bream and roach. It was interesting to note that our barbel had a higher average size than David's catch. As dawn broke I had a slack line bite that I struck.

'I've got a snag – no, it's moving,' I commented.

It was obviously a bigger fish as it fought hard, hugging the bottom all the time. Slowly I could feel it tiring, and it was netted after a ten-minute fight. It was a large, fat barbel, which weighed 10lb 4oz. We had reached our target.

Although I have always spent some time fishing for Thames barbel, I must admit that I have lost some of my enthusiasm because I found that large barbel were so much more easily caught from the Hampshire Avon and the Kennet. Another important factor is that I believe that there is a basic change in fish populations in the lower Thames. I suspect that carp have in the last five or six years increased tremendously in numbers, whilst the barbel population has decreased. I am now regularly catching carp in with my barbel catches. These carp appear to be getting larger every year, with fish to over 30lb reported on the grapevine by the few carp fanatics fishing for them. But the barbel could be dropping in average size. I too am impressed by Thames carp and will be concentrating my efforts on these magnificent fish in the future.

The Tributaries

Whilst barbel populations in the lower Thames itself are in decline, the tributaries – particularly the Wey and the Colne – have in recent years started to improve as barbel fisheries. Could some of the Thames barbel have migrated up the tributaries, pushed out of the main river by an upsurge in boat traffic and carp, or is it just a natural cycle?

About five years ago, Tony Myott took me to a section of the Wey near Byfleet to fish for barbel. We arrived at dusk to fish for three hours using block-feeder tactics with maggots. Tony suggested that I should fish a fast run below a deep hole and in front of a large weedbed, while he fished upstream. I was confident that the swim held barbel as it was similar to swims I had fished with good results on the Kennet. My feelings were more than justified as in the short session I caught barbel of 6lb 1oz and 4lb 2oz, together with a chub and an eel. Tony enjoyed similar success. We returned a week later to enjoy more barbel catches, which gave us the confidence to put in a more determined effort. This in turn rewarded us with more and bigger barbel.

The following year I went in search of other sections and swims for Wey barbel. I found a likely swim behind a fallen tree which forced the water into the far bank, creating a fast-water swim with a large weedbed between the angler and the swim. This weed provided excellent cover for the fish. The fast water eventually entered deeper water and lost its pace at the end of the swim. This was a virgin swim and I had to cut away nettles before wading into the water to take up a position on the near side of the weedbed. I tackled up with an 11-foot custom-built carbon trotting rod with all-through action and

Bill Rushmer shows this superb 10lb 3oz Wey barbel to the camera.

a handleless centrepin. I thought the swim would respond to a bait trotted down with a 'pin as I could make the bait travel slowly across the bottom and coax it over any snags, ridges and weeds to drop into any hollow.

The reel had a large diameter to help line recovery and a wide drum with no handles to cut out tangles, improve control and aid line drying. The line came off the top of the drum rather than the bottom to give better line control with less chance of tangles caused by wind. I used a modern reel rather than the traditional Allcocks Ariel because it had less than half the weight. This reel was loaded with 4lb line.

The terminal tackle consisted of a swan-necked balsawood float holding the equivalent of 7BB, with an olivette placed 18 inches from the hook. I used an olivette rather than bulk shot as it is neater and offers less resistance to striking. The remaining three no. 4 shot were evenly spaced between the olivette and size 14 forged hook. A no. 8 shot was placed under the float to act as a depth mark if I wanted to experiment with the depth.

I waded out to plumb the depth and found an even 3 feet throughout most of the swim. The swim was then fed with 6 droppers of hemp and 2 of casters by means of the bait dropper with extra weight that I have already described. I started to trot through whilst holding back with the float set 6 inches over depth. I immediately caught two dace followed by a good roach of 1lb 9oz, but there was no sign of any barbel. I repeated the heavy feeding sequence as I was convinced that barbel were present. This produced in the following twenty minutes three fair chub to just over 3lb. I then doubled the amount of feed in an effort to overfeed the other species present. This worked and I soon had a violent bite and was playing a fair barbel which when landed weighed 6lb 9oz. After another twenty minutes I caught another barbel, followed by three others taken at about twenty-minute intervals.

I thought that I had caught most of the barbel present when I had another good bite. I struck into solid resistance. This was a much better fish. I had to give line but played the fish very hard in the limited swim for seven or eight minutes before it decided to bury itself in the comparative safety of the weeds directly in front. I walked downstream to apply steady pressure to force the fish to leave the security of the weed. As the fish left the weed it was obviously tired and I was able to net it with ease. I looked at the fish and quickly waded ashore to weigh it. Two youngsters were just arriving to fish at night.

'That's a good barbel – the biggest we ever seen,' commented the taller angler.

'Yes, it does look good. Let's weigh it,' I replied.

The taller angler read off my Avon scales: '9lb 6oz.'

The lads helped me photograph and return the barbel. They commented that they were surprised to see such a large fish taken on float tactics rather than legered luncheon meat at night.

'Well, I am not. I have caught fish of this size and larger with a fair degree of consistency from the Hampshire Avon. I'm sure that trotting is a very under-rated method of catching barbel. Also, there's no boat traffic on this section, and that improves daylight chances,' I explained. 'I do catch a lot of barbel on legered meat baits, but I prefer to float-fish. And float fishing with a centrepin can present a bait in a way the barbel find irresistible.'

That year I caught a lot of barbel from the River Wey, but none to beat that 9lb 6oz specimen. The following season I moved to another section which was generally deeper and which I thought contained fewer but better-sized barbel. This appeared to be the case as I caught fewer barbel but with a much higher average size. The best was a 10lb 3oz specimen that I caught on float-legered hair-rigged hempseed with the centrepin reel. This fish and a 1lb 3oz roach were the only fish on a very hot day when the river was very low and stale.

The Wey is not an easy river to fish for big barbel as it suffers from flash floods and is at present experiencing an explosion of mini-barbel. On many sections there is a marked increase in the number of smaller barbel being caught, whilst other sections are now producing the odd fish which in the past were noted for their lack of the species. I believe that the long-term prospects on the river are excellent as the barbel spread out and mature.

The Colne is another tributary that is

producing increasing numbers of barbel. The Boyers Angling Scheme section is well known for its large barbel, with the recapture of one of its barbel being reported most seasons in the angling press. I do not fish this section, preferring to give my attention to the lower reaches. In the past I have concentrated my efforts on the large roach that inhabit some of these sections. The roach fishing has been excellent, with many 2lb+ roach to 2lb 10oz falling to my rod. During my roach-fishing sessions I have taken several medium-sized barbel but did not start to fish for them until last season, when I saw two very large barbel spawning. Naturally, I tried to catch these specimens but all my efforts have produced a few barbel mixed with carp. These carp have presented a problem and I am determined to find a way to catch one of the specimens that I saw last season. However, I am convinced that, like the River Wey, the long-term prospects for barbel on the Colne are also excellent.

I have concentrated on float tactics as I feel that other contributors will have more than adequately dealt with all aspects of legering with various baits. I hope that my experiences on the Thames and its tributaries provide the reader with the information that he requires to do well on these venues. At present I would recommend that he should concentrate on the tributaries rather than the main river, as barbel appear to have declined in recent years on the lower Thames. This could be because of the upsurge in boat traffic, or carp, or even as the consequence of a natural cycle. Larger barbel appear to be more common on the tributaries such as the Colne and Wey, which have the added advantage that many sections offer excellent sport for those using float-fishing tactics.

The Middle Severn

JOHN DARBY

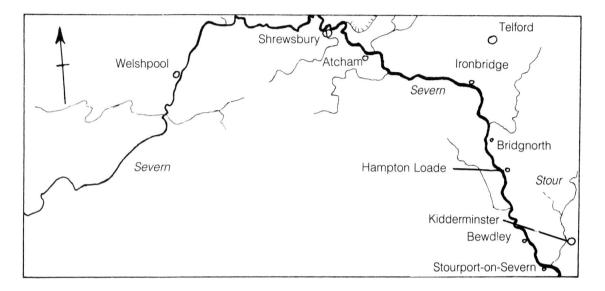

History tells us that the Severn was named after the beautiful Sabrina, who was drowned on her stepmother's orders in the cold upper reaches. Today, as we pursue the numerous barbel in the river, we can only hope that she looks down favourably upon our endeavours. Whether she does or not, it is generally recognised that barbel fishing on the Severn to all intents and purposes ends after the first sharp frosts, usually around November time. Apart from the odd occasions mentioned later, it does not present much of a prospect for the rest of the season, although the tail end in March can sometimes produce if the weather is mild.

From its source shared with the Wye at Plynlimon to its mouth below Chepstow, the Severn is 220 miles long and as such is the longest river in England. It is navigable to Blackstone Rock between Bewdley and Stourport. The area has been referred to as the very essence of the heart of the English countryside. This will raise no arguments from me because, as one of the most happily biased anglers the Severn ever produced, I agree that this most beautiful spot epitomises the pleasantness of these middle regions in general and the Severn valley in particular. This huge rock of sandstone towers above the Wribbenhall waters to a tremendous height and stretches for a thousand yards like some silent sentinel from the beginning of time guarding against the inevitable oncoming boat traffic. There is a cutting through the rock which is manmade and is credited to the Romans, who made much use of this waterway to get to their largest inland port at Wroxeter. There is a salmon pool immediately at the foot of this magnificent rock with a deep cone-shaped chasm, which Tony Hart, a well-known southern-based angler, and I plumbed to a depth of over 40 feet. This hole shallows downstream to rapids of just a few inches, which gives some idea of the diverse contrasts to be encountered on this river.

The changes of moods above and below this rock are most noticeable. Below and downstream, the river is more featureless and overtopping of banks occurs at regular intervals in high water. Lakes form in the fields as the river splits and reforms half a mile or so further on; one such area a mile below the rock is known as Mucky Meadows because of this. During such times, fishing the tributaries such as the River Salwarpe between Holt Fleet and Worcester can produce some pleasant surprises. From the rock upstream, the river is made up of quiet rush-lined salmon pools and an abundance of delightful small islands interspersed in turn with the rapids made up of weeded gravel beds and slow, sullen stretches.

One of the main features of the river is the gully which runs almost its total length from above Wroxeter down as far as Worcester. In some places it is little more than a slight depression following the course of the river; in others it can be as deep as 25 feet. These gullies

are given names by local anglers. The water temperature can vary considerably within a few hours; a drop of 2°C in 90 minutes is not unusual, depending on the time of year. When this temperature drop occurs, it heralds the kiss of death to barbel catching. Several hours before temperature changes, barbel seem to become aware of them and will go off their feed. A check on the level of the marker stick pushed into the river bank on arrival – always a wise precaution when fishing the Severn – will reveal nothing, and re-checking the water temperature will show the same. Nothing has changed, nothing seems different, yet suddenly the barbel show no interest and obviously know that their environment is affected. Several hours later the water level starts to rise and the temperature falls – obvious reasons why the barbel activity ceased, which goes to prove the sensitivity of this species to the environment. The temperature drop is usually caused by the run-off of compensation water from the Llyn Clywedog regulating dam built above Llanidloes in 1964. This huge accumulation of water, some 11,000 million gallons, covers 615 acres. Llyn Clywedog is only ten miles from Plynlimon but the river has already tumbled from 2,000 to 500 feet.

The water – which is released from the bottom of the dam at 96 m.p.h. – is very cold indeed and, at this point, de-oxygenated. However, this is not the only consideration, for the rainfall in Wales probably affects the Severn more than any other single factor. The average annual rainfall at its head is 90 inches, and rain falls for 286 days of the year. As much as 5 inches in an hour has been recorded and this, without any other rain further downstream, can cause a rise of 18 inches an hour in the Severn valley; lower down, the river will rise 15 feet, overtopping the banks in the process. This water is much colder than that of the lower districts and has a devastating effect, especially in winter when snow water makes the river unfishable for several days at a time. Terry Fish, a committed barbel catcher and a good all-round angler, has always maintained that the gravel beds shift with every severe winter, making it appear to be a different river to fish each season. It is certainly true that snags will move and new ones form after bad winter floods. Winter temperatures can drop below freezing-point and high summer can bring the mercury above 23°C. However, the temperature usually ranges between 3 and 21°C. Normally, barbel will not be taken in temperatures below 7° and fishing is seldom rewarding in anything below 9°. Similarly, difficulties will be experienced in temperatures above 19°. The most profitable temperatures are between 12° and 18°, the higher ones being the optimum.

On the brighter side, when winter fishing is a struggle, there will be occasions when after a good spell of mild weather heavy rain will bring an unexpected bonus. If this rain is restricted to the Midlands it is warmed on its way to the feeder streams by ground heat which has been built up by the winter sun, and this in turn can raise the temperature of a dour, unyielding river and bring the fish on. This effect can last for a few days, sometimes until the river again cools naturally or rain falls in Wales. This rise in temperature takes between 18 and 48 hours to reach down

as far as Worcester, depending on the amount of rain, where it fell, and the river levels at the time. Under these conditions the opportunity must be watched for and taken if winter barbel are to be won. Throughout the year Severn-Trent Water Authority officials give a very useful daily report of water levels and temperatures, which makes it possible to forecast fishing prospects.

The start of the season is generally poor until around mid-July, when barbel will begin to 'crash out', which lasts until about September or October. This rolling or basking is often the only way of spotting barbel on this river; there is little other chance of seeing them in the Severn except on the rare occasions when spawning can be observed. Barbel spawn on the gravel shallows when the water is low and warm. This normally occurs during the early part of May and lasts only a couple of days. It is an extremely rare sight which few are privileged to see, especially on a mostly coloured river such as the Severn. To witness it one virtually has to live on the river during this time or be extremely lucky. In some years river levels and temperatures are not conducive to spawning and it does not occur.

The fish pair at the bottom of a pacy glide, about two to three feet wide and fourteen inches deep, between long fronds of streamer weed. They swim up together, the males obvious by their smaller size. At the head of this pathway they turn across the weed to another parallel glide, usually closer to the bank. Sometimes the female is so large that her dorsal fin and back are out of the water as she literally bullies and breaks her way through the weed. Broken weed will often float off downstream because of this activity – the weed is thick and she has to be quite forceful to break the fronds. Oblivious of any observers on the bank, the male gently eases and presses against the female. As many as three or four pairs will be spaced out in these glides. They will regroup at the bottom of the first glide and if necessary repeat the procedure until spawning is complete, after which they will lie quietly at the bottom of the glides. Sometimes several males may be involved with one female, and after being chased she may well end up with bruise marks around the wrist of her tail which are easily recognised as spawning marks. Next day none of the shoal will be visible at all. It will be as though they were never there.

Basking occurs during hot summer days and will be most prevalent from half an hour before dusk until dark. This activity coincides with feeding during the early and high summer. Daytime feeding is not particularly keen, especially on hot days, but before dusk feeding rises to a peak. Normally bites will stop abruptly with the coming of darkness as though their interest has been switched off, even if up until this time the sport has been frenzied. It can only be presumed the barbel have moved off or stopped feeding – the majority, anyway. This happens irrespective of the amount of groundbait fed into swim.

On the other hand, night fishing – as on any other river – is an experience not to be missed. The problem on the Severn is getting permission for there are few places where it is willingly allowed. The Birmingham Anglers Association and other large associations control a good deal of the fishing and naturally enough much of it is match-oriented. Match men, not generally being interested in night fishing, see no reason why others should be, so don't bother too much to stick out for these terms when negotiating leases. Landowners don't particularly want people tramping about in the night and in all fairness in some instances individual anglers only have themselves to blame. It's the same old tale of the majority of thinking people suffering for the few thoughtless ones that unfortunately exist within our ranks. There is some night fishing to be had but a great deal of time, effort and, frankly, respect has to be put into acquiring it – legally, at any rate.

A further observation is the regular feeding pattern encountered. Three or four fish will be taken, then there will be complete inactivity. Then feeding starts once more, the pattern will be repeated over and over again. Terry Fish and I have experienced this phenomenon many times when fishing at Wroxeter. The angler downstream has been the first to catch as the shoal has moved slowly upstream, then the next angler, and so on. As the shoal moves on past, so the first angler has stopped catching again while those upstream continue to catch for a while longer. We have both come to the conclusion that these nomadic shoals patrol a given stretch and back again, a regular route, and are maybe slowed by the amount of groundbait laid down. But at the same time they will not stop indefinitely, irrespective of food availability, as it seems they must instinctively always be on the move. It is possible to sit it out with a solitary bait for many hours without a bite, then another angler will groundbait with particles and will catch almost on the first cast. However, once the barbel are feeding there are times when any bait will be taken without hesitation. All the usual baits will take barbel on the Severn – bread, paste, meat, tares, maggots, hemp, worms and cheese. I have tried to put these in my own personal order of merit, bread probably being the most overlooked and underrated. Salmon anglers often take big barbel on dead gudgeon, on prawns and, of course, on salmon lures. Bernard Sage, who has become a purist barbel angler and whom I have fished with for several years, concentrates on fishing prawns on a salmon pool in the hope of winning his double. Particle baits such as seed baits are often necessary attractors – in order of value, casters, hemp and maggots. Maggots are probably the least commendable as they often attract eels, which can become a nuisance. Particle baits will attract other species, chub and roach being the most obvious. Also the smaller barbel can be a nuisance if big barbel are sought, but this is one cross that has to be borne.

Barbel will be taken from the identical spot where they crash out, which may be a small area sometimes no bigger than a yard or so, and a feeder is a good method for this situation. Accurate casting after the spot has been found is most essential and this can be tricky at distances. A yard either way can render the angler fishless while the barbel feed close to the hookbait. This is where finding that running channel referred to earlier before starting to fish will pay dividends. This gully may be

at some distance and can make bite detection difficult. Some anglers consider that a bending rod is the only indication a barbel will give, whilst others advocate the use of touch legering to feel the tiny plucks given by the fish. On the Severn both of these extremes are correct, though consideration has to be given to prevailing conditions. The pace of the current, the bait and the eagerness of the fish all have their effect. A lot of false bites occur because barbel lie on the hooklength as they take loose feed from the feeder. When an indication is struck at, the hooklength is drawn between the pectoral fins and the hook is partially set in the underbelly between the fins. Last season I foul-hooked a fish in the pectoral fin and we counted sixteen tiny wounds where hooks had pricked the fish recently. To avoid this I suggest shortening the hooklength.

In general the fish that can be expected will be smaller than in many other rivers. Doubles are present and normally at least one is reported caught every year, but these are few and far between. The Severn has been referred to as one long barbel swim. While this statement is rather frivolous, over the past 27 years since their introduction the stocks have multiplied beyond all expectations. Match men on occasions criticise barbel because they tend to be a great leveller when confronted with the feeder, but there is no doubt they enjoy terrific publicity because of this fish. Most match anglers look forward to fishing known barbel swims and obviously these middle stretches are a paradise for this type of situation.

In their formative years barbel inhabit the fast shallows where spawning took place. Here many fish can be taken but in general they will necessarily be small. When they grow and start to rove they will move off, after spawning, into deeper, slower water and tend to inhabit salmon pools and snaggy areas with good cover. This will occur around mid-July and shoals made up of 2–3lb fish will move through the swim, their place being taken in turn by another shoal.

This is most noticeable when the shoal consists of larger-sized fish. One such shoal was located the season before last and with individuals all around the 3lb mark. Last season they were relocated and almost without exception weighed 4¼lb. From marks on certain of these fish it was clear that it was the same shoal. The one exception to this standard size was a fish of 5lb 2oz. Whether it was a faster grower, a fish from another shoal or a female, I cannot say. So far this season this shoal has not been located. Perhaps it has already split up into smaller groups and odd solitary fishes. In some cases these shoals will range up to 6½lb in weight, but by this time the weights will be more diverse – for example, some fish will still be only 4½lb while others have continued to grow. One can hazard a guess that the larger fish are females and will become the solitary fish that one locates in salmon lies, perhaps because they are large enough to coexist with salmon.

Although the average weight of barbel caught has increased over the last several years, the top weight seems to have declined. During the early summer when the fish are shoaled on the shallows cleaning themselves after spawning, if the water is low and clear

it is possible to see the backs of so many fish that they give the impression that the bed of the river moves. At such times the shoal must run into many hundreds. Therefore, the huge bags of almost 200lb of barbel which are reported from time to time are not so amazing as they first seem. In these shoals the fish used to vary from 12oz to 2lb. Normally fish under 12oz are seldom caught. When they are, one can only presume there has been a breakdown or a shortage in the food chain. Today the normal average weight to be expected is between 4 and 6½lb.

A noticeable feature of these fish is the colouring. I have heard it said by an eminent angler that a barbel over 5lb undergoes a colour change from the silver of the recognised small Severn barbel to a gold bronze associated with fish from rivers that produce a better standard of inhabitant. Although this is most certainly correct, this change begins from about 3¾lb onwards. A strange fact is that fish caught after several days' flood appear bleached and colourless. There is little doubt that this is due to daylight being kept out of the water by suspended silt and it is obvious that the fish has been deprived of light. The relevance of this statement is that sometimes fish are caught in clear conditions from salmon pools and have this particular colouring, which leaves one to wonder whether these fish live more deeply than their fellows and so get less light.

The explanation for the decline in the top weights reported may be greater understanding and knowledge on the part of the better class of barbel catcher and a more honest appraisal of catch weights. Another possible reason is the effect of the summer of 1976. It was pitiful to walk along the banks from Bridgnorth to Bewdley and see the very large barbel and chub dying in the slacks. During one such time in the company of friends I came across several barbel in one such eddy where all the fish were close to death. Three of them we estimated to be over 9lb and one of those was almost certainly a double. I have never seen such fish on the Severn since, not on the bank at any rate. It is my belief that the best fish were largely destroyed, which allowed the lesser fish in the shoals to take their place; being so numerous, these never reached their full size potential. Another spin-off of that drought summer is that the year was ideal for fry survival – their predators were cut down and of course food was prolific. Nature has a way of redressing the balance; at one end of the scale we lost the bigger more susceptible fish; at the bottom end she overcompensated.

In recent years Severn barbel have certainly received better treatment at the hands of increasingly knowledgeable anglers. The early days saw many atrocities committed in the name of 'barbel bashing'. It was not unusual to see the pathetic sight of barbel strung out by their dorsal fins in a keep-net after a match or an individual session; they were laughingly referred to as Christmas trees. To prevent this occurrence I have even heard the less informed advised by those who should have known better to cut off the leading ray of the dorsal fin. Thank heavens for micromesh and the increasing knowledge of the specialist barbel angler! Another practice from those times was the tagging of electro-netted fish.

Whether this served to tell us anything, apart from the fact that barbel could swim 28 miles, is obscure. What is certain is that it caused extremely bad bleeding sores on the fin and the associated parts of the flesh of the fish, in extreme cases causing death. To my certain knowledge the tags were removed in disgust by most thinking anglers.

Match Tactics – Mal Storey

Things have certainly changed from the heavy tackle of the early days. A rod of 12 feet is ideal for swimfeeder fishing, the most successful method for catching barbel on the Severn from the start of the season until mid-November, when weather and water temperatures drop. A swimfeeder is basically a plastic tube with holes in to allow the bait to escape and a strip of lead down one side to keep it in position on the riverbed. It is capped at each end to stop the bait dropping out, and is attached to the main line by a loop of nylon and a swivel. For years I searched for the ideal 12-foot swimfeeder rod, never finding the precise tool to satisfy my needs until the British company Tri-cast made a rod exactly to the specifications I required and the Mal Storey Severn-Trent feeder rod was born. Over the last two years sales already have reached 4,000. What is so special about this rod? First, its length. There was not another feeder rod on the market at 12 feet, which in my opinion is an essential length, for two main reasons. On the Severn during the summer months there is a terrific amount of weed growth along the margins on many swims and a 12-foot rod is ideal for playing barbel round and over this weed. Typical leger rods of up to 10 feet in length are really a waste of time for this purpose. Second, when fishing a far-bank swim it is important to keep as much line out of the water as possible to avoid drag and a 12-foot rod enables one to do this with ease. Of course, on the strike this length of rod picks up line far more quickly than a shorter rod. Third, to cast medium-sized swim-feeders, with or without extra lead, to the far bank on rivers such as the Severn and Trent a powerful rod is required, yet it must retain enough sensitivity to show a bite clearly. This task was left in the hands of Tri-cast and they per-formed to perfection. Fourth, a most important factor is that the action of the rod must spread throughout its length for playing a barbel on small hooks. In my opinion, a rod that has some give down into the butt section is essential to absorb those sudden fast, hard runs that barbel produce, and this in turn helps to prevent a small hook from pulling out of the flesh in the mouth, and also helps eliminate line breakage.

The choice of reel is much less cru-cial. As long as you use a reel that you feel happy with, and that has a reliable clutch system, the choice is yours, be it closed-face or open-face. My own reels are Abu 507s. They are no longer made, but they suit me down to the ground for the Severn style of fishing.

I carry two spools – one loaded with 5lb line, which I use for casting a standard 1½oz swimfeeder with up to ¾oz of extra lead; and another with 6lb line for casting the same swimfeeder with 1½ or 2¼oz extra lead. This I have found to be the best balance of lines, for the thicker the line you use the

greater the water pressure and conse-quently the more lead is needed to hold the feeder still. For example, a 1½oz feeder fished on a 5lb reel line holds the river bed nicely, but the same feeder fished on 6lb reel line would need an extra ¾oz lead to hold. My aim is to use the minimum amount of lead pos-sible to hold the bottom and the minimum thickness of line to cast it.

The best swimfeeder to use is the medium-size block-end feeder available at most tackle shops. I use a type I market myself. This differs from some of the normal shop-bought ones in that both end caps are domed in shape, which makes them more streamlined – and come through the water with much less resistance than the ones with flat caps. The strip of lead which runs down the side of my feeder weighs 1½oz – twice as much as many normal shop-bought feeders, and necessary to hold in the faster rivers such as the Severn. Another feature is the way the strip-lead goes over the top of the cap at the top of the feeder (the end you put your bait in). The lid is specially cut, and when the strip of lead is fitted in position the lid becomes hinged. Not only is it now very simple to fill your feeder quickly – an important time-saving exercise for a matchman – but the lid cannot come free while you are fishing, which prevents annoying tangles caused by the hooklength pull-ing through the feeder cap.

The feeder is attached to the main line by means of a nylon loop which is fixed underneath the strip-lead where it folds over the top cap. To this loop a barrel swivel is attached by threading the nylon loop through one of the swivel eyes and then pulling it over the top of the opposite end and back down, securing it firmly in place. I carry extra ski leads in ¾, 1½ and 2¼oz sizes. When fishing a faster moving swim than normal – for example, when the river is carrying extra water – one of these can be clipped under the strip-lead of the feeder. When you retrieve the feeder it planes up off the bottom of the river bed away from any snags, hence the name of ski-lead.

The holes in the swimfeeder really must be ³⁄₁₆ inch in diameter. If they are not enlarge them, otherwise bait may jam and be unable to escape. When using casters as bait, you may find that even holes of ³⁄₁₆ inch diameter need to be enlarged to allow the bait to escape, especially if the swim happens to be a little slower moving than average.

Attaching swimfeeder to main line is a straightforward task. The feeder runs freely on the reel line and is stopped by a leger stop – the shop-bought jobs are fine – about 2 inches from the end. The leger stop must not slip; tie a loop in the end of the main line and attach the hooklength to it loop to loop.

My hooklengths always start at 18 inches. Hook to feeder distance can easily be lengthened by moving the leger stop up the line. For middle Severn fishing I carry the following hooks to nylon: 14 to 4.4lb, 14 to 3.2lb, 16 to 2.6lb, 16 to 3.2lb, 18 to 2.6lb and 20 to 2.6lb. I never use a hooklength under 2.6lb BS because with the pressure needed to get those fighting barbel over snags and weeds it is all too easy to break off. On the lower reaches of the Severn, where the current is much slower and the weed and snag factors are much less, at times a 1.7lb hooklength is quite serviceable.

When tackling up I always start with a size 16 hook to a 3.2lb bottom – see how things go, and take it from there. If fish are feeding exceptionally well a step up to a size 14 hook is on the cards. But more often than not it turns out that a drop to a size 18 hook is necessary to encourage fish to keep feeding. The hook pattern I favour is a Mustad 31381, a crystal-bend forged hook. Similar patterns are Lion d'Or 8408 and Kamatsu B920.

For a day's fishing on the middle Severn the only factor left to decide upon is bait. Had I written this chapter in 1985, the deadliest of baits for barbel would no doubt have been casters and cooked hempseed mixed together at a ratio of about two pints of casters to one pint of hempseed, with casters used as hookbait, or sometimes maggots as hookbait only. The caster and hempseed mixture was always used in the swimfeeder, and about three pints of casters and two pints of hempseed would do for a five-hour match. Before casters and hempseed became the dominant bait on the Severn, maggots were used extensively and accounted for many big barbel catches. For the first time in eight years the 1986–7 fishing season saw a definite swing back to maggots as the major bait. There were still some matches won with casters and hempseed, but more were won with maggots used in the swimfeeder as well as on the hook. I think that the coming season will confirm a definite swing back to maggots as the major bait. A good guideline for maggot bait quantities is about a pint for an hour's fishing, with perhaps an extra pint taken in case of emergency. The only other bait I would take is luncheon meat, and this would only be used in a very coloured river. It would be fished on a paternoster ring with a lead big enough to hold out in the current – 2, 3 or 4oz. A size 6 hook to a 4lb trace tied to 5lb main line and leads up to 3oz would be used. With leads over 3oz I would use 6lb main line and a 5lb hook trace. Wide-gape size 6 hook would be baited with a lump of meat about the size of a pound coin broken from the block. This is a deadly method for barbel in coloured water.

Choosing a Venue

Much of the middle Severn barbel fishing is available to anglers holding appropriate licences.

The 15-mile stretch of water from Bewdley upstream to Bridgnorth is in the main fast and streamy, with lots of fords, gravel bottoms, rock gullies and natural bank life – a haven for barbel. The same pattern continues upstream from Bridgnorth to Coalport and then to the historic town of Ironbridge, where the river is characteristic of the middle Severn.

Upstream of Ironbridge the river changes somewhat: although there are still typical middle Severn stretches, they are broken by some deeper and slower moving water with much less character, and these deeper stretches are not really so good in terms of quality of fish. They do, however, produce some fish, and usually they are big specimens of at least 6lb in weight, quite often 8lb, and occasional fish of over 10lb. Several double-figure barbel have been caught over the years from the area of the power station downstream of Build-was. This is a slower moving stretch of water, of the type which I believe will eventually produce a British record barbel. Between Ironbridge and Atcham lies Cound Lodge, where I believe the very first barbel were introduced to the Severn in the 1950s. Downstream of Cound Lodge is the Leighton water, which overlaps with the top of the Buildwas water on the opposite bank. Atcham, upstream of Cound Lodge, is another area renowned for producing specimen barbel over the years. Another prime example of the slower moving stretches of this upstream area of the Severn which do not produce barbel in any quantity lies below Atcham Bridge, where for a few meadows this type of water prevails.

Just upstream of the confluence of the River Fern, at a swan's neck in the Severn, the river takes on once more what I call its 'middle Severn' character – faster, streamier water – and it is here that we find our barbel shoals. I have not fished upstream of Atcham, but I believe that from Atcham to Shrewsbury the water is similar, with the streamier stretches producing the better catches. These streamier runs certainly hold most barbel. The fish range from 1½lb to about 6lb, and average about 2½lb. When match fishing these stretches anything over 6lb is a bonus and a little unusual. From a specimen hunter's point of view, I would head for a slower stretch of river, where, although the barbel population is much smaller, the individual fish are bigger.

Choosing a Swim

With the river at normal height, there are several factors I would look for when assessing a swim. A mark just above a ford is nearly always a good holding area for barbel. Likewise, downstream of a ford – where the fast, broken water forms an unmistakable mainstream, usually cutting a channel in the river bed – is generally a good bet.

In rocky areas where you can see the bottom of the river, any black patch where the bed is not visible is a likely spot. This is where over the years the main current has worn a channel through the rock and more often than not formed an underchannel – a favourite barbel lie. Willow bushes growing on the river's edge and protruding out into the water indicate another excellent holding area for barbel, and extreme accuracy in casting a swimfeeder is needed to keep it tight against the bushes where the fish lie.

Quite often an uninteresting-looking piece of water can be a productive area for fish. If you look carefully at a piece of water you can sometimes see where part of the water is pushing through faster than the rest. This could quite easily be a holding channel for barbel. Likewise, you may look at the water and see part of it bubbling or rippling. This may indicate a snag in the water – another good holding area. The rippling may also mark a point where the river bed shallows up, and fishing where the river deepens on one side or the other of this shallow part quite often produces good catches of barbel. The so-called 'crease', where fast water joins slack, is often a good place to try, for it often indicates a ledge or underchannel, holding shoals of fish.

One feature I would always look for – especially when pleasure fishing with a free choice of swim – is a holding spot at least halfway out. This is because when you hook a fish it is easily picked off from the shoal without any great disturbance. If you are fishing close to your own bank, a fish being played out tends to disturb the shoal, which can disrupt feeding.

The Lower Severn and its Tributaries

PETE McMURRAY

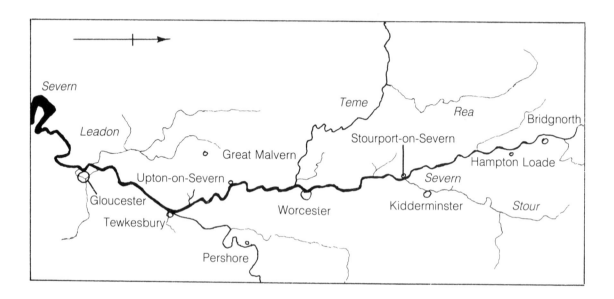

The River

When we look at the lower Severn, from Worcester downstream to the Bristol Channel, there is an enormous amount of water, a lot of which is still virtually unfished for barbel, especially the specimen-sized fish which undoubtedly exist. Many large barbel, fish over 10lb, have been caught from the river between Diglis weir and Tewkesbury. The largest I know to be substantiated weighed 12lb 3oz, and that is a huge fish from any river. So there is no reason why the lower Severn could not produce a fish of 13lb. There are many problems trying to sort out the larger than average specimen, but the first and probably the most important is location.

The Severn below Worcester very quickly becomes a big, wide, deep, coloured river and, surprisingly large boats navigate it up to Diglis docks. To be honest, it does not look a typical barbel river. Do not be put off by this. First appearances can be deceptive for there is a large head of barbel all the way down to Tewkesbury and below. The average size of these fish is 3–5lb and, being plentiful, they are fairly easy to catch most of the time. While they provide great fun and terrific sport, after a time these fish can lose their appeal and the thought of a large specimen becomes the challenge and driving force.

Two approaches can be used. The first is to try to catch as many barbel as possible, hoping that with the law of averages sooner or later you will catch a big one. Unfortunately, I have found that it tends to be later rather than sooner. The other way is to try to find a swim or stretch of river that seems to produce the larger fish. On the whole these swims hold fewer barbel, but what is lacking in quantity is often made up for by quality. One thing I am sure of is that many of the larger fish are roamers. Some appear to stick to one area, but a lot are capable of moving several miles if the mood takes them. They may be in a swim for only a couple of days, or may spend a couple of months in an area before moving on again. Really it is a question of what you want from your barbel fishing. I like to try for the bigger fish, but when things are too slow I will go looking for sport in swims where a fish over 5lb would be unlikely, but where possibly two or three fish can be caught in one session. One advantage of the bigger barbels' tendency to roam is that you never know what has moved into a swim and a noted small-fish swim can occasionally turn up a big surprise.

I have used this approach for several seasons now, splitting my time roughly between two-thirds on harder stretches for the bigger fish and one-third on the easier, more plentiful swims. Not only is catching these smaller fish fun, but it gives me renewed confidence for the leaner times on the harder stretches. By the end of the season you will have landed a fair number of barbel, with a sprinkling of larger fish. To be honest, I just love barbel and barbel fishing and the positive bite and hard fight from even a small fish is something I will never tire of.

Starting at Diglis weir in Worcester, straight away we are in a most productive area. Weirpools are synonymous with barbel and Diglis is no exception. They are different from most types of swim in that they seem to appeal to barbel of all sizes, so apart from being able to catch plenty of fish there is a reasonable chance of a specimen. The problem at Diglis is that the weirpool itself is now restricted to salmon fishing until the end of their season in October. This is a great shame because there is some terrific sport to be had there in June and July. Possibly the large female barbel move into the weirpool to spawn in the spring and there is a good chance that they will still be in the area on 16 June.

If you talk to some of the salmon fishermen they will tell tales of the huge barbel they have caught in close season. I have listened to these stories with an open mind, but experience has taught me to take them with a large pinch of salt. As not many salmon fishermen carry scales the fish are not weighed, and those not used to barbel find them difficult to estimate. I have seen barbel caught which for all the world looked as though they would weigh 10lb when in fact the scales said 7½lb.

Nevertheless, there is no smoke

A good example of a chunky lower-Severn fish, weighing 9lb 2oz.

without fire. I have caught two barbel, one of 3lb and one of 6lb, whilst salmon fishing with 3½-inch wooden Devon minnow. Both fish were hooked fair and square in the mouth, and many fish fall to the salmon anglers on bunches of worms and prawns. Friends on the Hampshire Avon have observed large barbel in the close season behaving very aggressively, pushing and butting salmon out of a lie; perhaps the spawning urge triggers this aggressive reaction to salmon baits. Suffice it to say that Diglis is well worth a try as soon as the salmon season is finished.

A mile or two downstream of Worcester, the confluence of the river Teme is another noted hotspot, particularly early in the season, and has definitely produced barbel to 10lb.

Locating Barbel

Locating the fish is half the battle in catching quality barbel in any river, and particularly this one, so perhaps now I should mention the type of features to look for on a lower Severn barbel swim. Here the river gets wider and slower, and the gravel bottom slowly disappears, giving way to clay and hard mud. With no shallow areas there is very little weed growth, so the water is very difficult to read in the classical way. Bends in the river, where the current is moved from one side to the other, or possibly where the flow is increased even if only marginally by a slight narrowing, are good places. Any deviation in speed or flow marks a potential swim. Another safe bet is to find some sort of snag. Barbel love cover and as there is virtually no weed they make do with whatever there is. Fallen trees, sunken boats, submerged fences – all hold fish. These snags do not have to be huge. The odd waterlogged branch, a few smallish rocks and all sorts of underwater rubbish will attract barbel. It pays to take the time and trouble to find these features, even if you have to resort to casting a heavy lead across the river until you feel it bump into them. Once located, swims of this type can be very productive, particularly if they coincide with any change in current speed or flow direction.

When a likely swim has been found it pays to fish it as much as possible so that a picture can be built of the barbel population. If you are catching plenty of fish in the 2–4lb range I would be inclined to rate the swim as unlikely to produce an 8lb+ fish. I look for a lot less action but hope that the first couple of fish will be in the 5–6lb range. If this happens, it is fair to assume that a better class of barbel inhabits the swim and it could hold a really large resident fish.

A little further downstream we come to what is the best-known barbel stretch on the lower Severn at Beauchamp Court and Clevelode. Quite honestly, the whole length here is one big barbel swim. This venue along with most others on the Severn is heavily match-fished, and, although being unable to fish some weekends can be inconvenient we can turn the situation to our advantage by locating swims with big-fish potential. Fifty anglers all fishing a stretch week in week out will soon contact one of the bigger barbel, so I make a point of talking to the match men about barbel. Most of them are very friendly and helpful, though sometimes a little optimistic with their estimates of the size of lost fish, which are inevitable, with the very fine tackle many of them use. Some match anglers and particularly the top ones are excellent fishermen and know the score with regard to the bigger fish. Their advice on location I have found generally to be sound. In fact, two seasons ago a local match star told me of a swim where he had lost a big barbel right at the net. It appeared a nothing sort of a swim, and it is doubtful whether I would have given it a second glance, but I am glad he told me for it produced several good fish to 9lb 2oz.

The weekly angling press and some of the local papers carry reports of the bigger matches and these should be studied for mention of captures of larger barbel. This approach is particularly useful from Upton-on-Severn down to Tewkesbury, where there are fewer noticeable features and obviously a lot of time can be wasted fishing the wrong areas. Another point which can help in finding swims is that barbel do sometimes roll on the surface, especially around dusk. This is a very good sign because it is my experience that a rolling barbel is a feeding barbel. Basically, I would say that from Worcester to Upton barbel are present in great numbers and you will not be very far away from them whichever swim you fish. From Upton to Tewkesbury, although there are plenty of fish, the stretches tend to be a bit 'swimmy', but as the average size is higher time spent prospecting is well rewarded.

Tewkesbury weirpool is the last well-known hotspot. There is a good head of barbel here both above and below the weir and this area has produced fish to at least 9lb. Barbel are undoubtedly present much farther downstream – in fact they have been reported as low down as Gloucester – but from Tewkesbury the Severn is tidal and loses all its character. Consequently my barbel fishing stops at Tewkesbury.

Fishing Methods

Having found the barbel we have still got to catch them. Most baits and methods work, but perhaps a point or two might be useful to the angler new to the lower Severn. Swimfeeding with maggots or casters is very effective but a large amount of feed is often needed to get through the river's population of chub and dace and a gallon for a day's fishing is nothing unusual. If the chub and dace are a nuisance, the bootlace eels can be a problem so bad at times that it is impossible to fish with maggots. Hemp or tares can be excellent hookbaits in the summer and are almost eelproof, although they do not seem to have the all-round appeal of maggots or casters for the barbel. Hemp, however, is superb for holding barbel in a swim. The relatively heavy grains sink quickly and get caught on the bottom, making the fish really work hard to get them. It

Pete McMurray with a superb 9lb 6oz barbel from the lower Severn, caught during a hotel spell.

is unfortunate that a lot of the effectiveness disappears with the onset of colder weather, but during the summer and autumn I nearly always lay a carpet of hemp in the swim, no matter what hookbait is used. Sweetcorn is another excellent bait which can be used very effectively in a swimfeeder and works especially well over a carpet of hemp. As with most swimfeeder techniques, you have to keep casting to the same place. It is no good spreading your feed all over the river, so pick your mark carefully and keep hitting it. Then be patient, as it can take quite some time to get the barbel interested.

There cannot be many barbel anglers who have not got a tin of luncheon meat in their bags at all times. It must be the number one bait, having accounted for thousands of barbel of all sizes. The beauty of meat is that it is so versatile. It can be chopped into tiny pieces and fished with a feeder, or cut into every shape and size right up to huge chunks the size of a matchbox. All will catch barbel. Meat can be so good on the lower Severn that the match men will use it in preference to maggots, particularly when the river is coloured. Sausage meat was a very popular bait a few years ago before the luncheon meat boom, and it still catches well, even more so where luncheon meat has been hammered to death. In fact the scope to experiment with baits is enormous. I have caught barbel on cat-food paste and on trout-pellet paste and in the future I think we will see a lot of developments in barbel baits along the lines of carp fishing.

When a group of barbel anglers are talking it is not long before the subject gets around to bites. Opinions vary, but I think it is fair to say that the majority of bites will be positive pulls on the rod top. My advice is, if in doubt, strike – it only takes a few seconds to rebait. One type of bite on the Severn which is frustrating is the very fast, hard snatch – suddenly without warning the tip is pulled over as much as a foot or more but springs back almost before you can react. Par for the course is about one fish hooked for every five or six bites. This type of bite seems to occur on hard-fished stretches when meat is the bait. Obviously the barbel are nervous of taking the bait properly into their mouths. They hold it on the edge of their lips before feeling the resistance of the rod and dropping it. A change of bait is not the only answer. Fishing with a bobbin on a long drop improves the number of hooked fish a little, but the best way I have found is to fish upstream as opposed to the more usual downstream or downstream and across. This slows the bite down nicely and, presumably, with no resistance from the rod top, the barbel feels confident to take the bait right into its mouth. Bingo – every one is a winner! The lead should be just heavy enough to hold without moving if the line is knocked by small pieces of floating weed. Paradoxically, the complete opposite of this rig – increasing the size of the lead by what would appear to be a ridiculous amount – sometimes works very well. For example, replace a 3-swan-shot link with a 1½–2oz coffin lead. What we are really doing is fishing with a bolt-type rig. Because of the extra weight, the hook pricks the barbel's lip. It panics and rushes off, giving you a very powerful indication. When setting up this rig, the hook point must be left proud of the bait. Also the hooklength should be fairly short, perhaps 9–10 inches or so.

Talking of leads, I would like to give the old-fashioned coffin a little plug, for it is much better than the universally used bomb where you need to hold the bottom hard. I know bombs can be hammered flat, but even so the coffin lead is more effective. I remember fishing the same swim as a friend who was having a job to hold with a 2oz bomb while I was holding using a 1oz coffin. By the same token, if a moving lead is required the drilled bullet being round is very good at rolling. Leads of both types should be fished on a link of lighter line so that if you get snagged with a fish on all you will lose is the lead.

Barbel are strong, powerful fish and this must be taken into consideration when choosing the strength of the tackle. Lines from 4lb to 8lb are what I use on the Severn, and for somebody new to barbel fishing I would recommend 6lb as a minimum. Hooks must be as strong as possible. I am still looking for the perfect model in the smaller sizes, but the Drennan Super Specialist is reliable down to size 14, as are VMC model numbers 8408 and 9284.

Barbel can be caught at every hour of the day or night on the Severn, but if I only could fish for two hours I would fish from one hour before dark until one after – the classic barbel feeding time. Despite this, many large catches on particle baits have come during warm, still afternoons when it is possible to get the barbel into a feeding frenzy. One glorious afternoon I took fifteen fish between 2 and 7 p.m. before running out of bait. And I used one gallon of maggots and a gallon of hemp! In situations like this it is almost impossible to overfeed. It is hard to generalise but roughly speaking my approach is to fish with particles in the day and larger baits after dark.

From the barbel-fishing point of view the river is at its best from August to October, and later in the year if there are no hard frosts. Unlike a lot of the southern rivers, the first really frosty day signals the end of consistent sport on the Severn, but a mild spell towards the end of the season can bring the fish on the feed. The floods which inevitably come in the late autumn have to be seen to be believed – ten feet above

normal level is nothing unusual. The water is the colour of cocoa, roars through, and as most of it comes from the Welsh mountains it is very cold. I am sure that this drop in temperature has a lot to do with the poor winter fishing; the fact is that for much of the winter the river can be almost unfishable. A little extra water before the temperatures really drop – say, a one- or two-foot rise with a bit of colour – I would rate as ideal conditions for the larger fish.

The barbelling on the lower Severn is undoubtedly good, with plenty of smaller fish to keep your interest and some much larger fish for anybody who wants a real challenge. There are also quite a few in between. My first experience on the river aptly sums up the lower Severn. It had just got dark as I settled into a swim on a sharp bend at Clevelode. Over the inky water came the sound of music, which seemed to be getting louder. As I was miles from anywhere, this was a little bemusing. As the music grew louder and louder I noticed the flashing lights, and there coming around the bend and right through my swim was a disco boat, complete with fifty John Travoltas and partners. I could still see them as the rod pulled over and I found myself playing a 5lb barbel.

The Teme

Rising up in the hills on the Shropshire–Powys border, the Teme starts its journey down to the Severn, flowing through some of the loveliest parts of Herefordshire and Worcestershire. Nobody fishing the river could fail to be impressed by its charm and beauty. The Teme is a lovely river just to fish; the chance of catching barbel is an added bonus.

A wide variety of wild life and birds abounds along the river banks. There are herons, owls, kestrels, and many kingfishers. On one magic occasion I actually had one land on my rod – sadly it flew off before I could photograph it. The Teme is basically fast flowing, with many shallow areas running into deeper stretches. I doubt if it is more than twenty yards across at its widest.

Although the river has never been stocked officially with barbel, the species is now well established and breeding successfully. Obviously Severn fish found the river to their liking and moved upstream. A barbel of 6lb was caught back in 1966 from a stretch of the Teme five miles from the mouth. Possibly this was one of the pioneer fish responsible for the now large stocks of barbel throughout the lower and middle river. They have been caught as high up as Ludlow, where the river is basically a trout stream, and they appear to be spreading further upstream every year. To find barbel in numbers I would recommend looking from Tenbury Wells downstream.

Locating the barbel is much easier than on the lower Severn – in summer the fish are visible in the shallower swims – but the same approach is used. First find the cover; barbel will not be far away. It is a shame that some angling clubs have a nasty habit of asking the river authority to clear the banks for them. Severn-Trent need no encouragement in this direction – because when they have finished

nothing is left standing; trees, bushes, saplings, even brambles and all those lovely barbel-holding snags are dragged out and burnt.

I talked recently to an official of the local club who was bemoaning the fact that their stretch was not fishing well for barbel this season. I asked him if he thought it was just coincidental that the river authority had recently finished clearing all the bankside cover – 'improving', they call it. I realise that some of this work has to be carried out, but they really go over the top. Luckily there are many privately owned stretches which are completely untouched.

The average size of the barbel is lower than in the Severn. There are large numbers of fish in the 1–3lb range, a fair few of 4–8lb, and in most years the odd 9lb fish is reported. The largest fish I am 100 per cent certain of weighed 12lb 13oz and was taken in early September from the lower Teme – in fact only a few hundred yards from the mouth. This casts some doubt as to whether it was a true Teme barbel or a Severn fish that had moved into the river – not that that matters, it was a magnificent specimen from either.

All the usual baits work but I have found hemp and tares particularly effective for taking a bag of fish in the summer. For most of my barbel fishing I use leger tactics in one form or another, but on the Teme there are several stretches where float fishing is very good. Surely running a large float with a centrepin down a fast gravelly run is one of the most pleasing ways to catch barbel. Even the smaller fish in this river fight well; because of its size they have nowhere to go so they tear off downstream as fast as they can.

I have landed smallish barbel with as many as four other hooks in their mouths. These were very small hooks, size 18 and 20, tied to line of approximately 1–1½lb. With this sort of tackle you are going to lose a large proportion of hooked barbel. Now I am aware that the fish can become line-shy in the daytime and anglers resort to the ultra-fine tactics in desperation. I feel that the problem is more one of presentation – baits attached to relatively strong line and a large hook just do not behave in the same way as the loose feed, the bait looks unnatural to the fish and is therefore rejected. To overcome this some friends and I have been using the hair rig for a number of seasons with very encouraging results, especially when using small particle baits such as hemp, maggots and corn. It's not the complete

answer but the hair does help tremendously with presentation.

Local anglers call the Teme the red river. Just have a look at it after a few hours of rain and you will see why. It rises quickly and gets the reddish colour from the clay soil. The river can rise three feet and turn red overnight. Try not to be put off by this. The barbel will often feed well in these conditions on large baits such as meat, cheese or worms. The advantage of the rising river is that it appears to put the chub off the feed, so every bite you get in these conditions should be from our whiskered friends.

The Warwickshire Avon

Joining the Severn at Tewkesbury, the Avon is officially classed as a tributary although it is very much a river in its

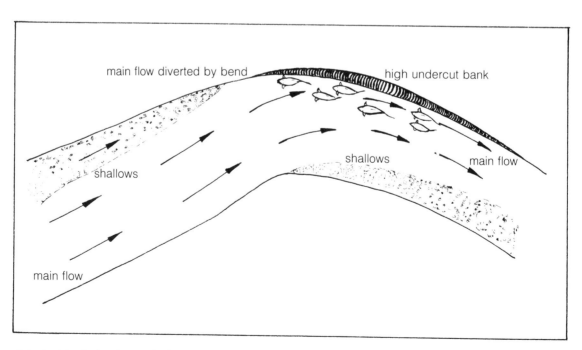

A typical barbel swim on the Warwickshire Avon.

A hard-fighting Warwickshire Avon barbel of 9lb 1oz.

own right. It differs from the Severn in that it is a lowland river winding across the basically flat county of Warwickshire and through the Vale of Evesham.

The Avon is best described as a fishy river. It holds a large head of most coarse fish, particularly chub, which makes it very popular with the match-fishing fraternity. The original stocking of barbel was carried out by the Severn-Trent River Authority in October 1964 with 117 fish from the Yorkshire Swale at Pershore, Fladbury, Hampton Ferry near Evesham, Offenham and Welford. Another 50 Severn fish were introduced in 1973 at Strensham weir and up at Warwick. At the same time the River

Stock at Clifford Chambers and the Alne at Alcester received a stocking. The barbel have established themselves fairly well in these areas – especially at Offenham and up towards Stratford, where they have obviously spawned successfully, to judge by the numbers of small barbel caught. There are large stretches of the river which at first appear unlikely to hold barbel, but some do, and where this happens the average size is high. Barbel, particularly the bigger fish, are great wanderers and I think that this is what happens on the Avon, with the larger fish moving to an area of their liking, perhaps to become permanent denizens or perhaps just to

93

stay a short time before moving on again.

For the pioneering angler the river has a lot of potential; much of it is unfished for barbel and I feel sure many productive areas are still to be found. Once again my approach with regard to locating the swims is to keep my ear to the ground for stories of barbel being landed, or more likely lost; to talk to anybody who fishes the stretches regularly; and to look out for cover in the shape of snags.

In the main I have found that the consistent swims in the Avon are on hard-fished stretches, where there are one or more swims with large permanent snags. I believe that the barbel hold tight to these snags in the daytime, moving out only after dark. It is possible to encourage these fish to feed on particle baits close to the snags in the daylight, but it can be very difficult to get them to take a large bait then. In normal conditions at night with the larger baits the fishing can be very much hit and miss; the fish travel quite considerable distances – several hundred yards – and it's a question of picking on the right swim at the right time. A foot of extra floodwater and the prospects are much better. The fish seem to feed harder and in these conditions the fishing after dark with

Two 7-pounders from the Warwickshire Avon, caught on swimfeeder and maggot tactics.

meat can be excellent. By fishing close to the snags in the daytime we can at least be fairly certain that barbel are close by, and, as mentioned earlier, by heavy feeding with casters or maggots, they can be persuaded to feed. The problem is that they are unlikely to fall to the cruder presentation you get when using tackle strong enough to land them safely.

The hair rig is the obvious thing to try first, but I have found it less effective with the more educated fish from hard-fished stretches. If this is the case you have no alternative but to scale down to lighter tackle than would be normally employed in such swims; if they are played very gently, larger fish can be coaxed away from the snags and then quickly landed. It is well known that the harder you pull the harder the barbel will pull back; even a smallish fish will pull remarkably hard if bullied. I suppose it is all a question of how light is light. What I am talking about is a 4lb hook link and a size 14 hook, which is about half as strong as I would normally use in snaggy swims – I have not lost any as yet. The secret is not to panic the fish by trying to pull it away from the danger area. If you do, the barbel immediately rushes in the other direction and into the snag. With gentle, light pressure it can be coaxed away from the problem until it is a safe distance away and then played out in the normal way. If the fish starts to panic and runs for the snag again, ease right off or if possible pull towards the snag. This seems to confuse them completely for they either stop or head in a different direction. There is a temptation to use even lighter tackle if you are struggling for a bite, but my absolute

minimum is a 3lb hook link – any lighter and the risk is much too great. I have caught too many barbel with tiny hooks to very light line still in their mouths. A top quality stretchy line, such as Maxima or Bayer, is best for the hook links and one of the super strong size 14 hooks mentioned earlier. For safety whilst playing a large barbel on these finer lines I like to use a longish, soft rod. My favourite has an 18-inch quiver tip build into it, and the test curve is about 1lb.

Having seen the damage keepnets can do to barbel I do not like to use them as a general rule, but where a fish is exhausted half an hour in a large knotless net or soft carp-type sack to make sure it has completely regained its strength has got to be better than releasing it too soon. They sometimes appear to have recovered only to roll belly up when you let go. If in doubt it pays to retain a fish a bit longer, it could well save its life.

In my opinion the Avon has the potential to become a big barbel river; the next few years will tell which way it is going. I fear that if there is a population explosion such as on the middle Severn the river will be unable to maintain the faster growth rates and higher average weights being enjoyed on some sections now. There is no way I can see this productive river supporting too many large barbel – not with the huge head of chub already present, which are on a similar food chain. The Severn and Teme have a very large barbel population but a low average size. I would like to see the Avon barbel thrive and spread out without losing the potential for quality. Time will tell.

Yorkshire Rivers

DAVID MASON

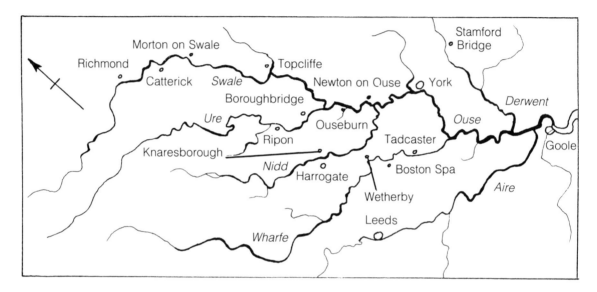

Any angler living in the Yorkshire area undoubtedly has a wealth of barbel fishing at his disposal. Such is the volume of water available that not even the most dedicated barbel enthusiast could hope during his lifetime to cover effectively all the rivers open to him. The main concentrations of barbel are to be found in the Yorkshire Ouse and its various tributaries, namely the Swale, the Ure, the Nidd, the Wharfe and the Derwent. With the exception of the Derwent, which rises in the North Yorkshire Moors, these rivers have their beginnings in the Pennines. The high rainfall experienced in this area and the various land drainage schemes at the heads of the Dales leave these rivers open to sudden influxes of floodwater – a factor that has a profound effect on the barbel fishing.

There are many established barbel fisheries in Yorkshire yet, strangely enough in a county where the barbel are indigenous, lengthy sections, even on the more popular rivers such as the Swale, are only lightly fished. This is even more relevant when applied to the Derwent, where literally miles of water never see a barbel angler and the river's potential remains largely untapped.

Although rich in barbel rivers, the Ouse system does not consistently produce the large barbel that are caught from some of the noted southern barbel waters. People tend to get a false impression of Yorkshire barbel fishing, thinking that our rivers are teeming with double-figure fish. Nothing could be further from the truth. Occasionally barbel large by national standards are caught – a look at the Yorkshire river records will confirm this – but these barbel of 10lb or more are so rare that the achievement in catching one cannot be overemphasised. The most competent barbel angler could spend his days in search of one of these fish and still not catch one. In comparison, it will be difficult to imagine any angler in a position to fish regularly the Hampshire Avon or the Dorset Stour suffering a similar fate. The Yorkshire rivers do vary in potential but a barbel of 7lb or more must be rated as a specimen, and to build up a tally of fish of this calibre would be the culmination of many seasons' hard work.

The Yorkshire Ouse

Wide, deep, and at times featureless, the Ouse rises a short distance below Aldwark Bridge at a point where Ouseburn Beck enters the main river. Here a signpost clearly denotes the termination of the Ure and the beginning of the Ouse. Barbel are found from this point downstream to the immediate tidal sections of the river below Naburn Lock, although it must be stressed they are by no means evenly distributed. From the upper city limits of York down to the weir at Naburn, barbel are conspicuous only by their absence. It is in the reaches upstream of the ancient city that the Ouse is best known as a barbel river. The most prolific section

of the river is centred on the Newton, Benningbrough and Red House preserves. The Ouse does contain other noted barbel fisheries, but they are generally known by past reputation rather than recent form. It is interesting to look back to the 1960s when barbel anglers enjoyed consistent sport in all the popular venues above York. Barbel are still taken from these areas, but reports are of a more isolated nature at present. Recent angling results suggest that although the Ouse still contains a good head of barbel there has been an overall decline in the number of fish present over the past decade. There has also been a gradual upstream movement of the greater part of the barbel population present in the non-tidal sections.

These reaches form what can be a most frustrating barbel river, one that appears to go through different phases. In what is generally a short barbel season due to the climatic conditions in the north of England, the Ouse can fish remarkably well over a period of two to three years during which time barbel feature regularly in match weights and some excellent specimens are taken by specialist anglers, particularly at night. Then invariably follows a sharp deterioration in the river's form. The decline can last for several seasons, when the most intensive effort can receive scant reward and blank sessions are commonplace even under the most perfect conditions.

Why this regular on-off pattern should occur is open to speculation. During the unproductive periods it is easy to assume that the barbel have moved from the previously productive swims and that the problem is basically one of relocation. This theory is partially true, but by no means the entire answer. During these periods barbel often betray their presence, particularly at dusk, by surface activity and it can be most disconcerting to have fish resident in your swim with an apparent reluctance to feed. The heavily fished match sections that take in all the known barbel reaches of the Ouse can see an entire season pass with virtually no barbel recorded. Most rivers experience off seasons, but the Ouse does seem to go through these pronounced phases more than most.

It is always wise to keep a careful eye on the match results, with particular emphasis placed on their locality. Once stories of barbel begin to filter through, that is the time to concentrate your efforts in search of these often elusive Ouse barbel. I was fortunate in that I first tried for these fish at a time when the Ouse fished remarkably well. This period, 1979–82, also saw a marked increase in the average size of the river's barbel. The majority of these fish were over 5lb with 6lb+ barbel there for the

taking. Local members of the Barbel Catchers Club also accounted for some tremendous specimens, including barbel tantalisingly close to double figures. The Ouse is rated as one of the better specimen rivers in Yorkshire, and has from time to time produced genuine fish in excess of the 10lb mark. It certainly holds more barbel in the 7–8lb bracket than most anglers would believe.

At first glance the Ouse represents a daunting task. This wide and unlikely-looking barbel river can, particularly when in spate, take on an almost intimidating appearance, yet with a careful eye for the river many various likely-looking barbel haunts can be located. Deep, slack swims near the bank, with the most gentle of back eddies, are usually reliable areas. These are mainly found where the river bends slightly, and the Ouse's current is deflected into mid-river. Being the big river that it is, the Ouse's features are much more gradual than its tributaries, and these holding points can easily be overlooked. The best time to view such

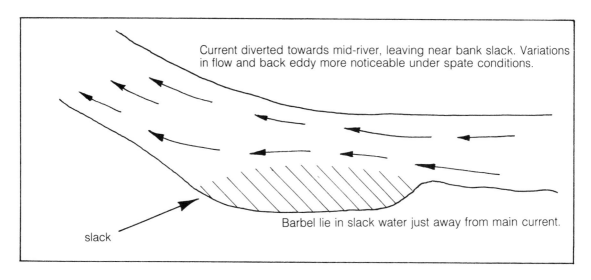

Current diverted towards mid-river, leaving near bank slack. Variations in flow and back eddy more noticeable under spate conditions.

Barbel lie in slack water just away from main current.

slack

areas is when the river is slightly above normal level. About a foot of coloured water highlights these variations in flow much more clearly. Any sudden increase in depth should be taken note of. These depressions are key barbel swims, although not too easy to locate.

Occasionally the marginal areas can be seen to shelve off abruptly, but most of these variations in depth remain undetectable visually. One such swim exists on an unlovely-looking stretch of the Ouse and has in past years accounted for some huge nets of barbel.

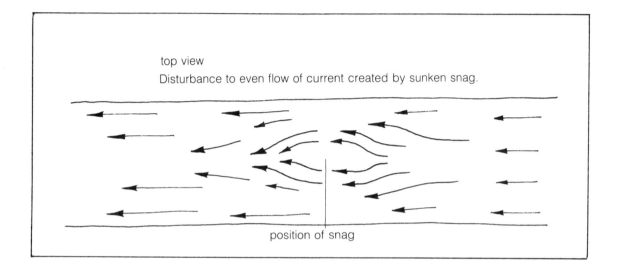

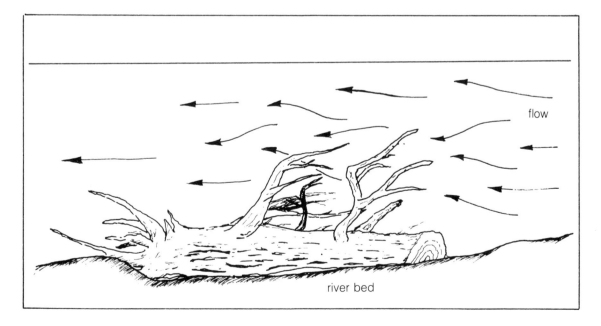

Sunken tree swept down by floods.

A bait cast outside the depression during daylight hours is a total waste of time, the barbel simply hole up in the safety of the extra depth provided during the day before moving up-river to feed at dusk. One wonders how many of these depressions will for ever remain undetected on this expanse of water. My old friend Simon Lush, now resident in Oxford, worked one stretch of the river by boat complete with echo sounder and his findings on the drastic increases in depth were interesting, to say the least.

Without doubt the best Ouse barbel swims are those that contain any form of sunken snag. The most obvious landmarks – such as bankside willows or rows of partially submerged pilings – are easily recognised. The latter also create a streamy effect to the current much favoured by the barbel. Always study the river's surface, carefully looking for any point where the current boils up. This may appear insignificant at first but it invariably denotes a sunken obstruction of some substance, as it would have to be to withstand the immense scale of the winter flooding. Other sunken snags, well submerged, are impossible to pinpoint – that is, until a barbel is hooked and promptly beds itself in one. It is most upsetting to be playing a fish in a comparatively clear stretch of water only to feel that sickening immovable resistance. I often follow the weighing in at the end of a match not just to assess the location of any barbel caught but more regularly to find where fish have been lost. A string of swan shot cast into the appropriate swim will soon betray the position of these sunken snags.

When fishing the river at night the areas that have a distinct edge on all others are those where the river narrows slightly, causing a tunnelling effect to the current. The barbel prefer to forage in these streamier areas after dusk. I will illustrate the point with the following example. During the 1981 season one near-bank swim, although hammered almost out of sight by daytime anglers, yielded good nets of barbel throughout the season. Those of us who fished the swim noticed the sport decline during the last hour of daylight, yet some fifty yards upstream where the river narrowed we would see some frantic action during the first few hours of darkness. The barbel had simply moved upstream to feed in the faster water. In the daytime swim it was a matter of sitting it out until the early hours of the morning before picking up the odd fish – in other words, waiting for the barbel to drop back after the initial night-time feeding spell.

One other aid to fish location on a river of little clarity is to visit the river at dusk in the hope of spotting any surface activity. This is always more pronounced during the evening and often continues well into dark. This disturbance can be quite hectic at times, although there is not always a correlation between this rolling and barbel actively feeding. At one stage when the Ouse was going through an inconsistent period my angling companion Philip Duston, who lives within easy reach of the river, regularly walked the river banks at dusk in the hope of locating any of these barbel. On one particular occasion, on a short section of river we had previously ignored, Phil saw a significant amount of disturbance and the following evening he capitalised on his initiative by taking three good barbel topped by a splendid specimen of 8lb 8oz. A good look at the swim during daylight showed not only that the current increased in pace but also that the area contained a submerged snag – a double advantage.

The Ouse is not generally regarded as an early-season river and it is usually mid-July before barbel begin to show. The best months are from August to the end of October. Occasionally barbel are reported during winter months, but any required mild spell is usually accompanied by torrential rain and it is not unusual to see the Ouse running 12 feet above normal, which makes the river totally unfishable. The condition most conducive to barbel fishing during the summer and autumn months is when the river is in spate. About two feet of coloured water is ideal. Providing the levels are acceptable barbel can be taken when the river is rising and when it first begins to run off, and a coloured river and a mild overcast night are as near perfect conditions as you can expect. I have caught barbel with the river 6 feet up and still rising, but under these conditions swim selection is restricted to the slack marginal areas. With a less severe flood most of the normal swims can easily be fished and, although fishing a coloured river in full flow may seem off-putting, it must be remembered that the current speed on the river bed is far less powerful than that on the surface. The river does not fish well under drought conditions. With prolonged low water levels the various barbel shoals become tightly packed and, although it is always possible for one angler to experience a red-letter day, it does give the rest of us

a false impression of the Ouse's form.

The most effective way to fish the river is to use one of the various legering techniques. Of these feeder fishing is undoubtedly the deadliest method. I prefer to use open-ended feeders and basically limit my choice to just two: the conventional open-ended feeder to which extra strips of lead can be added when fishing far-bank swims or during spate conditions; and the Drennan feeder link with one end removed and the link reversed with swan shot added to reach the required weight. As on any barbel river, the list of successful baits is extensive. My choice is governed by the various river conditions under which I expect to fish. By far the most consistent daytime bait during normal levels is caster, particularly when used in combination with hemp. Maggots and meat-based baits are more effective when the river is coloured. During night sessions the smell factor of meat and cheese paste pays off, while maggots come into their own as the season progresses and the eel activity dies down. During the hours of darkness it is noticeable that the bites on meat baits become more cagey during the autumn period, and a switch to maggots usually sees a return to the more confident bite associated with the barbel. For bite detection I rely on a range of quiver tips and adapt these to house isotopes for night-time fishing.

While one's first thought on the Ouse may be to cast well out into the river, many of the best swims are within a rod's length of the side, particularly those with any willow cover. However, the steep nature of the flood banking may necessitate a lengthy downstream cast to reach the required position.

Therefore, if it is possible to negotiate the bank tops safely, I set up a second rod complete with bait dropper and work myself downstream before depositing a carpet of feed over which my hookbait will be cast. It is critical to concentrate any feed into as confined an area as possible, especially on a river with no easily defined feeding routes.

The Ouse is an often neglected barbel river, possibly because its sprawling features lack the charismatic quality of its tributaries. This is unfortunate because the Ouse is capable of producing barbel in quantity and until recently this river was rated second only to the Derwent as being the Yorkshire river most capable of giving up a barbel large by national standards. I must admit that the Ouse is one of my favourite rivers and is certainly the most consistent night time river I have fished. The rapidly diminishing light regularly prompts a positive response from the barbel on a river that has appeared lifeless throughout the day. An awareness of the fish's presence is heightened as the barbel begin to break the surface with an ever-increasing regularity. This contributes to the attraction of fishing the Ouse, with the hopeful culmination being the capture of a specimen barbel from what is a most unlikely-looking river.

Kevin Clifford returns an upper-Ure barbel.

The Ure

A great deal of what is applicable to the Ouse is relevant to the lower Ure. The Ouse is purely a south-bound continuation of this river. The weirs at Newby Hall and Boroughbridge offer welcome relief on what is a typical lowland river, consisting mainly of long, deep stretches of water. Barbel frequent the streamy sections below the weirs and are dispersed throughout the river's course. It is to the river's final reaches before it joins the Ouse that the lower Ure owes much of its reputation as a barbel river. This section, taking in the lengthy Dunsforth and Aldwark fisheries, is a noted barbel water and one that is highly regarded for its ability to produce specimen fish. Like the Ouse, the lower extremities of the Ure are considered to be more productive during the hours of darkness, and the almost total night ban that now exists in this area has made the barbel fishing an increasingly difficult proposition. These restrictions exist on many other sections of the various Yorkshire rivers, and it is essential to ensure that night-time angling is allowed and the appropriate permission is obtained before starting to fish. The problems encountered on the lower river bear little resemblance to those experienced in the upper barbel-holding reaches.

The Ure in the Ripon area changes dramatically in appearance to a river consisting of alternating pools, glides and rapids. Aquatic plant growth is confined to mosses and in high summer to a blanket of algae which can cause severe difficulties to the coarse angler, particularly when leger tactics are employed. The bottom is made up of pebbles ranging from matchbox size to boulders. In common with other spate rivers the key to success on the upper Ure is to catch the river when it is carrying extra water, preferably as the river is fining down. The time of year also seems to influence the barbels' willingness to take a bait. At the start of the Yorkshire season barbel will probably still be occupying the spawning areas and in the period directly after spawning the fishing is difficult, especially so when the weather is dry. During high summer the flow rate decreases and the fish seem to feed only at dawn and dusk, the early morning finding the barbel ranging over the shallows where they can be stalked and a bait presented to intercept them. As the day progresses the barbel will retire to form tight shoals in areas of cover, usually in the form of overhanging willows or sometimes a deeper, steadier patch of water. Towards autumn the barbel begin to feed in earnest, with the best of the fishing being from September through to the first frosts. All this is of course subject to the whims of weather. The Ure is an extremely volatile river and can rise with an alarming rapidity.

The first issue confronting a newcomer to the river is fish location. The two major techniques for locating Ure barbel are by direct observation or by tapping local knowledge and concentrating on the established barbel swims. Many of these are close to the bank, under fallen trees or similar snags. Depressions are always worth a try and are often the result of floodwater scouring out the bottom because of a constriction caused by trailing or sunken willows. If you see a shoal of chub hanging around a snag, try feeding them with casters and maggots for a while. The feeding activity of the chub can often stimulate hidden barbel, which may betray their presence by flashing or giving a glimpse of their orange fins, which are easier to spot than the outline of the fish itself.

The barbel shoals comprise fish of all sizes ranging up to about 7lb. During the day the fish become tightly packed and I know of one angler who counted over fifty barbel lying in a solid mass in a slight depression, all refusing to take any offerings of loose feed. There are reports of larger fish but, as is often the case, they are more solitary in habit and do not frequent the known barbel hotspots.

Tactics on the Ure are much the same as for any other barbel river except that the feeder seems less effective on the upper reaches. With plenty of water coming through roving leger tactics tend to score, but when the river is lower, particularly towards autumn, float fishing can be deadly. Phil Glossop, who has fished the Ripon area extensively, and to whom I am grateful for much of my information on the Ure, accounted for over 70 barbel one season, with 41 of these coming in just three trips. On these occasions all the fish succumbed to a moving bait. This just shows the inconsistency of these reaches – the normal form was just to pick up the odd fish or two and achieving this often required switching swims and covering a considerable distance of river before the barbel were located. A friend of Phil's also experienced the same frustration, having to work very hard for his fish. He took over a hundred barbel in the same season, 84 of which fell in only four sessions. So despite a high annual return of barbel, the fishing is not as easy as it would first appear.

On the popular stretches, where the barbel see quite a bit of feed introduced by anglers, baits such as meat and casters are firm favourites, but on the little-fished or exclusive stretches lobworms are a must. These areas are run basically as trout fisheries and therefore the barbel see little of the more conventional baits. Here naturals are the order of the day, with lobs being an easily obtainable and proven bait.

The upper barbel-holding reaches of the Ure do not seem to fish well at night – possibly because of their northerly location and the resulting sharp drops in temperature. The dawn period is always considered to be the most productive time here. During the early years of the Barbel Catchers Club a couple of our members, including Dave Plummer, obtained permission to fish Brian Morland's syndicate water in the heart of Wensleydale and they certainly found this to be the case.

Their exploits in taking barbel often in exceptionally shallow water during the early morning proved to be fascinating, especially to those of us who had concentrated on other barbel rivers where fish spotting was impracticable. Here it paid to be as mobile as possible, searching out the different groups of fish. This proved to be barbel fishing in its most intimate form. On many occasions it was simply a matter of dropping a link-legered lobworm directly in the path of a barbel working its way upstream, and relying for bite indication on touch legering or, more often, seeing the fish pick up the bait.

The disturbance of playing a powerful fish in shallow water obviously disturbed other members of the shoal – hence the necessity for the angler to be continually on the move.

The alternating character of the Ure certainly offers the barbel fisherman a sharp contrast in his approach to the river. It is difficult to imagine that the crystal-clear water of the upper section of the Ure eventually gives way to the wide, sluggish reaches of the lower reaches.

The Swale

The Swale is the best known nationally of the Yorkshire barbel rivers, and holds a good head of fish. The species is present from below Richmond down to the river's confluence with the Ure at Myton. Most of the serious barbel fishing takes place on the lower river, this section coming under intense pressure during the summer months.

The river downstream of Topcliffe weir has long been noted as a prime barbel fishery and although it is difficult to imagine any area of the Swale not receiving the attention of the barbel specialist, the reaches upstream of the famous weir are lightly fished in comparison.

The upper barbel-holding regions of the river resemble a typical trout stream. Tumbling over gravel beds, the Swale at this stage is swift-flowing, mainly shallow and gin-clear, with the deeper glides proving to be the most consistent holding points. I remember fishing the Catterick section of the river, where the Swale is ideally suited to float fishing, and by 'trotting off the stones' – the term used popularly at the time – and loose feeding heavily with maggots it was possible to accumulate some outstanding catches in this type of swim.

The upper Swale is an excellent barbel water in its own right, but the

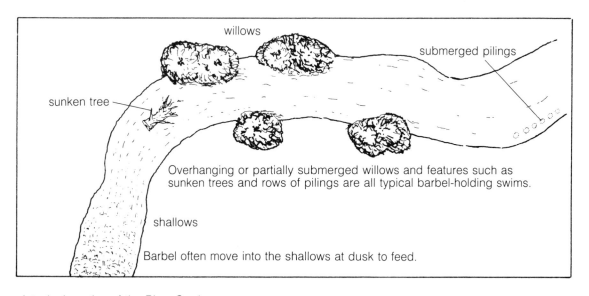

A typical section of the River Swale.

downstream reaches are more readily associated with the barbel angler. As it winds its way between steep flood banking, the physical characteristics of the Swale vary considerably, ranging from deep, slow moving reaches to the faster sections of water that make up much of the river. Even on the more sedate stretches the river is unlikely to cover any considerable distance before its flow is disrupted by areas of gravelly shallows. The margins are often bordered by dense willow growth and, although other lengthy sections contain little bankside cover, the Swale always retains an attractive appearance.

The shallows are always a good starting point when in search of barbel, especially at dusk when the fish move into these well oxygenated areas to feed. Here barbel can regularly be taken in just a few inches of water, often a tell-tale dorsal fin breaking the surface to betray the movements of a fish working its way along the margins. In daylight many holding points are close to these shallows, sometimes at the tail end of the fast runs, where the current is usually diverted along one bank, creating a deeper channel of water. The abundance of streamer weed present during the summer months provides the necessary cover. Once the pace of the current begins to even out and the weed growth largely disappears, barbel can take refuge in the various depressions in the river bed. These variations in depth can be just a few feet in length and only inches deeper than the surrounding area and yet are still capable of holding several barbel, the fish using the extra depth to rest from the rigours of the main current.

Alan Davies, who lived just eighty yards from the Swale, found three of these swims in a short section of river directly downstream of an area of shallows. He worked out the barbel's movements by concentrating in the slightly deeper swims during the day. A bait accurately presented in each swim in turn often produced a fish while one trotted down the wrong line invariably resulted in many wasted hours fishing. The barbel then moved upstream into the faster water at dusk and Alan proved this by catching barbel progressively nearer to the shallows as the evening progressed.

These streamier sections of the river, however, are noted for the quantity rather than quality of their barbel. To seek out the Swale's better fish a change

Dave Mason with an above-average brace of Swale barbel.

of mark is required. The river's specimen barbel are to be found in the much steadier, deeper areas, which often house some formidable submerged obstruction. Sunken trees, lines of pilings now in the river's main course as a result of bank erosion, bankside willows or, better still, willows actually growing in the river, all offer the chance of a barbel. The most snag-ridden spots are generally considered to be the best barbel swims. Many of these unfortunately owe their reputation to an unacceptably high rate of lost fish. With the bait anchored only a short distance away from any snag, the action is short-lived – a searing run of immense power results in the inevitable breakage. The line is usually badly frayed on a tangled mass of submerged roots and parts with only minimal resistance. What could be termed a standard snag-fishing gear – rods of 1¾lb test curve and 8lb line – can be totally inadequate at times.

Jon Wolfe, a member of the Barbel Catchers Club from the Halifax area, has concentrated almost exclusively on these snag-ridden swims and in recent years has achieved a consistently high return of specimen barbel from the river. The most successful of the various methods employed is one both Jon and I have had to resort to and requires the use of extra-strong tackle, so much so that it may appear totally out of proportion to the species. We use powerful rods of 2½lb test curve and lines rarely less than 12lb BS tied direct to strong eyed hooks. The innovation

Alan Slater at full stretch tries to dislodge a Swale barbel from a snaggy swim.

of the hair rig has become a most important extension to the barbel angler in these circumstances and allows a more natural presentation of the bait. This set-up may seem crude but any bite indication can be extremely violent and the risk of leaving barbel with hooks and lines trailing from their mouths is largely avoided. The power of the rod has to be utilised to the full to bully the fish into open water as quickly as possible, and with the river bed often littered with unseen snags the barbel must not be given its head.

These tactics have proved extremely efficient in what had previously been considered impossible swims; it really comes down to a brief trial of strength between one's choice of tackle at one end and the streamlined power of the barbel at the other, with the ensuing struggle over in a very short period of time. During a two-day session on the river I remember Jon accounting for a superb barbel of exactly 9lb, with a slightly smaller fish of 8lb 5oz falling to my rod the following day. Both these fish were hooked and landed in well under a minute. The rod at times took on an alarming bend but, apart from the discomfort of aching arm muscles, the barbel were landed with only minimal fuss. Other anglers fishing the same area had great difficulty in controlling even much smaller fish on their initial runs and the percentage of fish landed was very low indeed.

Occasionally, more balanced tackle can be used even in the snaggiest of areas, but this is totally dependent on the position of the snag. Take, for example, a sunken willow on the opposite bank. Rather than allowing your bait to rest just upstream of the willow, it must be dropped alongside it. The resulting strike usually sends the barbel hurtling down river into safer water, where with luck the fish can be played out before being netted. Barbel can be very stupid and they do have a tendency to pull hard in the opposite direction to the strike and, regardless of any nearby safety, set off on a long, raking run. When the river's flow becomes sluggish because of consistent low levels, the barbel often prefer to lie alongside these snags: the offending obstruction creates a much-needed injection of pace which allows any items of food to be easily intercepted.

With the exception of the shallows, night-time fishing can present more problems than those encountered during the day. As darkness descends on the river the barbel leave the cover of their daytime haunts in search of food and those anglers who select any of the noted daytime pegs may remain fishless for several hours, usually until the early hours of the morning. This period before dawn sees the barbel again take up residence in the more conventional-looking swims. A switch of swim immediately after dusk can pay dividends and the most unlikely-looking areas can turn up a barbel. The main advantage of fishing after dark is that barbel can be hooked well away from any snags, which offers the rare luxury of playing a fish in open water.

The Swale does have a reputation for producing specimen barbel but it is only in recent years that the river has lived up to its name. During the late 1970s Archie Braddock, then the records officer of the Barbel Catchers Club, wrote a series of articles in one of the angling monthlies and made refer-

over 9lb recorded from different areas of the river, particularly from the lower reaches. Jon certainly underlined the improved capabilities of the river by landing a truly memorable fish of 11lb 4oz in the autumn of 1985. Providing a common-sense approach to location is adopted, the Swale at present must be one of Yorkshire's best bets for anglers fishing selectively for specimen barbel.

The Nidd

This is a lovely little barbel river and an undoubted joy to fish. From time to time barbel are reported from upstream of Knaresborough, but realistically the barbel fishing takes place from this point down to the river's confluence with the Ouse at Nun Monkton. The river is attractive throughout its length and these lower barbel holding-regions are no exception. The Nidd at this stage runs over a series of weirs and, while it never attains any great width, the river narrows noticeably as it nears the Ouse. Snaking its way across the Vale of York, the Nidd alternates in character. Steady glides lined with willows are broken up by areas of gravelly shallows rich in streamer weed.

Locating fish is not a difficult problem as the river's good looks inspire confidence. High banking built in aid of flood prevention provides a good vantage-point for viewing any likely-looking area. The most productive sections are in the vicinity of the river's many bends. Look first for any darker areas of water that signify a sudden increase in depth and then for any feature that provides the overhead cover that all barbel love. This usually comes in the form of one of the Nidd's numer-

Dave Mason cradles a chunky 11lb 6oz Swale barbel, a club record for the river.

ence to the fact that Swale barbel had relatively poor growth rates. Earlier, scale readings taken from fish in both the lower and middle reaches of the Swale showed that barbel weighing more than 5lb were old fish of thirteen years or more, and at that time they were considered specimens for the rivers. Occasionally much larger barbel were reported, but with certain sections of the river very heavily fished the odd good specimen taken amongst many other smaller ones gave a misleading impression of the river's potential. The river has gone through a distinct change and at present is producing some tremendous barbel. These are often reported from areas that gave up fish of only modest proportions a few years ago. There is a good head of 7lb+ fish present and each season sees barbel of

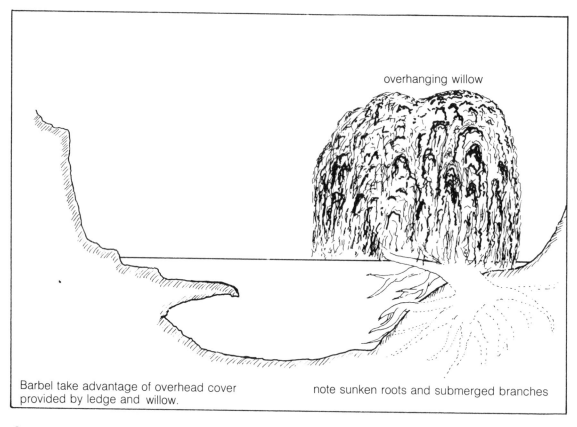

Barbel take advantage of overhead cover provided by ledge and willow.

overhanging willow

note sunken roots and submerged branches

Cross-section of a River Nidd barbel swim. This may contain overhanging willow or an undercut ledge, or be a combination of the two.

ous overhanging willows or undercut ledges, easily visible on this small Ouse tributary. These are without doubt the most consistent of swims and a combination of the two provides the classic Nidd barbel holding point, though they should never be fished to the exclusion of all other areas.

One example, and a particular favourite of mine, was at the end of a fast section of water. Here the river widened considerably, leaving a sheltered glide on either side of the main current. This proved to be a most consistent swim during the summer months, with the fish lying just inside the steady water away from the main flow. Not even the continual casting of a large block-end feeder into what was a relatively shallow glide seemed to diminish the barbel activity.

Many of the river's noted barbel swims require a sensible choice of rod and line, particularly when you are confronted by an impenetrable line of willows. Fragile tackle has no place here, for the barbel when hooked will make several desperate lunges towards the safety of the various sunken roots and branches so prevalent in these areas. A stepped-up approach is essential in many of the river's fearful-looking

Phil Duston nets a good Nidd barbel.

swims, especially when a legered bait is allowed to roll directly under the willow cover. One's outlook must remain flexible, methods should be changed when the features of any holding area dictate it. An isolated willow often offers a favoured swim and, if you position yourself well above such a point and revert to float fishing tactics, with plenty of loose feed introduced, it is possible to entice the barbel into open water. This gives those vital extra few yards to gain the upper hand on the barbel during its first explosive run. Several of the river's swims, however, can be extremely deceptive in appearance. Willows that reach well out from the margins, rather than penetrating the

water to any great degree, simply spread themselves across the surface of the river. The natural instinct of the barbel angler is to apply maximum pressure when a fish nears the willow but, if the rod is kept low and the terminal tackle free from any willow branches, a barbel can be played out in comparative comfort.

Typical of all Dales rivers, the Nidd displays many pleasing variations in flow yet the current speed directly upstream of certain willows can be almost static. Such swims are ignored by the majority of barbel anglers but always offer the possibility of an above-average barbel for the river. Like its parent river the Ouse, the Nidd benefits from an influx of coloured water, and with the reduced light penetration the barbel are more willing to leave the safety of their normal swims. The importance of fishing a narrow, snaggy river under these circumstances does not need to be elaborated upon.

There has been a marked increase in the average size of the river's barbel in recent years but even so the Nidd does not compare favourably with some of the other Yorkshire rivers in its potential to produce specimen barbel. At one time the best chance an angler had of picking up a big barbel was to concentrate on the lower reaches downstream of Kirk Hammerton, where Ouse fish entered the river to spawn. These barbel were generally of a higher average size and any exceptional specimen, usually taken during the early months of the season, was in all probability an Ouse fish caught before it dropped back into the main river. At this time of the year the lower Nidd held two distinct groups of fish – the resident barbel, fish that were mainly territorial; and good numbers of Ouse barbel. These fish, besides making inroads into the Nidd, covered considerable distances in the Ouse itself. Much of this information came from tagging and dye-marking carried out in the early 1970s.

However, the building of a gauging weir just below Skip Bridge, only a short distance away from Nidd Mouth, has obstructed the passage of most of these to the spawning grounds upstream. A spring flood is essential to ensure that the barbel can bypass this barrier. The recent construction of a second weir only a few yards below the original gauging weir, in an attempt to raise the river level, may have made this obstacle

less formidable.

The decline in migratory fish movements has led to a reduced demand on the Nidd's resources from this point up to the weir at Hammerton. This has coincided with increased reporting of quality barbel from this section of the river. Fish of 6lb are much more in evidence nowadays and, while the river contains far fewer 7lb+ barbel than would be present in the Swale, for example, such specimens are accounted for each year.

The fact that there has been a marked change in the barbel fishing on this river is apparent. Many instances clearly prove this point and one occasion immediately springs to mind. During the 1973 season I spent two evening sessions fishing a swim containing a partially sunken tree that covered two-thirds of the river's width. In this short period I accounted for seventeen barbel, all taken on float-fished maggots. The best fish scaled slightly over 4lb. The rest ranged between 1½ and 3½lb. This sort of catch, in terms of both numbers and size, would be most unlikely at present. The diminished influence of the Ouse and the resulting lower density of the barbel population have contributed to the escalating numbers of larger fish reported in this part of the river. Yet this trend of fewer but better-quality fish has been mirrored in many of the reaches upstream. Bearing in mind the Nidd's past reputation, the transition on this river has been quite remarkable. From Cowthorpe down to the York Amalgamation holdings at Tockwit, barbel nearing the 7lb mark are being taken on a level that would have been unthinkable a few years ago. A quite

Dave Plummer with his record Wensum barbel of 13lb 6oz.

(Above)   Jon Wolfe with a lovely
10lb 15oz barbel from the Derwent.

(Left)   Colin Woods gazing at a sleek
9lb Hampshire Avon barbel.

(Opposite)   A very happy Andy Orme
shows off his 13lb 7oz Avon monster.

(Above)   Ray Walton pleased with a
10lb 11oz Royalty specimen.

(Right)   Phil Duston with a good
6lb 14oz Nidd barbel.

(Above)   Dave Morphen with a fine
River Swale fish weighing 8lb 9oz, which
he caught in September 1986.

(Left)   Dave Mason holding a 9lb 11oz
beauty with a 7½-pounder on the
ground, from the Ouse.

Pete Reading admires his 11lb 1oz Avon barbel.

A beautiful 11lb 12oz Stour barbel returns to its water home.

Pete McMurray is delighted with this 9-pounder from the lower Severn.

A superbly proportioned and marked Hampshire Avon barbel, taken
on trotting gear.

Pete Reading holds one of the biggest barbel ever caught, a truly
huge specimen of 14lb 2oz. This is 6oz heavier than the British
Record Fish Committee best fish.

exceptional barbel of 9lb 7oz was taken in 1984 from one of these areas by Stan Latakowski, but I fear that the majority of anglers who may set their sights on such a fish will remain disappointed.

None of my friends fish the Nidd in the hope of landing an outsize specimen. A great deal of the pleasure is derived simply from fishing this intimate little river in the most pleasant of surroundings. The fighting quality of these Nidd barbel has to be experienced to be believed – pound for pound, they are equal to anything the barbel angler is ever likely to encounter.

The Wharfe

Barbel first began to appear below Harewood and are to be found at various intervals down to the tidal waters below Tadcaster. As far as its scenic value is concerned, the Wharfe is a river of two distinct halves. The tidal reaches could never be described as picturesque. The river certainly looks promising enough directly below the town weir at Tadcaster, but soon begins to lose its initial sparkle. Just above the new bypass bridge a series of groynes has been built in order to help stem the silting problem so prevalent in this area of the river. The Wharfe has experienced its share of problems in the past, with inadequate sewerage facilities leading to a deterioration in the water quality. However, the recent completion of a new treatment plant will undoubtedly benefit the river in future years. There are few bankside willows in evidence and, even though the Wharfe displays plenty of current variation as it meanders through the flat agricultural land, it does on face value

lack the appeal of the non-tidal reaches. When you take into account that the predominant species hereabouts is the unwelcome eel you could be forgiven for overlooking the water as a worthwhile barbel proposition. This would be a mistake as the river's appearance often belies its potential.

The lower Wharfe is a productive coarse fishery and holds a good head of barbel. These are found mainly between Tadcaster and Ulleskelfe, some five miles of water, with occasional fish reported below this point. Barbel of 5lb would be classed as good for the river but a sprinkling of much larger fish is present, and only recently local bailiff, Dick Gott, witnessed and weighed an outstanding Wharfe barbel of 9lb. At this stage the Wharfe is heavily match-fished and heavily pleasure-fished, and few anglers devote their attention towards the barbel. Intensive angling pressure does mean, however, that the locality of any productive barbel swim soon becomes known. Lines of submerged stumps and areas of weed cover are usually the most reliable points. In places there are dense banks of marginal weed, which create a noticeable increase in the current speed, channelling out the favoured deeper glides.

The upper barbel reaches are a more attractive proposition. There is improved water clarity and far more bankside cover, and what weed growth is present in the lower extremities of the non-tidal areas has a more luxurious appearance. Directly above Tadcaster the river is wide and deep with only a negligible flow. It is at Easdyke that the Wharfe takes on a more familiar appearance, varying between shallows and deeper, more even-paced areas of water. Barbel are present in this section of the river but not in any quantity.

It is just a short distance upstream that the Wharfe's most prolific barbel fishery is to be found. This extends from Boston Spa to just downstream of the papermill at Newton Kyme. Barbel nearing 8lb have been reported here, but it is for its capabilities of producing fish in numbers rather than for their individual size that this area is best known. Some quite outstanding catches of barbel have been accounted for, particularly by float anglers. The barbel are never far from any available willow cover, but many of the better swims are provided in the deeper channels in what is basically a shallow section of water. On this virtually weed-free section of the Wharfe much of the river bed can be seen clearly and you could be forgiven for thinking the water devoid of fish life. The barbel are pocketed away in the deeper, less visible areas, or – as is often the case – crammed tight under the overhanging willows. A steady stream of loose feed catapulted to drop short of these willows can often draw the fish into open water.

The Wharfe in many ways typifies the type of barbel fishing one would have experienced on certain Ouse tributaries not so long ago. Then the backbone of our fishing was made up by barbel in the 3–4lb range, with the emphasis being placed on the numerical rather than the specimen style of angling.

The Derwent

The Yorkshire Derwent must be regarded as one of the country's most difficult barbel waters. Compared with the other Yorkshire rivers, the Derwent holds few barbel and what specialised fishing takes place tends to be localised. Possibly more barbel anglers concentrate on the short streamy section of water below Stamford Bridge weir than on the remainder of the Derwent's barbel-holding region. Indeed, these shallow areas of water downstream of the river's weirs are one of the few sections of the Derwent that resemble a conventional barbel river: for the major part, the river is deep and mainly even-paced. Totally different in character from the Dales rivers, the Derwent really is a most beautiful river with much of its banks lined with alders and willows. The margins at times contain dense weedbeds; bordered with rushes and lilies, they present an idyllic picture during the summer months. However, the river's inviting looks do not extend to its barbel fishing. I have known anglers catch a Derwent barbel at their first attempt and give up after months spent trying to catch a second.

The main problem is that you are fishing for a small head of barbel on a river which contains few textbook barbel swims and hardly any consistent ones. The fishing in the shallow, gravelly runs near the river's weirs can never be described as easy, but in the deeper, more typical Derwent reaches the barbel fishing can at times be almost impossible. The only certain thing on this river is that the blank sessions will far outweigh the productive ones. A successful outing usually means the capture of just one barbel, and this is always a notable occasion in my book.

Location is a difficult problem. The

Dave Mason caught this 10lb fish during floodwater conditions on the Yorkshire Derwent.

barbel appear to be mainly nomadic, so providence usually plays a more important role than actual swim selection. Other Yorkshire rivers contain noted barbel 'holes' – areas that consistently produce barbel season after season. The Derwent is almost totally lacking in such swims. Likely-looking features like those found on other barbel rivers *can* produce fish but catches are so infrequent that these areas could never accurately be described as barbel swims. For a great deal of the time you

are fishing blind, hoping that your choice of swim coincides with the barbel being present and in a feeding mood.

The only section of the river I know that could loosely be described as consistent harboured a huge sunken snag. I was put on to this area by two Hull anglers, Kev Clifford and Bob Goodison, both of whom had enjoyed undoubted success there in the past. It is doubtful whether barbel were present there all season, but it did appear to be

115

one of the few holding points on the river that a barbel angler had been fortunate to locate. The swim may have contained a few resident fish, but I suspect that the majority, particularly the larger fish, were travellers.

Therefore, rather than fish a fairly lengthy section of river and risk missing out completely, I would concentrate on this very short section of the Derwent, knowing that eventually the barbel would move into this area. This is not really a purist approach. After all, the sign of a successful angler is an ability to anticipate the best time and conditions. But I never did meet or hear of an angler who came anywhere near to working out these Derwent barbel. When a barbel was landed it was best to exploit the situation fully, by fishing as hard as possible over a relatively short period before the barbel invariably moved on. This typified the best approach anywhere on the river. A friend of mine decided to concentrate his efforts on a section several miles upstream from where I have done the majority of my barbel fishing. He was lucky enough to catch a 7lb barbel on his first trip and his mate took a fish of 8lb the following day. Subsequent sessions over the next two months resulted in a total blank. This just illustrates the importance of a concentrated effort over consecutive days. A casual approach would almost certainly have ruled out the second fish, a splendid specimen for any Yorkshire river.

My favourite swims are the steady, deep glides usually just upstream of the trailing branches of a willow – the sort of place ideal for laying-on tactics. When looking at these gentler areas of water it is difficult to imagine the drastic variations of depth that occur on this river. One such swim is 9 feet deep less than a yard away from the bank and slightly further out into the main flow the river plunges almost an extra 3 feet. Therefore, when fishing such swims the use of a bait dropper is essential to ensure that you are accurately groundbaiting the area where your hook bait is. It is virtually impossible to loose feed with any degree of accuracy. Your offerings could be deposited on an unseen ledge well away from where you intend to fish. When feeder fishing near bank swims I also make use of the dropper, depositing an initial carpeting of feed before starting to fish.

The barbel fishing on the Derwent can at best be described as slow; the only way to achieve any form of consistent catch rate is to put in as many hours as possible. I cannot think of another Yorkshire river where having the right temperament is so vitally important. You have to accept the inevitable blanks and yet remain as positive as you would on any other river, varying tactics and baits to suit. Always keep an open mind because the river can often show a complete reversal of form; in one season the barbel may be more inclined to take a bait at night, while in the next the daylight hours prove the most productive.

I feel most confident in periods of high water, although I must stress that my experience of floodwater fishing is based on one short section of the Derwent. This area is in the vicinity of the previously mentioned snag swim, and sees the main current running on the far bank. The much steadier near-bank swims seem to attract the barbel when

A well concealed angler tackles the Derwent above Stamford Bridge.

the river is up and running through powerfully. Barbel can never be guaranteed during these conditions, but the odds are drastically improved. Two or three days of floodwater fishing can be more productive than literally weeks of fishing the river at normal level. So begrudgingly does the Derwent give up its barbel that these ideal conditions usually appear no more than a couple of times during the summer and autumn months.

On one such occasion two friends and I fished this area over a period of four days and, although the fishing could never be described as hectic, each session producing just one barbel, the fish ranged from 7lb 12oz to just over 9lb – exceptional barbel fishing by Yorkshire standards. Once in flood the Derwent does take longer to run off than its Dales counterparts, and more recently the river gave up a barbel to either Phil Duston or myself on every evening of a five-day spell. The fish included a big 8lb+ barbel to Phil and my long-awaited Yorkshire double – two examples which illustrate that, caught at the right moment, the Derwent can at times almost be described as predictable.

The average size of Derwent barbel is

117

high and of the fish we have recorded just short of 50 per cent are over 7lb. A careful study of the photographic evidence does show a good number of these barbel to be recaptures, and by collating information with other members of the York specimen group we have ascertained that individual specimens do cover considerable distances. One obliging barbel of 9lb 4oz was taken by Alex Chrzanowski some 2½ miles upstream from the point where I was fortunate enough to recapture the fish the following season. In the next twelve months the barbel was reported on three further occasions from different swims between these two areas, with the fish reaching a top weight of 9lb 12oz. This in itself gives a misleading impression of this particular stretch of the Derwent. The casual visitor could be under the impression that the stretch had produced several different fish over 9lb when in fact it was just one barbel caught five times, a large split on the tail fin easily identifying the fish. Even so, the Derwent is the home of some very big fish – a result of the classic combination of a rich river and a very low density of barbel.

Barbel appear to be distributed mainly below Stamford Bridge, with possibly more fish reported from this section of the river because of the slightly greater angling pressure. However, fish have been reported at several points upstream. Recently a huge barbel of 11½lb was taken by a match angler between the weirs of Buttercrambe and Stamford Bridge, and I know of other isolated catches from this length, including fish to just short of 9lb. Barbel are present in the reaches above Malton and in the areas below the weirs at Kirkham and Howsham. It was at Howsham that the Derwent received a consignment of Swale barbel several years ago. Barton Hill Beck, which enters the river a short distance below the weir, has produced the occasional fish during the early months of the season, which suggest the stream is being used for spawning. The Rye, which joins the Derwent north-east of Malton, also holds a few barbel, as does its tiny tributary the River Seven. So, while they are thin on the ground, the Derwent network holds a widely distributed head of barbel. The upper and middle reaches are hopelessly underfished and, therefore, extremely intriguing.

While no one could ever realistically plot the downfall of a double-figure barbel, for those with the resolve the Derwent must be regarded above all the other Yorkshire rivers as the one most likely to produce such a fish. Jon Wolfe and Trevor Dale decided to concentrate on a section of the river that was hardly ever fished for barbel. The fishing was typical of the Derwent, very hard going, yet not even the fact that both anglers were rewarded with the same double-figure barbel could detract from the capture of such a splendid and rare specimen. This is just one example to stimulate those who desire such a fish but are deterred by the river's reputation. Little is really known about this enigmatic river, and the Derwent must be regarded as the ultimate challenge to the barbel angler in this part of the country.

The Hull

The River Hull is some twenty miles long and a natural chalk stream in its upper reaches. Over the years there have been several attempts to stock this river with barbel. Evidence of the fish's presence appears in Jim Bazley's *Fishing in Yorkshire*: 'Barbel were introduced from the River Yore [Ure] by kind permission of Lord Bolton in 1935; there is reason to believe the species will do well.' In 1961 fish again originating from the Ure were released at Hempholme and in the tributary West Beck. Other consignments of barbel include an introduction by the Yorkshire Ouse and Hull River Authority of 64 barbel between 1 and 6lb from the Upper Swale in 1966 into the river's tidal reaches, and an occasion in the early 1970s when the river at Wilfholme received stocks of both chub and barbel, again from the Swale. A few fish were caught in the tidal areas during a five-year period after the 1966 stocking; one most productive area was the weir at Hempholme and barbel were reported as far downstream as Beverley. There has been a gradual decline and the barbel now seem scarce indeed. Barbel have been progressively transferred from West Beck to the Hull at Hempholme and it is possible that any fish caught in this area are those transferred from the upper river.

Any barbel resident below Hempholme weir are thought to move upstream to West Beck to spawn. Observations on barbel activity carried out during a survey spanning three years witnessed successful spawnings in 1973 and 1974. In 1975 fish gathered on the spawning areas but failed to spawn, due to low water temperatures. The very low number of small barbel present indicates that the survival rate after spawning is exceptionally low. Further evidence of the lack of young fish was found during annual electro-fishing to remove grayling from the West Beck. What were thought to be the same shoal fish – thirty barbel with estimated weights ranging between 6 and 9lb – were netted each year. As recently as May 1986 Steve Jacques spent many hours observing barbel on the West Beck. Of the fish he saw only a very small percentage weighed around the 2lb mark. The unfortunate conclusion is that many of the larger barbel present may be fish originally stocked. With few fish reaching maturity as a direct result of successful spawnings on the river, the initial optimism over the barbel's future may not be fully realised.

The Yorkshire rivers can differ quite dramatically in character yet all share certain similarities with regard to the best conditions for fishing and the location of barbel. Barbel swims may be obvious on some rivers but much less so on others (compare, for example, the Nidd with the Ouse). Most of the barbel rivers have experienced an increase in the amount of specimen fish reported, especially the Nidd and the Swale. Even though the gauging weir at Skip Bridge on the River Nidd represents an unpredictable barrier to fish movements, one wonders how many of the better-quality barbel so much in evidence on these two rivers at present are fish from the Ouse and lower Ure which have failed to drop back into the main river after spawning. These and many other facets of barbel fishing in Yorkshire remain open to speculation, and even though our knowledge of the species increases each year there are still many questions that remain unanswered.

The range of barbel fishing in York-shire rivers could not possibly be encompassed by one angler's experience, and much of the information in this chapter has been drawn from members past and present of the Barbel Catchers Club. My thanks to those who have contributed their hard-earned know-ledge – especially to Phil Glossop (River Ure), to Kevin Clifford and Steve Jacques (River Hull), and to Den-nis Linley, who has supplied several of the photographs.

The Kennet

TONY HART

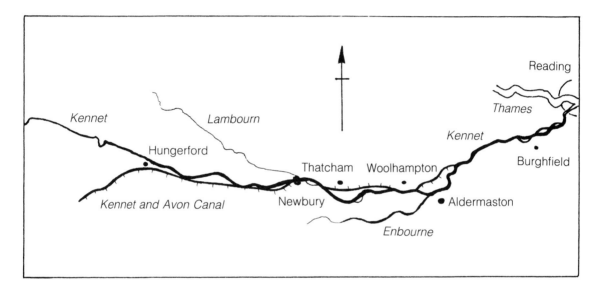

As one of the many tributaries of the Thames, the River Kennet has the distinction of being one of our native barbel rivers, its stocks being used over the years to populate many of the premier rivers of this country. The mighty Severn and also the Dorset Stour, which in turn has indirectly given the Hampshire Avon the barbel for which that great river is renowned, are among those to have received at some time or another batches of fish taken from the Kennet's middle reaches. So it would be fair to say that the Kennet has more than played its part in the growth of barbel fishing in this country.

The river rises west of Marlborough and flows on through some of the most delightful countryside, passing through the small rural towns of Hungerford and Kintbury before eventually reaching the busy town of Newbury. This part of the Kennet has long held the reputation of providing the fly angler with trout fishing second to none, while below Newbury and for the remainder of its course through to Reading the river can claim specimens of just about every species of coarse fish you could think of – superb roach and dace fishing, as well as exciting sport with more powerful fish such as chub and barbel, while in some parts of the

121

river carp, bream and tench can be found. But then the Kennet is no ordinary watercourse. Back in the early part of the last century the river was finally linked to the Bristol Avon by a canal system that became the Kennet and Avon canal. This operation took over eighty years to complete, joining the canal to the Kennet below Kintbury and then at frequent intervals right through the river's course to Reading and the Thames. Commerce has now forsaken the canal in favour of the busy M4 motorway and the A4 which follows the course of the Kennet from Reading through to Newbury and beyond and gives the angler easy access to the banks of the river.

From Newbury to Thatcham

From a barbel fisherman's point of view, Newbury marks the upper limit for any serious fishing. Although there are barbel above the town they are extremely thin on the ground, leading one to wonder if the area might produce one or two good fish. Location would be the major problem, of course, and would require a lot of groundwork. I would seek out areas of weedy shallows dropping off into deeper water, or perhaps undercut banks over a reasonable depth. But perhaps the best advice I can give is to consult anglers who fish the area regularly. While they may never have seen a barbel caught, they might know of someone who was broken in such and such a spot, or of someone even catching one from a certain swim. Common sense will usually tell you which information is useful and which to disregard. Once the decision is made

where to fish, a little prebaiting might be useful wherever possible. As for bait, I would probably look no further than luncheon meat or sweetcorn, perhaps using hemp as an attractor with both. Obviously, this sort of an exercise would not be an easy one, certainly not one I would recommend to the angler out to catch his first Kennet barbel. However, for the specialist who enjoys a challenge what could be more rewarding than catching a big barbel from an unrecognised part of the river?

There is little in the way of free fishing on the Kennet, so Newbury Town provides us with a bonus, for much of the fishing in the town is free, with the opportunity of catching the odd big fish. Once again, though, barbel are very few and far between and mainly localised in pockets throughout the stretch, so location is the major key to catching them. One does occasionally hear rumours of enormous barbel coming from this town water, although usually they are unsubstantiated. The last I heard of was a fish of 12lb 2oz taken from the lower part of the town water in 1982. I have no doubt that in parts this free stretch has the potential to produce very large fish, although it may not look classic barbel water. Definitely in its favour is the lack of night fishing restrictions throughout the town water, which reinforces my belief that a big barbel from Newbury town is a distinct possibility.

It is not until we begin to move out of the town that we find a gradual increase in the barbel population. The White House pub water on the A4 below the town, while it couldn't be called consistent, does have a slightly higher concentration of fish. In the past this fishery has produced some superb barbel, including more than a few doubles. It is a difficult water, though, with the most likely period for barbel being around dusk. Day tickets can be bought from the pub at modest cost on a dawn-to-dusk basis.

If we follow the towpath downstream the river turns left and goes through the sluices of the local mill, a private area, while the canal is left behind to make its own slow way. Flowing more swiftly now, the river, shallow in most parts, flows under the Hambridge on the outskirts of Thatcham town. I have always found this a particularly attractive part of the Kennet, with its lush beds of ranunculus and streamer weed wavering over a bed of hard golden gravel. As a stretch it has always epitomised for me everything I like about the Kennet. It is even possible around late May if the weather is warm to spot barbel spawning around the area of the bridge. As anyone who has seen barbel going through their nuptial rites will agree, it is a fascinating sight, with barbel of all sizes milling around the bottom. But it also has a more practical side as it gives the added bonus of being able to see at first hand the size of barbel in the area. Having whetted your appetite though,

Pete Tillotson is delighted with this Kennet club record of 10lb 12oz.

most of the fishing from below the bridge is controlled by the Civil Service Angling Club for members and their guests. In fact they control the fishing rights on the right bank for the next two miles downstream and probably half the left bank.

The top part of the fishery is fairly shallow and, if you are cautious, you can spot the barbel as they lie under the weed or marginal cover. I find that by introducing a steady stream of particle baits on a little and often basis before and as I begin fishing I can usually get the fish interested. When I am fishing in this manner I like to use the minimum amount of lead to hold bottom so that just a gentle lift of the rod will be enough to start the bait moving again. I find that by casting just upstream and holding the rod the line can be kept off the water and the bait can easily be manoeuvred through the swim. Bites can be anything from a slack line, when the bait is in the upstream position, to a full-blooded pull, but in any case I prefer to feel the line and generally strike at anything suspicious.

Half a mile or so below Hambridge the river becomes narrower and noticeably deeper. Here a short stretch on the left bank is rented by the Thatcham Angling Club for its members. Although fishing can be arduous at times, some very good fish can and do turn up occasionally, including the odd double-figure fish such as the 10lb 10oz barbel caught by Alan Slater in 1978, or the three doubles caught from the same area by Pete Tillotson in 1978 and 1979. A fine water although a temperamental one, and one that lends itself more to winter fishing than the earlier part of the season.

After some 200 yards we come to the boundary marking the end of the fishery, and once again the river begins to shallow up again. After a couple of bends the Kennet and Avon canal joins from the right at Bulls Lock, and Kennet and canal flow together again for perhaps the next half mile or so downstream. Needless to say, the Civil Service still have the right bank, while the left bank is rented to the Newbury Angling Club for the local anglers. Once again it is a generally deep area, and, typical of deep water on this part of the river, the fishing can be slow. However, it does on occasions turn up some fine barbel. The largest I have seen was a 9lb 15oz fish to a local angler in March 1984, but the odd double does make an appearance from time to time.

At the boundary of the Civil Service water the river makes a sharp bend to the right, parting from the canal as it does. Following the right bank it is not long before we find ourselves approaching the first stretch of water under the control of the Reading and District Angling Association, which controls the bank rights to much of the fishing on the Kennet from this point downstream. Their permit gives access to some of the best fishing available on the river, from the point of view of both the pleasure angler and the big-fish man. While I am told it is possible to obtain a permit direct from the association, I understand there is a long waiting list, so it would be advisable and certainly easier to join one of the many clubs affiliated to the RDAA. I would say that for anyone considering fishing the Kennet on a regular basis it would be worth looking at the fishing they have to offer.

The River Kennet meets the Kennet and Avon Canal at Bulls Lock, Thatcham.

Chamber House Farm is the first water we come to on the permit. Split into two sections, upper and lower, the stretch includes areas of both shallow and deeper water. The top section opens for fishing from 1 October due to the popularity of the local trout and it is reputed to hold some superb barbel. However, it is a mainly shallow piece of water and the big barbel either tend to have moved into deeper water or are difficult to locate by the time coarse fishing commences in the normally chilly month of October. The lower water, however, generally holds more depth and opens earlier, on 1 July. As with the top stretch, there are some superb barbel to be caught, with doubles being recorded. It is a very popular water, too, and one that lends

itself to many forms of fishing. One of the more popular methods is to trot the far bank, beneath the branches of the marginal bushes and trees. I find that due to the loose feed that goes into the water the barbel have become quite used to maggots, and whenever I can I prefer to use a light feeder. I find it scores better and I can get away with heavier tackle, just in case a better barbel comes along. Another method worth a try, particularly on the shallow upper water, is a freelined or lightly weighted piece of luncheon meat that is allowed to trundle through the weed. Although it tends to catch more chub than anything, the odd barbel does turn up, particularly if the bait is slowed right down.

From Thatcham to Woolhampton

Leaving Chamber House Farm behind it is not long before we are standing on the river bridge at Thatcham. The river and canal are only a few yards apart here, with the Kennet and Avon canal flowing swiftly at this point just to our left. As a matter of interest, there are some good barbel to 9lb+ in the lower part of this canal section. It is strictly private, though, and controlled by the Reed paper group, the owners of the factory that skirts the bank. Meanwhile, the course of the river takes us on and after a short distance we come to the RDAA Crookham Manor fishery. The Kennet is relatively shallow in places here, with the streamer weed growing in thick profusion everywhere. This part of the river supports quite a large head of barbel and the early part of the season sees some good bags of fish being taken. As the season progresses, however, the fishing becomes harder. This is no doubt due once again to the popularity of the fishery but can partly be overcome with a good pair of polarising glasses. Start by introducing small particle baits as free offerings into the gaps between the weed – hemp and sweetcorn are particularly good – and fish a light leger over the top. The barbel can be seen after a while moving over the feed. My advice is to watch the bait if you can, as often a bite is not signalled on the rod top at all. Alternatively, if conditions are such that fish cannot be seen, move a couple of yards downstream of the desired fishing spot and leger upstream with barely enough weight to maintain position on the bottom. Bites are usually recorded by the line trembling where it enters the water, or a slack line bite, but in either case watch the line and not the rod top.

From the boundary that marks the end of the Reading and District water, we continue downstream in the direction of Brimpton Mill. It is plain to see that the depth has decreased dramatically, with the average swim now only perhaps some 3 feet or so deep and with plenty of weed about. There are also plenty of barbel, although the average is smaller, at around 3lb. Most methods will take fish here, with trotting being popular where the weed permits. The fishing rights are held by Newbury Angling Club on the left bank and right through to just above the mill at Brimpton and the roadway that passes its door. It is quite a picturesque little spot this, with the river flowing under the bridge and through the estate below. However, most of the fishing for the next mile or so is strictly private and syndicate-controlled. Having seen the water, I can say that it is charming in appearance. The river is skirted by woodland with plenty of deer about. As for the fishing, I would have thought it to be typical of the area with lots of barbel of a smaller average weight. Emerging from the trees at the end of this section, we see the canal over to the left about to join the river again. As it does so the depth increases accordingly. We are at Woolhampton and we find another road bridge. Over to the right is the Rowbarge, a pub that has been known to save the life of many a thirsty angler in the past. To the left is the railway station at Midgham. It is quite an accessible spot, with the A4

A typical upper-Kennet swim.

just a couple of hundred yards away.

Below the bridge the river flows powerfully on downstream and is listed on the RDAA permit as their Woolhampton water. At one time some superb barbel were being caught from this fishery, with the average easily exceeding 7lb. Alas, though, in the winter of 1976–7 the dredger was brought in to stop the surrounding land being flooded in times of high water and it has never been the same since, although I am reliably informed that the fishery is making something of a comeback of late. Certainly before 1976 a double was always a possibility and I have no doubt that this is probably still the case, but the swims are nowhere near as blindingly evident as they used to be and the odds of tracking down that elusive 10lb + barbel are that much longer because of it.

If I was intending to give the water a

try I would stay away until later in the season, late autumn or winter, when we can expect a few periods of heavy rain. A rising river can make location so much easier. I tend to forget what the textbooks say about fishing a river fining off after rain. In my opinion, at that stage the best of winter barbel fishing would have passed me by. I like to give the river two days of heavy rain to get the Kennet rising and coloured, and if the conditions still prevail I forget all of winter's discomforts and go fishing. In my mind these are without doubt the best conditions the big-barbel man can find. My only reservation would be if the rain contains sleet. Sleet has the effect of lowering the water temperature and usually puts the barbel down. Generally, though, in winter a steady deluge of rain for an extended period starts a chain reaction as far as barbel are concerned. The combination of extra flow and debris being brought down by the current gets Old Whiskers on the move seeking out more comfortable quarters. Also, some big fish which may have lain dormant for some time are on the move and expending energy – energy that has to be replaced! With natural food not so plentiful, the barbel tend to become less wary and are then more likely to accept a bait they might otherwise have left alone. If you consider this chain of events it is easy to understand why some very big barbel tend to end up on the bank towards the back end of the season and sometimes they are fish that are not located again.

It is at times like this that bankside slacks come into their own as swims. Even some of the smallest areas of slack water can contain barbel at some time during a flood, and as long as the swim has a reasonable depth against the bank I am confident of catching fish. Nothing could be easier than lowering a couple of droppers of finely chopped luncheon meat down to the bottom,

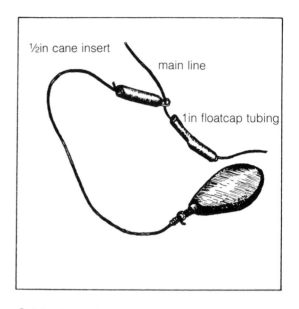

Quick-release rig.

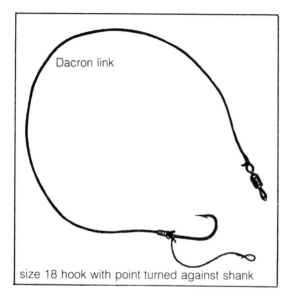

Hair rig for maggots.

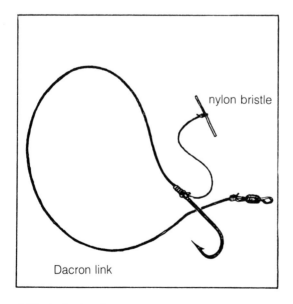

Hair rig for luncheon meat.

while remembering of course to keep back from the bank edge. For it must not be forgotten that the barbel can be practically at your feet. Then all that remains is to sit back from the water's edge and gently drop the baited hook into the water. The bites when they come are usually a slow confident pull down of the quivertip or rod top, but once again I strike at anything suspicious. This sort of fishing is all a matter of confidence really – believing that barbel can be caught from so close into the bank. I have caught countless barbel to 9lb 10oz from the Kennet using this method and, believe me, some from as close as two feet from the bank. It can be a deadly method – almost tailor-made for parts of this Woolhampton fishery – and it could produce one of the larger barbel that inhabit this water.

From Aldermaston to Reading

Before we reach our next port of call on our journey downstream, we once again see the canal part company from the main river and move over to the left, as we take the right bank. Stepping over the stile, we find ourselves on the well-known Old Mill restaurant stretch of Aldermaston, one of the few day-ticket waters on the river. The fishery consists of two weirpools and one mill-wheel outlet that joins the main stream, plus some fishing below the bridge. As you might imagine, being a day-ticket water it is inclined to get rather crowded at times, particularly in the summertime and at weekends. It is a very popular water, and part of its popularity is no doubt due to the large head of barbel in the water. Some really good bags of fish are taken from time to time, with most of the usual methods taking fish. Trotting, link-legering and the feeder are all good, with perhaps the latter in my experience being the most effective. Big barbel from the Mill are few and far between and doubles rare fish indeed. Occasionally big barbel that I think are travellers stray into the fishery, probably from Woolhampton, and compete for food with the large head of their smaller fellows. These larger fish can end up being caught a couple of times or more before they move on. One example is the 11lb 2oz fish that was caught in June of 1984 from the area of the road bridge, only to turn up again in the August at 11lb 8oz. But what the water lacks in quality fish, it makes up for in quantity.

A prolific day-ticket stretch at Aldermaston.

The fishing at the Old Mill probably sets the pattern for the next six or seven miles of river. It is here that the old adage 'the Kennet is one long barbel swim' really applies, so dense is the population of barbel at times. I prefer to fish this part of the river when I need a morale booster after having blanks on the other, more difficult stretches of the river. It is nice to get a few fish under your belt, so to speak, before trying for the big fellows – it is certainly very enjoyable fishing.

The river now takes us on to Padworth Mill and Padworth road bridge. Above the bridge is a half-mile stretch of water rented by the Thatcham club for its members, while below is the prized RDAA water, the Benyon Estate. It was from around this area that Pete Tillotson caught 73lb of barbel in a long afternoon session back in 1976. A total of 23 fish made the average about 3lb, and this is about the stamp of fish you could expect from this part of the Kennet. The same fishing would probably apply right through to Ufton road bridge and, to a large extent, beyond for the next couple of miles to Theale, although there are some pockets of water where the odd large fish might turn up. Generally, though, the barbel found in this part of the Kennet are smaller fish.

The river and canal seem to be meeting quite a lot now. In fact it tends to get rather untidy at times, with the canal leaving the Kennet for a short space of time only to return after a short interval, almost as if it resents being pushed along by the river and decides to take the occasional breather. Often we read reports in the angling press of double-figure barbel turning up from

around the area of Theale, so there are obviously some good fish to be caught. Once again location is the all-important key to success, as there are also a number of smaller barbel about.

At Theale the tiny Holy Brook leaves the company of the Kennet. It rejoins it a few miles downstream at Reading. For the best part the brook is a fairly shallow stream with an average depth of some 4 feet or so, but there are also a number of deeper pockets to be found throughout its length. Summertime will find this tiny fishery thick with streamer weed and the barbel sheltering underneath the waving fronds. As a rule these Holy Brook fish don't come very big and a 7lb barbel could be considered a fine fish from the water. But be sure you can expect a fair old tussle and a few anxious moments before pulling them over the net. Every so often, though, rumours start to circulate of the odd big fish being caught. I personally would not discount the possibility of a double from this little stream, but I have yet to see one or meet anyone who has caught one.

Our next destination, Burghfield Mill, is only a short walk across the fields at Calcott. The canal and river part company above the mill and flow parallel downstream before rejoining after a quarter of a mile. Between them they create a small island, which, although very narrow, can be almost impenetrable in the summertime with its thick growth of trees and vegetation. The only point of access to the island is by a couple of lock gates that lead to the lower part of the fishery, where the river is deeper, giving some ten feet of water in places. The thick growth of trees gives plenty of cover behind –

which is ideal for the angler, as the lower part of the fishery can provide some really good barbel fishing, with some fish of better than average size. When I am fishing Burghfield I prefer to use a feeder, an ideal way of providing a steady supply of hemp within a confined area on the bottom to attract the barbel. Used in conjunction with meat, I find it is as good a method as any. A word of warning though – maggots and casters should be avoided in this deep water, as the area abounds with hordes of gudgeon that devour the bait almost as soon as it hits the bottom. However, there are some fine barbel too. I have had numerous sevens and fish to 8lb 2oz from this water, but I suspect that there are larger barbel to be caught. Upstream along the island the river gets progressively shallower and the average barbel become smaller, with most of the fish taken from the pool being very much the same. Taken on the whole, though, this is a delightful fishery, particularly for the man who likes his solitude. There are plenty of barbel about with some good fish to be taken and once again all under the control of the RDAA.

A short walk from the Burghfield Mill fishery brings us to the road bridge at Burghfield and the very popular Cunning Man public house which stands beside the river. Beneath the old stone bridge the canal and river divide again, the river to the left and the canal beneath our feet to the right. They rejoin just a couple of hundred yards downstream. This area has in the past produced some outstanding barbel. To my knowledge a 10lb 2oz barbel was caught above the bridge in 1978 and another of 10lb 4oz locally about the

same time. While there were also reports of a couple of 11lb fish coming out within a few days of each other in the mid-1970s, these were very likely the same fish. They came from below the bridge during a period of really inclement weather and high water. We don't find a lot of barbel along this section but, as is the case along many of the stretches where canal and river join forces, the fish tend to be of a high average size for the waterway.

We are only a couple of hundred yards below the road bridge now and past all the boats and barges moored in line along the far bank. Once again, the river becomes our companion as she sweeps in from across the far bank to join forces with the canal. On our own right bank, we find the river tumbling over a weir into a deep pool. This weirpool is one of the few on the Kennet that I would fish with any confidence of a big barbel. My experience of Kennet pools has always been that they seem in the main to support small fish, contradicting all I have read about them in the past. This weir and where the river runs off below is all controlled by Leisure Sport and can be fished for the price of a season ticket, giving about half a mile of river fishing through to the point where the Kennet joins the next weir and the canal at Southcote.

It is easy to overlook the canal when thinking of big barbel, particularly when the river can look so inviting. Surprisingly, though, the canal, in areas where it has some flow, can produce really good barbel. One stretch in particular, from Burghfield for the next couple of miles downstream to Fobney pumping station, is capable of giving

131

up some excellent specimens – better in fact than the nearby river, which is a good deal shallower. While I would be the first to admit that it is not the nicest form of barbel fishing, these fish are almost totally neglected and catching them must hold a certain appeal in itself. My own preference is for the half-mile section that runs through to the pumping station. I have taken barbel to 8lb 1oz and have seen others of 8lb+ caught from the water and I do believe that larger fish are there for the taking.

In the pool below Fobney pumping station, the river and canal unite for the last time before entering Reading on a course that will take them through to the Thames at Caversham. This deep pool below the turbines of the pumper has seen some enormous barbel caught in the past. A young Alan Slater saw what was a very large fish caught here in the late 1960s. When Alan asked its captor, an old fellow, its size, he was told that it weighed 15lb. Now, while we all might tend to be sceptical, including Alan, of the weight quoted, Alan is convinced that it was a very big barbel indeed and just one of many memorable fish that have come from the pool over the years. Alas, progress being what it is, a memory of what the pool once was is all that remains. The swims that used to produce such marvellous fish are now gone, dredged

Fobney Pumping Station – home of large barbel.

away in the mid-seventies along with the next mile of bank downstream. Whether the water will ever return to its former glory only time will tell. There is a small consolation, however: the dredged section of water on the right bank is now almost all free fishing, and there are barbel to be caught, although they are difficult to locate.

Reading and Downstream

The left-bank towpath, rented by RDAA, brings us to the outskirts of Reading. On the opposite bank we see rows of back gardens that reach down to the water's edge, while behind us is an industrial estate with the ever-present noise and the smell of spent diesel fuel. My pen does not paint a pretty picture and it is hard to believe that this is the famed 'jam factory' stretch, or Beat 5 as it is now better known from its number in the RDAA permit. It could never rival the upper river for beauty and clarity of water, yet at times its fishing can match anywhere on the river. The water does tend to get abused, though. During the course of a year all manner of things are thrown into the river from the bordering back gardens. Everything from bicycle frames to table scraps find their way into the river. However, over the years the barbel have become used to the constant 'baiting' of table scraps and for this reason the barbel on Beat 5 have a more catholic taste than anywhere else on the river. At times the fish will accept just about anything, from plain bread to bacon rind, and one of the local anglers even makes a practice of catching them on chicken skin. There are times, however, when the very

same barbel that will accept the most unusual of baits become frustratingly difficult to hook. I have lost count of the times when the rod has pulled round hard with an unmissable bite and yet the resulting strike has met only thin air. When this happens it is likely to recur several times in the same session. One way to combat this situation is wherever possible to leger upstream with lightly balanced tackle and strike at the first sign of the lead dropping back towards you. Another method, of course, is the hair rig, with either meat on the hair or perhaps a feeder with maggots and maggots as the hook-bait. I have had some success with both, but prefer to use these methods as a last resort when all else fails.

A good tip I picked up from a friend who fishes the occasional match on this water. He recommends feeding the swim all day with either maggots or hemp. Towards the end of the session he removes the float and puts out a feeder at the tail end of his swim. This ploy has given him some good barbel of 7lb or so. In a way Beat 5 is a contradiction to the rest of the river, for, while the experienced Kennet barbel man usually knows the size of fish he can expect to catch from a fishery, in the case of Beat 5 you can never tell. One session will provide a catch of barbel of perhaps 3lb or so and the next you could find yourself playing a big fish. The water does contain some very big fish, although they are not often caught. An example is the 11lb + barbel taken from one of the back gardens in recent years which was photographed and reported in the angling press. An absolute monster of 13lb 2oz was caught from halfway along the fishery in 1975 by a policeman. That fish had several witnesses. More recently, in the last few weeks of the 1984–5 season, Alan Slater took a fine fish of 10lb 1oz.

About halfway down the stretch a small bridge crosses the Holy Brook as it rejoins the river. The RDAA fishery boundary lies just beyond the road bridge at Berkeley Avenue. As we walk on, the sound of traffic soon becomes masked by the sound of rushing water, and we round the curve of the river to find the County Weir in our path. The few swims available for fishing are to the right bank now, with the left bank sectioned off. Most of the barbel that are taken are caught by casting into the fast water on the left side of the weir, where most of the current has been diverted by the gradual curve in the river. The bottom here is absolutely littered with snags, so tackle losses must be expected. I personally fish with a lighter link to the main line. It's better to lose the weight than a hooked barbel.

The fishing from the weir right through the rest of the Kennet's course to its confluence with the Thames is free, but the river is murky and uninviting for the next mile or so before joining the Thames at Horseshoe Bridge. My knowledge of the river below County Weir is very limited, but the condition of the Kennet at this point, as it flows through the industrial part of the town, is such that any serious fishing would be hard to imagine.

Finding the Bigger Fish

To anyone who knows anything about barbel fishing, the river Kennet is syn-onymous with barbel. The river certainly holds a good population and generally fish can be caught with relative ease. There are so many, in fact, that there are times when the river tends to leave the angler bemused and disappointed, particularly after a good day's sport, when, despite the number of barbel caught, bigger fish never seem to turn up and five or possibly six pounds is the upper limit. The reason is that few large fish exist in these over-populated areas of river. The large head of fish competing for the available food precludes the sort of growth rate needed to produce large barbel. As a rule the resident fish in these areas become stunted in growth. It is nature's way of making the food go round. However, big fish do turn up from time to time – fish which are travelling from other stretches and wander into these heavily populated areas. It seems that when they do they tend to be caught a few times over a short period, while they are competing for the available food supply, before finally moving on, usually not to be seen again.

So, if we are looking for better than average barbel, the answer must be to look to other parts of the river with a much smaller head of fish, where lack of pressure on an abundant food supply produces the right living environment to support the bigger fish. If we look at the Kennet from that point of view, both the top and bottom parts of the river would fit the bill very well, as do most parts of the Kennet where the river and canal meet. It is probably true to say that at almost every point where they join the Kennet produces, or has produced in the past some very big barbel, including doubles. Unfortunately, though, the Kennet big-barbel angler has one disadvantage that is not wholly shared by his Hampshire Avon and Dorset Stour counterparts. Most of the areas likely to produce the goods are too deep for spotting fish. Taken on this basis, the angler has to resort to delving into the history of the water to assess its potential and, once satisfied, to rely on watercraft to sort out productive areas. I usually use a plummet to discover the contours of the river bed – usually the river is narrow enough to do this with quite good effect. All the usual barbel swims are worth a try – undercut banks, snags, slight depressions in the river bed (a particular favourite of mine when there is a good growth of streamer weed nearby), or perhaps deep slacks for later in the season. But usually anything found out of the ordinary will be worth a try at some stage, for it is always worth making the effort to locate your fish before starting any serious fishing. Both the method to be used and the bait will always form a very poor second best on my list of priorities. I would say: get the area and swims right, choose the right method for the swims in question and the bait being used, and persevere within that area.

Perhaps the biggest advantage when seeking larger barbel is the ability to fish a water at night. I always feel as I am sitting on the bank that the more the light fades into darkness the better are my chances. That is not to say that there will be a staggering increase in the number of bites. Generally with these lesser populated waters it is a case of sitting out an evening session for one fish, with the larger barbel having a habit of turning up later and into the early hours of the morning. Fish can be located either by moving from one lightly baited swim to another or by sitting it out in one swim waiting for barbel to move in. Both methods will catch fish. However, I would definitely advise against using a moving bait after dark. Instead, give the fish time to find your bait and be patient.

I suppose the possibility of a national record fish from the Kennet must be slim, although one could never rule out the chance of it happening. The river has so much else to offer, though. Depending on the mood of the angler, a pleasant day can be had amongst some very attractive countryside, fishing for the shoals of Kennet barbel that make the river so popular. Or, for the more single-minded angler, there is the opportunity of catching the one big barbel to be recorded in his diary as something special. Doesn't that sum up this glorious river?

The Wensum

DAVE PLUMMER

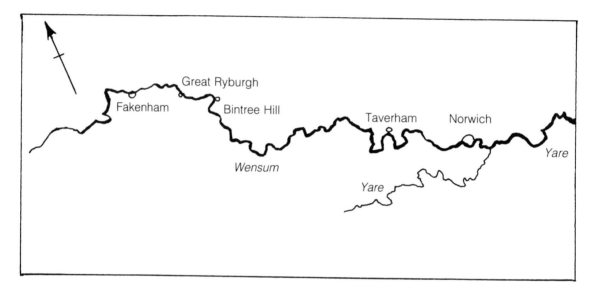

It was always an ambition of mine to catch a really huge barbel, ever since the mid-1960s when I first made trips to the Yorkshire rivers for barbel. It took about ten years of fishing them before I caught my first double-figure barbel of 10lb 4oz from the Yorkshire Derwent.

The lack of really big barbel in Yorkshire was something which I accepted reluctantly; a 5lb Yorkshire barbel was a specimen and anything over 7lb could well be the fish of the season. In the early seventies I contacted some big barbel on a day-ticket stretch of the Yorkshire Ouse, on a method common today – the swimfeeder and maggots. My first really big barbel weighed 9¼lb

from this stretch and was caught during the day when the river was high and coloured. As the years went by I tried new stretches of rivers until eventually I moved to the Derwent. Although the barbel were less numerous on this river, I felt that the chances of a big barbel were greater, as I proved with my double there in September 1975.

Then, with the industrial decline in my home town of Rotherham in the late 1970s, I made the move to Norfolk. I transferred my job as a train driver with British Rail to Norwich. Many people believed that I moved simply for the fishing, when in actual fact it was a joint family move which was decided

136

between my wife Linda, my son Neil and myself.

For the first nine months in Norfolk I lived in lodgings until the house was sold in Rotherham and we moved into one in Norwich. So the first summer in Norfolk was spent looking at waters which I felt had potential for big fish. Top of my list was, of course, the Wensum.

This river was reputed to hold barbel, but very few big ones. This theory was expounded by quite a few local experts, who genuinely felt that only three double-figure fish existed in the entire stretch of river which held barbel. The stretch in question was from Costessey Mill down to Hellesdon Mill, a distance of some three miles or so. I later found this theory to be totally inaccurate, as were some of the other reports.

I am a great believer in struggling on myself, learning about a new water, so I started to explore this particular stretch of the Wensum. Using polaroids and an eyeshield I quickly discovered why the Wensum barbel were wary of anglers and baits. The water is generally gin-clear with lush beds of streamer weed in summer which at times reduces the flow down to a very steady pace. Any sharp or sudden movements would certainly send the fish off to the sanctuary of overhanging bushes or beds of streamer weed. Big fish were at that early stage very hard to locate and that first summer, although I caught a few fish to over 6lb, I felt sure I wasn't really getting to the main reasons why the barbel were hard to catch.

The following close season was once again spent wandering along the Wensum, spotting fish and preparing several swims. As the season opened I was fishing for another species, rudd, but had made plans to visit the Wensum during the first week of the season. The river that week was carrying about six inches of extra water and spotting fish was quite difficult. I walked the entire river until I found a raft which seemed to be deflecting some of the floating weed which was now starting to come down as weed-cutting operations were under way somewhere well upstream.

I climbed an overhanging branch and I looked hard into the slack behind the raft, where about 4 or 5 feet of water gradually gave way to a very deep hole of about 7 or 8 feet. After about twenty minutes I caught a glimpse of three large shapes with orange pectorals fanning out on either side – barbel! I slipped back to the car and got my gear. My first job was to prebait the raft with hemp and sweetcorn, which I did with the aid of a bait dropper. I went back up the tree branch ready to watch any movement from the barbel. It was fairly obvious that the disturbance from the prebaiting was going to alarm the barbel so I anticipated quite a wait before the fish returned. But to my amazement only about five minutes had gone when the three huge barbel returned. I gently slid down the branch and picked the rod up. A simple link leger with two grains of corn on a no. 8 hook was my set-up. I gingerly lowered the bait into the gap behind the raft. Immediately the smallest of the three barbel worked up to the line of bait and then made a beeline for my hookbait.

The rod slowly went over and I struck simultaneously – it was only

A 12lb 2oz barbel and a 5lb 5oz chub taken in the same session.

then I realised that if the fish made a determined effort downstream I would have problems. This of course is what the barbel did, and although I tried hard to turn it from ploughing off downstream past the overhanging tree, I made little impression. If I played the fish upstream there was a fair chance that it would run into the branches which were protruding well into the water. The only other solution was to jump into the swim and go around the tree into the slack below. I know it was a drastic decision to make, but it was obviously a big barbel and I certainly didn't want to lose it. So I eased my way into the river, keeping the rod and line well clear of the bush. At first I was surprised just how much flow there was

in the swim and I must admit that it caught me a little off balance. As I neared the deeper part of the swim I felt my feet being swept from under me, but I quickly swam around the bush into the slack, pulled myself ashore, laid the rod down to fetch the landing net.

The barbel had been really obliging and had just lain out in mid-river while all this fiasco had been going on. I wound down to the fish and eventually played it to the waiting net. It didn't go into double figures but at 9lb 7oz it was my best Wensum barbel to date. A couple of days later a local angler had one of the two bigger fish I had seen and it weighed 11lb 4oz.

As that season petered out I was already making plans for the following season. I had made my mind up to have a real concerted effort right from the off.

As the start approached I was continuously prebaiting all the swims I felt would produce with sweetcorn and hemp. I even went into the river to clear snags from the river bed. Swims that were becoming heavily weeded were gently pruned as I cut a channel through the weed. One swim needed some work doing on the bankside trees and branches. Everything looked perfect, especially when the river came up a few inches and coloured nicely.

The first week produced several barbel to over 6lb, then disaster struck. I lost a very big fish at the net due to the hook straightening out. I couldn't believe it. The hook was a new type which had been recommended to me by a carp angler for use with particles. Thinking it may have been just one bad hook I persevered, but to my horror I hooked another big fish only to have the same thing happen again. To lose two potential doubles was indeed disastrous. Eventually, though, I changed back to my favourite brand and the next big fish I hooked I landed safely. This was a superb fish of 11lb 12oz.

That season turned out to be quite a turning-point for me on the Wensum. I caught a lot of barbel, thirty-five to be exact, with five doubles, and I learned that there was more to the river than people realised.

Trefor West joined me on the river and after a couple of seasons struggling like me eventually he mastered the river and caught some big fish. It was as though you had to serve an apprenticeship before a big barbel could be caught. Both Trev and I estimated that at one time, some three seasons ago now, there were at least seven or eight

Returning a handsome 11lb 4oz barbel.

doubles in the Wensum, with quite a few between 8 and 10lb. Several big fish just were not getting caught and, although we would occasionally see them in our swims, we could not tempt a take. I did eventually start to fish the river in winter and, provided I picked the right time – that is, high water and mild weather – then I could virtually guarantee catching barbel. I also had the advantage of having the river to myself apart from the odd chub angler. It was winter time that eventually produced my biggest Wensum barbel, a fish of 13lb 2oz in December, and the same fish again in March at 13lb 6oz.

Many people believed that this was the biggest fish present in the Wensum, but I can assure them and other anglers that at least one bigger fish exists. Both Trev and I can testify to that, having seen it several times, and for my own part I have hooked the fish twice only to lose it.

It is easy to get carried away with such a small stretch of river but potentially the Wensum has all the make-up to support far more barbel than are present at the moment. The reason why the present head of barbel haven't exploded like the Severn population is, I feel, a direct result of an uncooperative water authority's weed-cutting operations in stretches where the barbel spawn. Fortunately, in the last three or four years, restraint has been used and, thanks to several local anglers like myself, the spawning areas are left intact. Now the barbel have an uninterrupted spawning session, and surviving fry also enjoy the benefit of the extra weed cover.

I have campaigned through the Norfolk and Suffolk Anglers' Consultative

Committee for the introduction of further stocks of barbel into Norfolk rivers, but the water authority's negative attitude has meant that no alien fish will be introduced into their rivers. It is a sad state of affairs when long stretches of the Wensum, which would be ideally suited to barbel, are barren of fish.

Following on from this, many conservation-minded people cannot fail to have seen the 'Save the Wensum' campaign. This campaign has begun since the planned abstraction of the river near Taverham to supply drinking water for Norwich. My feelings are that with the resulting abstraction directly above the stretch which contains barbel the river will deteriorate very quickly. The water authority's assurances that the abstraction will not affect the levels I find unconvincing, and we live in gloomy anticipation.

For such a short stretch of the Wensum to have produced barbel in excess of 13lb is no mean achievement and many anglers like myself have had many happy hours tracking down and catching these magnificent specimens. Let us pray that abstraction does not ruin what I consider to be one of the top big-barbel rivers in this county.

The Great Ouse

PAUL WOODINGS

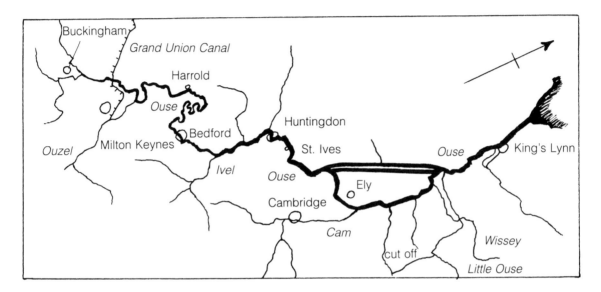

The object of this chapter is not to instruct the reader how to tackle up for his quarry or how to approach barbel fishing with advice about techniques. These subjects are dealt with adequately in other parts of this book. In any case, 'approach' is largely personal in angling and I would hope that anyone intending to fish for Great Ouse barbel already has a reasonably thorough grounding, and as much experience as possible with the species. What I have set out to do is to give the reader a general feel for the river and to provide some guidance about which areas to start on.

I also hope that this chapter will give the angler the impetus and confidence to stick at it if he has already tried and failed on the Ouse. Moreover, there may be anglers local to the river unaware of what they have on their doorstep. Hampshire and Dorset do not have a monopoly on barbel fishing!

The Great Ouse and its Barbel

The river itself flows eastwards through some of the country's most intensively farmed arable land in Bedfordshire and Cambridgeshire. Because of this, over the years and particularly since the last war, the river has felt the full effects of modern-day agricultural methods. Anyone with a concern for the

141

countryside should be fully aware of what these problems are. Suffice it to say that the river (and surrounding landscape) has been ravaged by land-drainage schemes prompted by farming interests, has been polluted by silage, has been abstracted excessively, and – probably worst of all – has been saturated by a multitude of toxic substances such as nitrates, insecticides, pesticides and chemical fertilisers.

In years gone by, before these vested interests began raping our countryside, the quality of the fishing on this river was superb. The chub fishing in particular was legendary. To all intents and purposes, however, the mid-1970s saw the death of this superb river as a mixed fishery. Now it is only a shadow of its former self.

Given the troubled history of the Great Ouse, it is nothing short of remarkable that today the river is actually *improving* all the time as a barbel fishery. And, considering that barbel are indigenous to the Ouse, it seems especially strange that even in the river's heyday very few were caught anywhere along its course.

It seems that only in the past ten years has the river really shown what it can do in the way of barbel fishing. The species seems to have filled a niche in the ecosystem of the river and, although some minor stocking programmes carried out since the mid-1950s have surely helped to boost the numbers, it is clear that at least some of the original stock have come through and have now colonised certain stretches.

Strictly speaking, the only rivers which can be said to hold indigenous stocks of 'original' barbel are those east-flowing rivers, like the Ouse and the Thames, which millions of years ago formed tributaries of the ancient great Rhine river, before Great Britain was separated from the European land-mass. Populations in other rivers are the result of official or unofficial transfers. In other east-coast rivers, such as the Nene and Welland, which undoubtedly held barbel for many many years, the populations appear by now to have died out almost completely. One can, of course, fish for barbel on various European rivers, such as the Danube, to this day. I must admit to being attracted by the idea of fishing for barbel which could well be direct descendants of the ancient original stock. Perhaps I'm a purist at heart.

As far as the Great Ouse is concerned, however, there can be no doubt that numbers of fish are very small when compared with many other barbel fisheries, especially in its middle reaches. This can probably be at least partially attributed to the fact that there are relatively few spawning areas, such as gravel shallows and weirpools, compared with such rivers as the Thames, which is probably the most similar in character to the Ouse. Whatever view you may take, there can be no doubt that if the river was left alone by man things would improve greatly.

Barbel Fishing Today

During the past ten years or so the situation with barbel on the Ouse has changed dramatically – basically, from a period where very few fish were caught to a time around the mid-seventies when barbel began to show in both the upper and middle reaches, not

Roger Baker with one of the elusive Great Ouse doubles, at 11lb 6oz.

in large numbers but on a fairly regular basis. It was at this point, in 1977, that I personally began to take an interest in what was being taken, mostly accidentally by match anglers, from the middle reaches of the river. The upper reaches were, I believe, very occasionally producing the odd small fish but the real drama was taking place in the middle reaches, with several double-figure fish being reported. So, describing the barbel fishing on the Ouse today, I shall deal with the river in two parts as there are some major differences.

The Middle Reaches

First, then, the middle reaches of the river, which in terms of barbel fishing can be considered as the river between Bedford and St Ives. Even when the middle reaches were producing barbel regularly, they were never caught frequently and, although I and two friends fished many times around the St Ives area, we had very little success. By far and away the most outstanding and successful angler on the river at that time, and possibly the most successful barbel fisherman of all time as far as big Ouse barbel are concerned, was Roger Baker of the Barbel Catchers Club. We fished quite a few times with Roger and I know that in order to catch the fish that he did, he spent a phenomenal amount of time on the river bank.

I always remember crossing the large

meadow where we usually fished, normally on a Saturday evening or afternoon, and casting my eye across the field and along the flat, featureless banks. The view was always the same, and from where we stood we could just make out two shapes; one was a bankside bush and the other was Roger Baker. I swear he must have taken root, just like the bush.

In the early eighties, however, there was some kind of mysterious pollution along the stretch that we fished. This resulted in the death of what must have been at least a high proportion of the resident barbel along that particular stretch and this, to quote Roger, 'really screwed it up'. Since then the middle reaches have been very quiet as far as barbel are concerned, and I haven't fished these reaches for about six or seven years. However, I don't think there can be any doubt that barbel are still present in the river somewhere between St Neots and St Ives and a true pioneer might well give it a crack. It's a matter of deciding whether or not the odds are too long. All the evidence suggests that if one caught a barbel on the middle reaches of the Ouse it would more likely than not be over 10lb in weight.

The character of the Ouse in this region is in the main very uniform; it is generally of even depth and such features as bankside vegetation, cut-out banks, sharp bends, trees, undercuts and rafts are at a bare minimum. The river itself also lacks the kind of features found in many other rivers (and, indeed, the Ouse in its upper reaches), such as clay boulders, lodges, streamer weed, cabbages, gravel shallows and sunken trees.

In some ways, however, this makes potential barbel swims more conspicuous, because where there is an obvious feature such as a narrowing of the river or a weirpool it is very likely to be frequented by barbel, assuming that they are present in the first place. I suggest, therefore, that if you intend to try your hand on the middle reaches, swims directly below a weirpool – say within 700 yards – are as good a place as any to start. You should also sound out anyone else who fishes the stretch you intend to fish, as you will need as much information as you can get. But be cautious. Do not necessarily believe everything you read or are told. There have been instances in the past, and the middle Ouse is one example, where reports of fish have been made that are to say the least highly dubious. You know the sort of thing: five barbel in an afternoon from Offord weirpool, no witnesses or photographs and no barbel reported there before or since. As it happens, Offord weir would be a good place to try, but don't allow false information to lead you up the garden path.

One other feature of the middle Ouse is the large number of boats, particularly in the summer months. While I don't necessarily think they bother the barbel, they certainly don't make the fishing any easier. They can be avoided completely in some areas – for example, in backwaters and directly below weirs and in their run-offs. Should you wish to fish a stretch where boats do pass through, however, I would suggesting fishing from about 5 p.m. in the summer until perhaps 2 a.m., depending on conditions and temperatures.

Another double for Roger – at 11lb 3oz!

The Upper Reaches

As far as barbel are concerned, the upper reaches of the Ouse are those between Bedford and Newport Pagnell, and maybe even a little higher. I apologise for being a little vague, but the situation with barbel in the upper Ouse is at present one of constant change and future events may indicate further barbel movements upstream. One major factor to consider is the size of the river above Newport Pagnell, as it does start to become very tiny in places. This makes these 'upper, upper' reaches more vulnerable to the whims of the land drainage department of the

Anglian Water Authority and less able to tolerate farm pollution such as silage. In the end these may turn out to be the governing factors in the progression of barbel upstream in the Great Ouse.

The upper as opposed to the middle reaches really do offer far and away the greater chance of a few barbel and some of these do definitely reach double figures. The past couple of seasons have shown this, with a handful turning up to some fortunate anglers. The upper reaches are improving all the time, and are very well worth fishing if you get the opportunity.

The character of the river here, in the main, is much different, with extensive

145

gravel shallows, streamer weed, dense reedbeds, onions, cabbage beds, sharp bends, sunken trees, snags, rafts, islands, deep holes and bankside trees and bushes – all in all, everything you need, and even the barbel! The barbel population on the upper reaches must have been 'bubbling' away for years, but since the early eighties their numbers have swollen out of all proportions. Some people have even expressed fears of them taking over completely!

Do not get the idea that these upper-Ouse barbel are easy to catch – this is far from the case. There still appears to be lots of dead water as far as barbel are concerned, but they have formed quite strong colonies here and there right up the river. The task, therefore, is to find a suitable area and get stuck in, and this is where rivercraft comes in, together with a grounding in barbel fishing and its problems. Once you get out there it is up to you to pick the best-looking swims and fish them. They are not difficult to spot and any or all of the previously mentioned features can add up to a potential swim. Stick at it and success should not be long coming.

The best times to fish are any time during the day, with the usual emphasis on evenings and after dark, but mainly in the summer and autumn. As far as winter fishing is concerned, don't be afraid to try it as the occasional fish has been caught when the conditions are just right (even on the middle reaches). The usual guide to the winter conditions is a river carrying a good bit of extra water, preferably fining down after heavy rains with air and water temperatures settled for several days. Look for water temperatures of 42°F or more, and weather as mild as possible.

To summarise, the upper reaches are more attractive to the prospective barbel angler than the middle reaches, but the middle reaches have historically produced most of the really big fish and therefore offer the biggest challenge.

Access in the main on all of the river is by day ticket or local club membership. These clubs are fairly easy to locate and join and are really very cheap. £10 should gain you membership of just about any of the local clubs that control stretches of the river.

Any of the accepted and generally practical techniques employed in barbel fishing today will work on their day, and the bigger your repertoire the greater your chances of success. The same goes for baits, except to say that in my opinion particle baits have the edge over larger baits, at least in the summer. Should you intend to fish in winter, however, you may want to concentrate on larger, smellier baits.

The Trent

ARCHIE BRADDOCK

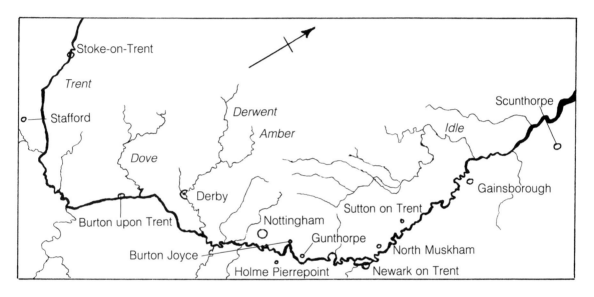

At midnight on a Friday late in August 1973 my phone rang. It was a very excited fishing pal, Ray Longland. 'Arch, we got six!' From that moment my fishing was never to be quite the same; the Trent had once more become a barbel river. What had happened was that Ray and two pals had gambled on an evening just trying to catch a Trent barbel, and had succeeded beyond their wildest dreams. Six fish to 2½lb is pretty small beer by any standards, but those barbel were probably the first for forty years or more to be taken by anglers deliberately fishing for them. Of course, everyone knew the Trent used to be a great barbel river in the dim and distant past, but those fish had all been killed off by pollution, hadn't they?

With the river barely a mile from my doorstep you can imagine I got pretty excited by all this, and the result was that not only did I really get down to catching these fish, but I also delved into the history of barbel on the Trent. Fortunately there are books still available by two of angling's great forefathers – Nottingham Bailey, a leading exponent of the Nottingham style of trotting with a centrepin; and J. W. Martin, known as the 'Trent Otter'. Bailey fished the river from about 1840, while Martin came on the

147

scene in the second half of the century. They fished together several times, and what days they must have been! Through their writings I had a glimpse of another age, a bygone world, and, of course, those bygone barbel.

Strange to say, they were never as big or as numerous as I had expected, and it took a very good angler to catch them consistently, as indeed it does today. Yes, both men caught doubles but to them a ten-pound barbel was just a good fish, not the ultimate of the season. For instance, the Trent Otter wrote of a catch of several barbel taken by an old angler, presumably in the early 1800s. What surprised Martin was the high average weight of 7lb per fish; the fact that individual barbel ran from 3lb to *15lb* didn't really interest him. There were still very big fish in the Trent in Martin's era; he mentioned the capture of one of nearly 13lb. He also reports 'seeing and handling' a fish of 16lb 10oz, taken on a night-line baited with lamprey. Obviously these giants were few and far between, as elsewhere he quoted that for every fish over 3lb caught you would catch four under that weight. Bailey mentioned that 10lb fish could be taken from many spots along the Trent, but his chapters are sprinkled with quotes of 4lb fish, and nowhere is the capture of a fish above 6lb described. Yet it must be remembered that the river was already in decline; as early as 1840 Bailey was complaining at the disappearing grayling, always the first fish to fall victim to pollution.

These anglers of yesteryear almost always float-fished, considering 'plumbing' (legering to us) as unsporting. Trotted lobworms were the order of the day, feeding chopped lobs by hand, much as the modern angler uses maggots. And who is to say that it wouldn't work today? Who, indeed, has ever tried it on the Trent? Not me, although it's something I'm always meaning to do. Perhaps one day I'll have the courage to do as the Trent Otter did. I'll make a huge cork-bodied float, capable of carrying 4¾oz of lead. Yes, *4¾oz*! I'll take it to a swim on the tidal water that is thirty feet deep at high tide, and trot this deep hole with slider rig and lobworm. Perhaps then I'll only catch barbel of over 5lb, with the better fish at 6 and 7lb or more. It will take me at least twenty minutes to land each one in such a heavy push of water. Yes, that's how they used to do it, and every time I read that particular piece it makes me realise that perhaps we modern specimen hunters still have a lot to learn. The present day carp-fanatics use 2oz leads to hurl a boilie into the blue but, I mean, 4¾oz – on a float!

That class of barbel were well above the norm for those days, and it may be that legering would have produced a higher average; we shall never know, but those anglers certainly had the edge over us when it came to large catches. Ninety fish in a day and three hundred in a week were two examples quoted. They also had one other thing going for them – a closeness to nature and an appreciation of their fishing that seems to be vanishing from our present-day world. Martin summed it up beautifully when he wrote:

It was a lovely morning in mid-September, with here and there browns showing among the greens . . . lap-wings were busy on the big meadow, and a couple of curlews kept wheeling round uttering their strange cries. A heron on fishing bent is gliding his slow flight towards the backwater known as the old Trent, and a couple of mallards quack out in alarm as they sweep over the boat. Under our feet the water gurgled and eddied and, as if to invite us to make a start, a barbel hurled himself from the water and came down with a resounding splash some twenty yards from us. Old Charlie made a sarcastic remark to the effect that he guessed I had fallen asleep, but I never could resist drinking in the beauty of that spot, and silently communing with nature.

And then came the dark ages.

Not long after these great anglers left the scene for ever, the Trent reached rock bottom. By 1920 barbel catches were falling dramatically, and by 1930 most of the chub and bream had gone as well. I arrived on the scene in the fifties, and what a scene it was! A river that permanently ran the colour and texture of soup, and with an acrid tang that could be detected half a mile away. We young teenagers used to pray for the wind to be on our backs. If it wasn't, the giant icebergs of foam sailing majestically down the river made life nearly impossible for the budding float angler. Legering was right out; all you got was coating of jelly-like slime on the line. Yuk!

But the old river still fought back, and on the good days it was a roach a cast trotting wheat. Remarkable, when you consider the filth that was being poured in from the potteries at Stoke, the breweries at Burton, and the grossly polluted river Tame. Where did

our captains of industry ever get the idea of piping their rubbish into the nearest river? And why didn't an outraged government immediately ban such practices? Good questions, my friends.

So I and my generation turned away from the Trent, seeking other rivers, and other barbel. Until that fateful phone call of 1973. Now, fourteen years later, the river is recovering as fast as it declined. From the tidal waters of Gainsborough and beyond to the narrow reaches above Burton-on-Trent, it's barbel and more barbel – a hundred miles of barbel! Hanging on in small pockets through the worst of the pollution, they are repopulating the river by successfully breeding in large numbers every year. They've been doing this since at least 1968, as has been ascertained by scale reading. Unfortunately, many of those early fish had diseases such as eye fluke, fin rot and pomphorynchus, which is an internal parasite. This was a legacy from the bad old days, but I'm happy to say that the current generations are clean, healthy fish.

So what class of fish can today's angler hope to catch? For the moment, at least, it's back to Martin's quote: four under 3lb to every one over. But don't let it worry you. They fight like tigers, and time after time I've been fooled into thinking I'd hooked something special, only to find a fish of a few ounces over 3lb. Yes, there are bigger fish to be had; my friends and I have taken several over 5lb, and a couple of 6lb+. The biggest capture I have been able to track down is a fish of 8lb 8oz, and I think there may be one or two such fish about. If we're lucky, just *maybe* one a

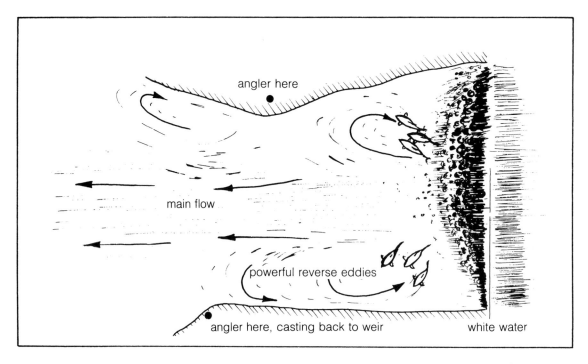

Beeston Weir, near Nottingham.

good deal bigger will turn up. There are many rumours, but a barbel can be a very deceiving fish due to its length. Odd times I have weighed fish for anglers who claimed them to be 'well over 5lb.' The best of these went to 3lb 1oz.

It also depends a lot on where you fish. Taking my home town of Long Eaton as a divider, it's fair to say that upstream of here there are far more barbel than lower down. With mile after mile of shallow, gravel-bottomed runs, it is in effect one huge barbel swim. The catches can sometimes be spectacular – 50lb of fish are often taken in matches. Most of these are on the small side, and one of my own bags totalled 17 fish with not one above 1½lb. On another occasion I had 16 between 2½ and 4¾lb. That's about

what to expect on these upper reaches, and it takes some hard fishing to improve on that. Downstream of Long Eaton I get the impression that the fish are not so numerous but of a higher average size. Of course, this may change as the seasons pass.

How to catch them? One has only to scan the match results in the angling press to read of 55lb on the feeder, 45lb on the float, etc. It all looks so easy – until you realise that a hundred anglers fished every peg on a mile of river, and only one caught barbel in any numbers. You go rushing down to fish that very swim, and an angler a quarter of a mile away is catching all the fish. Yes, they've moved! So forget about chasing swims and find your own. Look for a gravel bottom and a moderate or fast flow, not a crawl. Depth is not important, so long as current speed and bottom make-up are right. Aim to fish it in the evening and on into the dark for an hour. This is the key time, and the advent of betalights means that fishing in the dark is no problem.

Start by using a bait dropper to carpet the swim with at least half a pint of hemp, and repeat this as the light fades. The aim is to have a good 'taste' wafting down the river, and to perhaps feed off some of the nuisance fish, like chub. Use a minimum 6lb line; if you don't you'll be sorry. The first time you catch several good barbel in a session will make you realise just what punishment your line, and other tackle, has to put up with. For that reason always

use a soft-actioned rod, to help cushion the powerful lunges of the fish. Any make of strong hook will suit but don't go too small. I generally use a size 6, and I'll go larger when it's needed.

Use as heavy a lead as the swim needs, but if in doubt err on the large side. I will use a 2oz flattened bomb if I have to, and that is sometimes what it takes to hold in midstream on a wide, deep stretch of the lower Trent. Failure to go heavy enough is the biggest mistake of the barbel hopefuls I see on the river; they just never get the bait near the fish. Remember Martin, and his float.

The rod is propped high in the rest to keep as much line as possible out of

An average summer barbel, caught on sweetcorn.

the water, and it takes on an alarming curve due to current drag. Don't worry – when the bites come they'll often drag the rod off the rests. For that reason, never leave the tackle; I've seen one rod go into the river. Obviously, a near-bank swim doesn't need such extreme tactics, but always be prepared to up the size of the lead and fish further out if no bites are forthcoming.

No special baits are needed, but ringing the changes will often bring more fish when it seems that bites have ceased. So always take three or four different baits with you, as the fish will also change their preferences with rising or falling water levels, and take different baits at different times of the season. During the summer, while levels are constant, sweetcorn and maggots work very well. Fish with 2–3 corns or 8–10 maggots, leaving the point and barb of the hook fully exposed. This will help deter the chub but doesn't bother the barbel at all. Later in the season luncheon meat or cheese may well score best. In coloured water, lobworms come into their own, with meat as a very good change bait. Sometimes the fish will accept one bait only, scorning all others; at other times only repeated 'new' offerings gain their interest, so be prepared to experiment.

There is one more very important point and that is barbel movements. A rise in the river level of only an inch can mean that the fish have moved yards away, while a foot of extra water could shift them half a mile. Even in prolonged normal conditions a great deal of movement goes on. Imagine the fish lying up in their chosen area most of the day. As evening falls they start to move, often upstream, hoovering the bottom as they go. On reaching the end of their beat they drop back downstream again. This is a very simple pattern, and it can often be far more complicated, but it doesn't take a genius to work out that the angler sitting on the 'turn-around' swim will get a regular supply of fish. Upstream of him will be dead, and downstream a bit hit and miss. On just a few trips I have had that key swim, happily hauling them out, with anglers nearby scratching their heads and wondering what they're doing wrong.

More often, though, the catches will be about equal. I'll get a couple of fish, a few moments later my upstream companion gets one, and so on. Clearly a case of all of us missing the hotspot. That's exactly why the match men score; they've got an angler in *every* swim. It's really all about the current speed the fish like best, so when you are catching try and imprint the swim on your brain for future reference. After a while you will instinctively find yourself picking the right swim, more often than not.

On re-reading all this, I'm very conscious of all the things I haven't said, but at the same time I hope enough *has* been said to give the angler a good start. When the blank sessions come, and they do for all of us, don't lose heart. One day it will all fit together, and every cast will produce a battling Trent barbel. When that happens, you'll never want to fish for anything else.

The Bristol Avon

NIGEL MILBOURNE

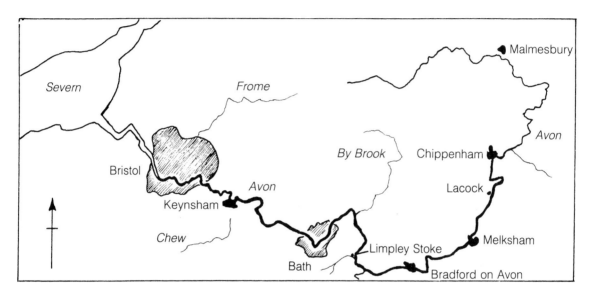

Fortune smiled on me during my salad days, for my father, a keen angler, saw to it that wherever the family went rods and reels were always put into the car boot. Consequently I have been privileged to watch seals herding shoals of finnock in the mouth of the River Spey in the north of Scotland during April snowstorms. In contrast, I've stared, unblinking, at the winking and dithering of tench-worried isotope floats in dark Devon claypits during sultry May nights. However, my angling apprenticeship was chiefly served fervently hoping the bright-finned roach of the River Yeo in north Somerset would find my flake baits acceptable.

There was always a healthy mixture of fishing and fraternisation with the fairer sex in my grammar school days, and one old flame's brother, Nigel, used to take me along on some of his trips after those roach. In retrospect, it is little wonder that I struggled to catch the better class of fish with my combination of tank-aerial rod, 6lb Platil line and either bubble float or coffin lead. But I used to set out for the riverbank with fresh hope every trip, in much the same way that I do today, albeit that I now enjoy a more enlightened outlook.

One day, Nigel asked if I would like to go to fish the Bristol Avon at Limpley Stoke with him. I looked through

153

my Golden Carp AA tab, thought of the 'Big River', read the long list of species waiting to be caught, and just had to go. Here, I felt, was to be a new adventure. Looking back, memories of that day still linger – the little copper-and-brass-trimmed tank engines trundled past along the riverside between Bath and Bradford, while carp basked under far-bank lilies and casually tossed sandwich crusts were torn into by quicksilver dace as they floated off downstream. The biggest impression of all was made by Nigel's throw-away comment that barbel were rumoured to be in the weirpool we were walking past. Little did I know that some twelve years of schooling later fate would see me return, quite by chance, to the same spot.

During the mid-1970s, an old college friend told me of a job vacancy which brought me back to Bristol from Plymouth, via a period of exile in Scotland, and it was a short step to befriending some new work colleagues, and planning a fishing trip on the first day of the new season. An afternoon beside a lake proved fruitless, so we went down to the Avon for the night in pursuit of chub. I sat on a stone all night in quiet solitude and caught my first chub, or two, but with failing batteries in my torch I didn't dare risk the climb down to the weir to see my mates hidden in the darkness. As first light crept over the rim of the high, wooded valley, I sat transfixed by the rolling and leaping of fish dancing as if in some ballet orchestrated by the gathering crescendo of the dawn chorus. Indeed, it wasn't until the voice of another early-season hopeful startled me back to reality that I decided to venture forth and find out how my companions had fared. Sure enough, they too had caught some chub, and – wonder upon wonder – three barbel, the first I'd ever seen. Dawn that Saturday morning instilled a new resolve in me – I wanted to catch one of these enigmatic creatures.

After work one evening during the following week, I leapt on my motor-

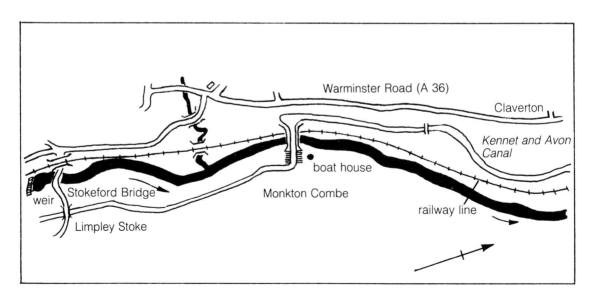

154

bike for the 35-mile round trip down to the weirpool to catch that barbel. It wasn't long before my rod hooped over and I played out my first. Here was a very agreeable alternative to summer nights spent fly fishing for sea trout on the Liddel, the Scottish border haunt of my teens, and boy, did these barbel scrap! The remainder of the season saw me to-ing and fro-ing on my motor-bike at every opportunity, whatever the hour and weather – September nights, heavy with drizzle and the smell of creosote from the old mill-yard; bejewelled, moonlit December evenings; and barbel, barbel and more barbel. I was punch-drunk.

During the next year, I read a letter to the angling press calling for the re-formation of the Barbel Catchers, and decided I had to get in on the action. I drove through torrential rain to Packington, in the heart of England, for the inaugural meeting and arrived sopping wet just as the first few words were being spoken. Since that day, I have struck up friendships with fellow barbel anglers the country over and revelled in our mutual interest and camaraderie. I've fished many rivers by kind invitation, but could never get back quick enough to try out new ideas somewhere along the 74 miles of the Avon with my Yorkshire-born angling companion Bill Robinson. However, when Bill decided to turn his attentions to the trout and entomology of Chew Valley and Blagdon lakes, some years later, I was left to soldier on alone.

One afternoon, during another bite-less club match, I chanced to be nattering to Paul Hollyman, who had drawn a peg I thought might produce a barbel, and persuaded him to join me for a session or two later that month just to prove there really were some fish in the river. Paul was able to bring his Kent carp-fishing experience to our new partnership and his viewpoint certainly helped me to keep an open mind on barbel angling because today eleven seasons have passed since that first Limpley Stoke barbel charged off downstream. Whilst the tendency is to get a bit set in one's ways without such exchanges – you know, the box fits so snugly into that well-worn hole in the bank – picking one another's brains sees each season bringing a fresh challenge somewhere along the river.

My thoughts turn towards the Avon during May, after a brief sojourn on the banks of Chew and Blagdon in April. Surely here is a time when the valley upstream of Bath is a treasure as rich as any in England, and this is when I happily walk along much of the river, pausing to sit and stare into likely-looking runnels for tell-tale signs of barbel over gravel. A golden flash or a pair of coral-pink pectoral fins is often the first indication that I have been unaware of their presence under my very nose all the while, lying doggo or playing follow-the-leader as they emerge on to a shallow bar to root and grub before sliding down into deep-water obscurity. Those early weeks of roach skittering on to weed as they procreate in gay abandon and the grey chub scarred and beaten about by their own excesses, only serve to build the drama as I keep my vigil for the flag-ships of the fleet. It is usually around the third weekend of the month that the female barbel move on to the spawning beds, each accompanied by a flotilla of smaller males, to lay their eggs. An unseasonal storm may delay the event, but it is possible to gain many suitable vantage-points between Malmesbury and Bath to watch this fantastic rite. Downstream of Bath the boat traffic gets under way with the warming of the weather and the spectacle is lost.

Distribution and Location

Since their first introduction into the river in 1955 at Stokeford Bridge, barbel have prospered and spread. The initial stocking of fifty-four fish has been supplemented by further introductions at seven sites during the 1960s and 1970s, totalling some six hundred barbel mostly from the Thames tributary, the Enbourne. How grateful I and many other anglers are now to Wessex Fisheries officer Mike Amey for his enterprise and enthusiasm in the project.

At first, several distinct populations resulted from the stocking, but it is now evident that this situation no longer holds because barbel have been reported from Malmesbury right down to the tidal section. Chief concentrations of fish exist around the Wiltshire market town of Chippenham and the valley immediately upstream of Bath, but more than the odd pleasure angler has been surprised by catching a barbel many miles from either of these two centres. A few years back an autumn match at Lacock, well downstream of

A patient wait for an early-season barbel.

Chippenham, ended with an unforeseen result when two barbel were caught on size 18 hooks by J. Raines. Each pulled the scales off the end of their range at 8lb. During the early 1980s several somewhat smaller barbel have shown up around the Keynsham chocolate factory, the upper limit of spring tides; and, indeed, as the decade has progressed, eight-pounders have been captured here too. The spread of fish is all the more remarkable when you consider that there is barely three miles between any of the numerous weirs over which the Avon tumbles.

The thrill of spotting barbel at sites where I haven't seen them before is ample reward for time spent peering through polaroids instead of capitalising on the annual slaughter during 'duffers' fortnight' with Bill, trout rod in hand. Now is the time to contemplate the coming season and try to decide where I'm going to attempt to get to grips with these bewhiskered adversaries. Not for me will the new season mean a tumble out of bed and a headlong rush to the better known swims, but, rather, a leisurely stroll to a likely-looking stickle at dusk. My weeks of river watching have kept me in tune and I'll know just where to go for the season's first capture.

Season tickets worth buying are Chippenham AA, Bath AA, Bathampton AA and Bristol Amalgamated, though it is certainly best to concentrate on one stretch which offers summer fishing on shallows and winter sport in deeper water until you become familiar with your quarry and their location. For example, restricting yourself to Claverton on Bathampton AA waters or to Limpley Stoke on Bath AA waters will cut ticket outlay to around £10 for the season.

The upper river flows east out of the oolitic limestone of the Cotswolds and is a preserved trout stream for many miles. This is a haven in which barbel can live virtually undisturbed in isolation pockets and there are bronzed leviathans seemingly out of all proportion to the riffles and glides which they frequent, some recorded during netting operations to 11lb+. I hope they remain an untenable dream. Where the stream slows and flows under the M4 motorway near Seagry Mill, barbel become a worthwhile proposition, and it is between here and Chippenham that I so enjoy spending summer evenings stalking my fish. Here you are best advised to travel light and spot your barbel before trying to tempt it, or you may spend seasons without success walking right past them, cunningly concealed under the bank. My most pleasurable capture came, on one of the Avons few day-ticket waters, as I was working my way downstream one evening. From the corner of my eye I spotted a sizeable swirl on some shallows. Thinking this could be one of the good chub which live hereabouts, I baited with bread flake and quietly approached to cast. The first swing was typically overcautious and fell short of its mark, but the second was taken immediately, and several anxious minutes later, with a little help from some friends, the prize was won – 7lb 6oz of quintessential barbel, right underneath the road bridge at Christian Malford.

There is often pain mixed with pleasure and to this day I wonder what might have been one early autumn evening downstream of Lacock. A barbel it certainly was, but I hadn't even seen it when it weeded itself at my feet as I turned around in panic to see my companion for the trip sliding down the bank towards me. Two or three jars of ale later in the Red Lion couldn't ease my sense of loss, for we'd planned that campaign without even seeing a barbel, trudged miles weighed down with angling and photographic equipment, and I even suffered the indignity of jumping down the river bank into a bed of nettles when a bull saw fit to take advantage of my lack of mobility.

In 1978 I joined Chippenham AA and spent the summer as if I were on commando manoeuvres, crawling up to the river's edge before flicking a natural bait in front of a feeding fish, or flitting from bush to rushbed in order to approach another which had given its whereabouts away with the typical roll and slap of the tail fin as it turned down. I must say that of all my seasons in the quest of barbel that summer ranks alongside the first in my memory, for, although the fish were on average small, each was a hard earned reward – and what compares with the delight of cradling the capture in the stream until it is fit to swim away, before you stand up and take in the evening's warmth and glow with satisfaction?

Summer fishing is equally well spent down through Chippenham, Reybridge and Lacock to Beanacre Dump near Melksham. Eight-pounders are specimen barbel from anywhere, but they are certainly present hereabouts. Indeed, 1982 saw the first claim for an

Harry Cook playing a Bristol Avon barbel . . .

. . . and satisfied with a fine 7lb 10oz catch.

Avon double ratified from Chippenham town waters. There have been several other doubles since the mid-seventies, and former Barbel Catchers member, Kenny Parsons, had a witnessed double back in 1978 from the middle Avon which he did not wish to publicise at the time.

Autumn and winter

When autumn comes and willow leaves float downstream, the flat Wiltshire countryside becomes a hard grey, desolate place. The first evening frosts see me heading further downstream to the sheltered Limpley Stoke valley; there is somehow a sense of intimacy with the river here. Barbel tend to take up deeper, more agreeably sheltered swims at this time of year, especially at the onset of the first floods, and presumably to get away from all the debris that gets flushed through. It is both a strange and a happy circumstance that very few anglers venture on to the banks when the river is pushing, because now is the time I like to be out most of all.

The ideal evening is a mild and windless one with drizzle in the air. If the river has colour in it, so much the better. Touch legering or quivertipping with an isotope on the rod top helps to keep one's profile low and disturbance to a minimum until the strike is met by a solid throbbing resistance as the barbel bids for freedom out in the swirling river darkness. A brief flash of the torch may be permitted to aid netting, but always be prepared for the 'one last dive' as the fish plunges away from the light at the surface.

The weight of the net lifted on to the bank brings feverish excitement as one stoops to peel the folds of green mesh away from the trophy. A quick weighing and a photograph as you gaze on the deep shoulder and well filled belly, and the fish is returned to the water. Remember that at this time barbel tend to come up from deeper water and must be capable of maintaining themselves upright before they are released.

Results over several seasons have indicated to me that barbel go on an autumnal blow-out and become somewhat easier to catch now, in the right conditions, than at any other time of year. Fishing during the day into smooth unruffled water can be rewarding, though dusk invariably brings greater recompense, especially as barbel will move close to the banks, and feed right under the rod top in coloured water.

Baits

There is no doubt that redolent baits will increase your chances of capture in autumn and winter flood conditions when feeding by sight is somewhat curtailed. I favour pastes at this time because they are soft and allow easier hooking in the cold water. A lot of the big old barbel of these middle reaches were blinded by the parasite *Diplostomum*, which last took a hold during the hot summer of 1976, so smell plays an important role in their feeding, not that their condition seems to have suffered.

My favourite 'smelly' baits are meat-based ones, and I often use luncheon meat, chopped ham and pork, sausage and pâté mixes. These can be made up as paste balls and particle-sized pieces using fine brown crumb to stiffen them, and various of the flavour additives available from carp specialists. I experimented a couple of seasons ago with Carptract 7 (liver) in meat pastes, and had a pleasing measure of success in coloured water. It was an instant bait because I tried it on the Severn in the autumn when fishing right under my rod top in a raging flood. I caught a chub of over 3lb and a barbel of 7lb on a stretch that doesn't regularly give up fish of such size. My good mate John Darby could not believe his senses when I made up some of the bait and split it between myself and his son Ian, who was eager to give it a go. In fact, I think John's wife has banned Ian from opening his tackle box in the house to this day!

Instead of turning to bait specialists, though, one can snoop about the kitchen cupboards and find several useful bait additives. Marmite, Oxo and Bovril have all accounted for their share of fish, notably better than average chub and some big barbel. Just don't mention my name when you have to account for their mysterious disappearance! It does pay to experiment with new baits in floodwater conditions if you want to catch the bigger Avon

Mike Stevens holds his magnificent Bristol Avon specimen which weighed 12lb 8oz, a record for the river.

barbel regularly, because like other members of the carp family the better ones become wary of big baits they have been caught on before.

In recent seasons coarse angling has seen something of a bait revolution, but it is worth pointing out that presentation is perhaps equally important. I have prolonged the effectiveness of a successful bait by using it in a variety of forms and offering it in different ways. Take 'pink inevitable', for instance. Once out of the can, it may be cut into large chunks and trotted on float gear, freelined, legered on a running link, or fixed as a bolt rig. The meat could be cut into much smaller pieces and used as a particle bait over which one might lay on, put it into an open-ended feeder with hemp, or if things get very difficult a hair rig might be used. Use imagination when the barbel get hard to catch, because contrary to popular belief they do not always pull the rod from the rests – they can give very subtle bite indications at times.

Early Spring

As the season draws to a close the days get longer, the water warms, plants begin a new growth cycle and life stirs on the river bed. Instead of the short, intensive feeding periods characteristic of warmer spells in winter, barbel feed for longer, replenishing lost weight and making ready for spawning. I like to go wandering along the river again at this time of year to see the changes wrought by floods and to choose some swims with shallow gravel bars flanked by emergent cabbage and onion weeds for some end-of-season sport. A pinch in the width of the river is often indicative of a good barbel swim, too, as there is usually a significant change in the depth.

When I decide to tackle one of the shallow swims at this time of year, I like to arrive about an hour before dusk and scatter some particle bait into the current over the shallow gravel bar, making sure that some washes down the slope into the depths, especially along the near margin. Casters, maggots, hemp and meat are all suitable, though this is about the only time of year that I will use maggots on the Avon, due to the problems of 'serpent wrestling' which I dislike enough during daylight, and like even less in darkness. I may then just sit and take the evening in, or, if the swim is well suited, I'll get the float rod out and lay on down the near margin until dark.

At nightfall, I'll put some more feed into the swim and cast in with a link-leger rig, positioning the bait on the slope. Later still, I'll cast my bait as close to the onion weed as I dare in the shallow water, listening for the characteristic kissing noise made by barbel feeding in shallow water around weekends. It is not unusual to catch a good bag of fish like this, thereby rounding the season off nicely, and leaving a feeling of anticipation through the coming months of enforced rest.

The Lee

ALAN HAYES

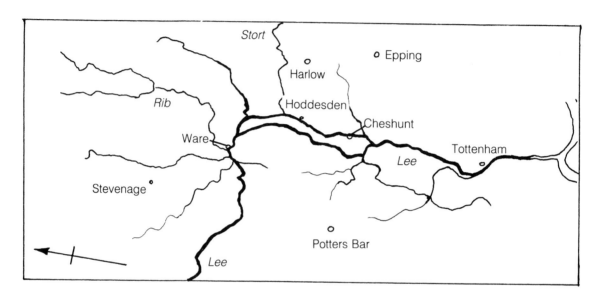

Although restricted to the innumerable weirpools and backwaters that are situated throughout the Lee valley, the barbel of this river have, over the years, proved themselves worthy opponents of many a skilled angler who has tried his hand at catching them. Indeed, over the past ten years the average weight has increased to the point that capture of fish between 5 and 6lb (of which there are many) is commonplace, although you will still find a fair share of fish between 1½ and 3lb that seem to make up the bulk of people's catches. The reason for this is that these fish are the survivors of a population explosion that occurred in the early 1970s. They have grown up in a cleaner river, with more natural food to enable them to put on weight. Another important reason is the fact that barbel are banned from being kept in keepnets, which cuts down the risk of scale and fin damage and, therefore, disease. Anglers, too, have treated the fish with more respect when landing them, and they also deposit up to 50 gallons of maggots per weekend on some stretches for them to feed on.

Rising just north of Dunstable in Bedfordshire, the Lee embroils itself with quite a few towns during its journey south towards London. The inevitable result of this is that the really natural sections of the river (the only ones where you will find barbel) have shrunk to the point of being in very short supply. Gravel extraction has also meant that the river has been diverted and re-routed, with the result that downstream from Hertford you will be hard put to it to find the original course.

But barbel, being barbel, have managed to live with this over the centuries, though the resultant pockets of fish that are left are under great pressure. There are, even now, still places where many an angler turns his nose up and walks on. If only they knew! From 12-foot deeps to 6-inch runs, the barbel are still there. You just have to know where to look.

During the early part of the season, the weed growth of the backwaters is quite phenomenal. Large banks of ranunculus, sometimes up to twenty feet long, sway back and forth in the current. Large beds of cabbage weed are also present, which provide excellent cover for the fish. Getting at the barbel through these weedbeds can be a very frustrating experience but the rewards are great. Strong tackle is advocated, though. I use an 11-foot compound-taper rod with a 1¼lb test curve and 6lb line straight through. In order to get through the weed, it is sometimes necessary to fix the lead so that you don't leave your bait hung up.

As to bait, I try not to use maggots this early in the season. Luncheon meat, sweetcorn, cheese and sausage meat can be just as good and a lot less expensive.

Once hooked, your barbel will try to tie your line in figures of eight in the nearest root of weed he can find. The answer is to always go downstream of your fish and never try to pull it across the weed, as many a good fish has been lost that way. So remember to look downstream before you start fishing – as trying to get around a 10-foot hawthorn bush can pose quite a problem!

Unfortunately, the weed does not last long on the Lee and by the end of July you would be hard put to it to find any capable of holding a good fish. This is sometimes a topsy-turvy time on the river; as the barbel look for new homes, they tend not to feed too well and fishing becomes difficult and patchy, to say the least. Fortunately, these backwaters are blessed with plenty of trees, particularly willows, which in many places overhang the river. These are classic barbel haunts but they attract the chub as well. One of my favourite swims on the Lee is where the river cuts into the bank almost directly beneath where I fish and undercuts the bank for about ten yards downstream. Barbel really seem to love this sort of swim, which is worth remembering when choosing where to fish.

At this time of year the float really comes into its own. In conjunction with the regular use of the bait dropper, you can have some real red-letter days. In the months of July and August, hemp and caster are really popular baits, whilst maggots, although a close second, tend to attract the small fry and the perch, which are reappearing in the Lee in ever-increasing numbers. Fishing with the float I have found to be an attractive and certainly more interesting method of catching barbel on the Lee.

As the flow is not all that fast (or non-existent), the stick float seems to suit, fished some 6 or 8 inches over depth, and allowed to drag through the swim. Bites on this rig, when they come, are really fast. One moment the float is there, the next it has flashed away and you're into a fish. Sometimes, if the fishing is slow, anglers like to lay on. This can be done with the same rig with the float pulled well over depth. This method is only really suitable for fishing close in, as the current will tend to pull the float under if fished out towards midstream.

When trotting, the centrepin reel is a

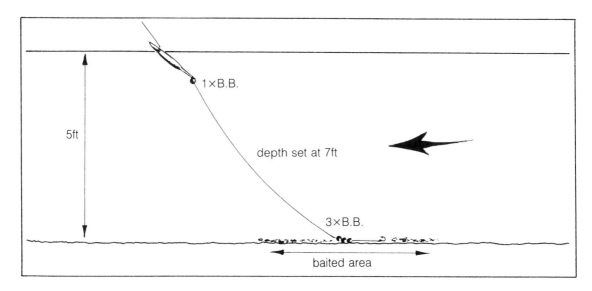

5ft

1×B.B.

depth set at 7ft

3×B.B.

baited area

Laying on rig.

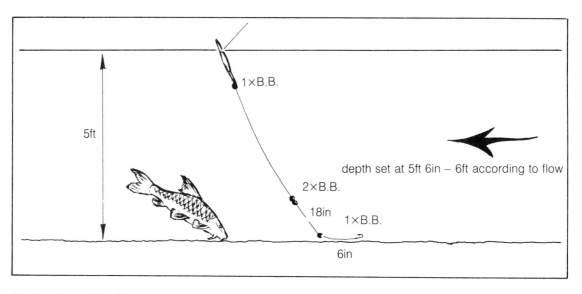

5ft

1×B.B.

depth set at 5ft 6in – 6ft according to flow

2×B.B.

18in

1×B.B.

6in

Trotting rig medium flow.

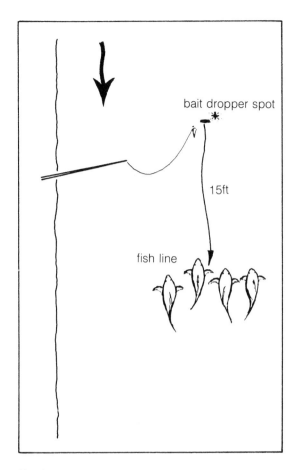

Trotting through.

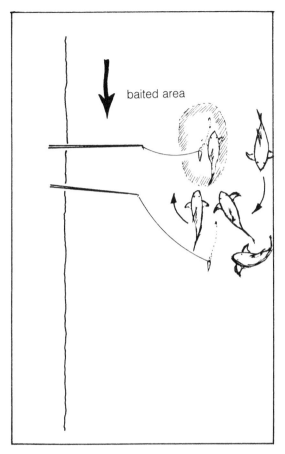

Laying on.

delight to use, along with a rod of 13–14 feet that has plenty of power. As for line, I'm very reluctant to go below 4lb. It's very easy to succumb to the temptation of using fine line whilst float fishing, but I have caught too many fish that have had hook to nylons (on one occasion, four in one fish) trailing from their mouths to give way to the temptation. The only big drawback of float fishing is that you tend to foul-hook occasional fish.

As regards legering, the swimfeeder is a firm favourite. I prefer to use an open-ended feeder and coarse bread-crumbs with either a maggot or hemp-and-caster filling in the middle. If you get the mixture of the crumb right, it should burst out of the feeder on hitting the bottom and settle in an area some four or five feet downstream. It pays to use a tail of about 16 inches. This keeps the small fry, which quickly home in to your feeder, from giving you those frustrating taps on the rod tip.

Barbel, I believe, feed in circular patterns. When they have moved upstream across your groundbait, they then move out into midstream and let the flow carry them down water until with a flick of the tail they position themselves downstream of the baited area. Then, if the coast is clear, they will again move up to start feeding again. This pattern occurs quite often, particularly if there are more than a couple of fish present.

A second rod fished some 10–15 feet downstream of the baited area can often account for fish if they are shy of the hookbait that is being fished over the groundbait. This is also a way of getting better-size fish as the big 'uns often seem to hang around at the rear of the shoal.

When the barbel home in on your groundbait, they normally force any other fish out of the swim. The only exception seems to be the bream, of which there are large shoals present in the Lee. They seem quite happy to feed alongside the barbel, so if you do start catching them you can be sure the barbel are not far behind.

Due to the silt that has built up in some swims, it is possible to see tiny bubbles appearing on the surface. These provide an early indication of the presence of barbel or bream in the swim. When you see this, a couple of dropper-loads of hookbait should be placed just upstream of your feeder (the second rod could be used for this purpose). This can tip the balance in your favour and entice the fish further into your swim. I cannot stress enough the importance of keeping the dropper going regularly, as barbel can consume vast quantities of bait in a relatively short time and they can lose interest if the food supply dries up. A further important point is to ensure that you cast to the same spot every time. It helps to pick out the shadow of a tree and mark the spot in

your mind, then stick to it. Sooner or later the barbel will turn up.

As regards the best time of day to catch barbel, I don't think that there can be any doubt that evening, just before dark, is the most rewarding. But it is very difficult to find fisheries that allow night fishing on the Lee and so we must look to other times.

First light in the Summer can sometimes produce the odd fish, especially with a piece of legered meat rolled under a favourite weedbed. But if, like me, you cannot always choose your fishing time, barbel *can* be caught on the Lee in day time if you are patient enough. In most cases, I believe that this is due purely to the density of fish in relatively small areas. They must quickly mop up food that is presented before other species get it.

However, I feel more confident fishing weirpools during the day as they can turn up fish at just about any old time. The weir pools of the Lee can, on their own, provide tremendous barbel fishing and they do hold some really big fish. Last year alone, one produced fish of 11 and 13lb – real monsters for the Lee. The pools also act as nurseries for really small fish and it is not uncommon to catch barbel of 3 inches in length. There are, I have found, two different approaches to fishing these pools.

The first is to get right in against the sill. These swims are often snag-ridden with large boulders or old timber piles, so strong tackle, able to withstand a lot of punishment, is required. Sometimes, if the flow is right, you are able to freeline a piece of cheese or meat right up to the sill by letting the underflow do the work for you. This is an excellent method of getting right into those bolt-holes favoured by the barbel. As soon as you hook a fish in these swims, it is vital to bully it out into the open water. This can prove quite exhausting. You literally must not give an inch or the fish will have your line wrapped round a boulder and that is that. Hence the need for strong tackle. Again, an 11-foot rod with a soft action, coupled with 6lb line, seems to do the trick, but it is worth checking your line every so often to make sure it hasn't frayed.

The second method is to explore the back eddies that surround the pool. Use of the plummet is important here as a sudden change of depth can prove a good spot to try. Don't be put off by the sudden surges of water that occasionally seem to come from the centre of the pool, because this is only a surface effect. On the bottom, the current is always flowing back towards the weir. You can always test this by putting some pieces of polystyrene in a bait dropper and waiting for them to reappear.

As the water under the rod tip is usually quite deep, laying on can be quite a good method for catching barbel, but most anglers prefer to use the feeder fished about a rod's length out. The only problem with fishing these pools is that they can be unpredictable. Swims which prove successful one day, can be devoid of fish another. So it sometimes pays to have a wander if nothing is doing and cast a rolling leger into the main flow and let it work its way around the pool.

During the winter, the Lee still produces fish. I have caught them in water temperatures as low as 39°F. During the

back end of the season, if the water is well coloured and the temperature slightly up, the barbel can come to the net one after another. This is also a time when big fish tend to show and one of the best baits for them, I have found, is the good old lobworm. They just can't resist them. Again, plenty of ground-bait with a few diced worms mixed in works well.

Fisheries

Being so near to London, many of these backwaters are easily accessible by both train and bus, although the upper reaches between Luton and Hatfield are rather more difficult to gain access to. These upper stretches of the Lee have been stocked with barbel by the Thames Water Authority and also illegally by anglers. Whilst I would like to see more barbel in these areas, the latter method should be avoided as disease could be spread with disastrous results.

At the county town of Hertford, the Lee changes from a pleasant chalk stream into the canal-type river that many of us know it as now. One reason for this is that the Rivers Beane, Rib and Mimran all flow into the Lee here, and contribute enough water to make navigation possible. Hertford is peppered with small rivers and weirs which, at first glance, look to have excellent prospects for barbel, but, alas, the fish are few and far between and have to be sought out.

Moving downstream to Ware, the Lee branches off from the canal and flows through three weirs, all of which hold barbel. Unfortunately, only one of these is available for public fishing. This weir has only just been built and bypasses Ware lock. It is quite an impressive structure and the water from the weir runs to about 8 feet in depth. This backwater rejoins the canal about a hundred yards upstream of the main road bridge in Ware, and the area around this bridge is one of the few places where barbel have been caught in the canal. There are some good slacks in winter when the Lee is in flood, and these are usually the best bet.

Just downstream of Ware there is another weir which, although built quite recently, feeds a backstream which could be considered to be the original course of the Lee. This backstream rejoins the canal after about three miles. Fishing on this water is controlled by Ware AC, except for one stretch which is trout fishing only. For some reason, barbel on this stretch are extremely difficult to locate, but they are there. It is really a river that needs a lot of reconnaissance to pick out the best swims.

Passing through Stanstead Abbots, the canal becomes the main feeder until we get to Rye House and Feild's Weir. This is where the River Stort joins the Lee and also marks the beginning of the Lee Flood Relief Channel. This weir has only recently been rebuilt and is designed to share the flow between the Relief Channel and the old backstream that feeds the canals and the weirs further downstream. However, when the water level gets below that of the concrete sill, there is only one sluice gate to allow water back into the canal and during the summer, when there is a great deal of boat traffic, this sluice seems to be unable to supply enough water with the result that the level drops and the weirs downstream cease

to flow. The fishing here is controlled by the West Ham AC, one of the very independent clubs which actually hold the freehold to their fishing rights. The backstream that rejoins the canal is only very short but there are some really good-looking swims in the pool area, along with some bad snags and a lot of depth, which can make fishing difficult.

Moving on downstream, we come to Dobb's Weir. On one side this water is controlled by the London Anglers' Association and on the other it is private fishing, although day tickets are available to fish both banks. This is also a picnic and recreation area (part of the Lee Valley Park Scheme) and in summer any serious intention of angling during the day must go by the board. The pool here is quite large and of uneven depth and it is about the most snagged-up area I have found. Barbel have been caught here up to 7lb+, but quite a few are lost in the snags. This is really a pleasure angler's venue and a good place to bring the family for a day out. This backstream rejoins the canal just downstream of Dobb's Lock but it is quite featureless and, again, winter is a good bet, when the floodwater creates the slacks. Careful use of the plummet will find a couple of swims with 12 feet under the rod tip. Enough said!

A mile or so downstream from Dobb's Weir, we come to Carthagena Weir. Fishing here is controlled by the much-famed Crown Fishery but tickets to fish the pool are extremely difficult to come by and there is a waiting list. This weirpool is one of the deepest I have found on the Lee, with depths plummeting from 6 to 20 feet. The tail of the pool is full of cabbage weed, holds a lot of fish, and is one of the few places where I have seen barbel jump on this river. There are also some large carp in this pool – up to and over 20lb – which makes it a much-sought-after venue. The river rejoins the canal just downstream of the pool and can be fished on a day ticket. Between here and the road bridge is a good spot to try, but it is advisable to check that there are no matches on the day you plan to go.

Moving on downstream to Wormley, we come to what must be the most famous barbel fishery on the Lee – King's Weir. This is without doubt *the* venue for any would-be barbel angler. It is quite literally stuffed full of obliging fish. To start with the pool, fishing is now available only from the bankside, with a maximum limit of six rods,

three on each side. This to me is a one-off fishery, and I have given up trying to anticipate what will be caught next. Barbel up to 9lb have been caught here but there are plenty between 1½ and 6lb.

Downstream from the pool, for about a mile, the fishing is controlled by Redland Angling on a season-ticket basis. These tickets can be obtained from the weirkeeper's house. Fishing on this stretch is done from the pegged swims, of which there are about seventy. There are swims to suit every angler – long deep glides, shallow gravel runs surrounded by weedbeds, deep holes, overhanging trees, quite a variation. Indeed, I have found that once you have found a good swim it is very difficult to give the others a try.

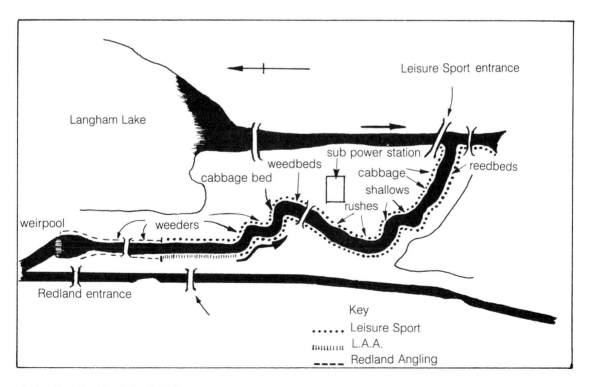

A detail of the King's Weir Fishery.

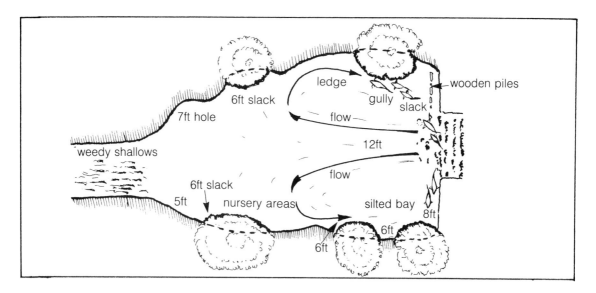

The weir pool at King's Weir.

One of the more productive areas is from the tail of the pool downstream to the footbridge. Immediately below the tail of the pool, the water is shallow and weedy; then the river deepens and widens, providing ideal trotting water. Further downstream the swims on the wall and around the big hawthorn are worth a try. Some twenty yards upstream of the footbridge, the weed growth is really thick and, as I have said previously, these swims are very productive in the early season. Downstream of these weedbeds, the river again deepens and overhanging trees provide ideal cover. The last two swims before the boundary fence are also very productive.

There has been a lot of development on this fishery. The most significant recently has been the use of a dredger to get rid of some of the worst of the silt that has been building up over the years. This is really exciting news as in some places (such as the wall section)

there is some 5 feet of water under the rod tip. The weirpool has also been dredged on the opposite bank from the house and a long cast from the bank with a rolling ledger could now prove necessary. This dredger has obviously left holes in certain areas of the river which only a few people will know about. The best way to find these holes is to keep a weather eye on where the bailiffs have been fishing – it won't take long to establish where they are!

From the boundary fence, the right-hand bank is controlled by the London AA for about two hundred yards and is open to full members only and clubs only on Sundays. The left-hand bank and the right-hand bank downstream of the LAA stretch are controlled by Leisure Sports Angling, and are classed as a 'special venue', but tickets can be obtained without too much difficulty. This stretch of the river twists and turns for a mile and a half and consists of a series of fairly deep pools connected by fairly shallow runs. At one time, the barbel on this stretch were genuinely thought to be smaller than those upstream, but they are now gaining weight fast and well worth fishing for. The 1986–7 season saw three double-figure fish from this water, with photographs of the fish to prove it. But I say again, it is well worth hanging on to the last possible moment before dark! The last hundred yards of the fishery before it joins the Relief Channel is a pretty good area for the better fish.

The Relief Channel has been flowing more or less parallel to the old river since they parted at Feild's Weir, below Stanstead Abbots. From Fisher's Green to Waltham Abbey, apart from a small stretch controlled by Metropolitan Police, the Relief Channel is available for public fishing. Day tickets can be obtained from the tackle shop in Waltham Abbey.

Halfway between Fisher's Green and Waltham Abbey, there is a sluice. This is home to a few barbel that have spread down from the King's Weir and they seem to be increasing in numbers. The channel around this area is pretty wide and the best swims I have found are those with a good depth under the rod tip. This stretch is also heavily match-fished and one of the best times to fish it is in the evening after a match has been held. At the back end of last season, barbel to 8lb + were caught around the road bridge area at Fisher's Green – proof that the fish are moving from the backwaters into the channel.

Getting back to the canal, the next weir downstream is at Enfield lock. This weir is strictly private as it is situated in the grounds of the Royal Ordnance factory, but the backwater becomes available for public fishing about half a mile downstream. This stretch is now well overgrown and silted up, sadly no longer the fishery it used to be. The barbel here are few and far between and difficult to locate. This backwater again runs into the Lee diversion, which by now has become encased in 8-foot concrete walls and a concrete bottom, but there are still barbel present up to around the 5lb mark.

The Lee diversion here is controlled by the LAA and is available only to full members. Every hundred yards or so there is a small sill weir to allow for the drop in level and it is these weirs that hold the barbel. As the river is only three feet deep it is quite easy to spot the odd fish, especially when they are spawning. This stretch was where I caught my first barbel, just above one of the sill weirs. Although it weighed only 4lb 12oz, the fight it put up hooked me on barbel and I have fished for them ever since.

The Lee diversion has started producing fish at Ponders End. This is good news if you don't like walking as most of the best swims seem to be about halfway between there and the Royal Small Arms stretch, which could involve a walk of up to a mile and half. Again, you must walk the river and plummet for the holes that are present. This is where you will find the fish.

Just to show that they can prove wrong our theories about where they can and cannot survive, barbel have been caught in the 'canal' stretch of the Lee around the Pickett's Lock area. This was at first almost unbelievable. But then, to back it up, a salmon was caught from the same stretch. Good news indeed for us London lads!

Farther downstream at the reservoir outlets at Tottenham Hale, we again find barbel living it up in crystal-clear water, brimming with daphnia, on which they feed at leisure all day long whilst three grains of corn sit forlornly on the bottom. I have been privileged to have caught a couple of 5lb+ fish from this stretch which were in superb condition, deeply bronzed on their backs and with pure white bellies. Believe me, it is well worth the wait to try and catch one.

Looking to the future, I hope that some of the lower stretches of the Lee will be stocked with barbel. There are one or two areas, particularly around Hackney Marshes, which I am sure could support them. It would indeed be a wonderful thing if once again barbel fishing were available in the heart of London and we could experience, as Isaak Walton once did on this once magnificent river, the thrill of landing Old Whiskers to the sound of Bow Bells in the distance. You never know!

Minor Rivers

The Ribble

Back in the 1960s the river Ribble was of no interest whatsoever to the would-be barbel anglers of Lancashire. Unlike the east-flowing Yorkshire rivers, one of which, the Wharfe, rises only a few miles away from the Ribble's source on Ingleton Fell, the Lancashire river was devoid of barbel.

Although the Ribble is primarily a game river in its upper reaches, the deeper, slower flowing middle reaches make an entirely suitable habitat for barbel. This fact was noticed by a few of the more pioneering type of local anglers and it wasn't long before the Ribble became yet another river to receive an illegal stocking of these fine fish. One has only to glance at a road map of England to find the obvious area where the first stockings took place. Barbel were caught in small numbers from the River Severn, transferred into large water containers and carried up the M6 by van or car. It is no coincidence that the main barbel-holding areas in the river today are still very close to the original stocking places under the motorway.

The spread of barbel in the Ribble since then has been steady. Very small fish are now found downriver as far as the tidal reaches. However, if bigger fish are the target then upstream of the motorway seems to be a better bet. Although the average size is nothing special, much bigger barbel are present and a small number of double-figure fish have been recorded, with the odd specimen going over 11lb. Standard barbel-fishing methods seem to work best – either feeder with maggot, or hemp and caster in an open-ended feeder. Where allowed, night fishing with meat is also successful. This method also allows the angler to get away with slightly heavier tackle – something to bear in mind, as some of the middle stretches of the river are quite snaggy. These snags take the form of largish boulders in some of the deep pools, or the sharp edges of deep channels cut through the solid bedrock which abounds in this area of the river. The river is very wide here but the barbel tend to lie up either in the deeper pools or in the deep channel, thus making location that much easier.

Whether these unauthorised stockings were right or wrong is a much-debated topic, but one fact that has emerged in recent times is that barbel are now well established in the Ribble and, as a consequence, the days of travelling in search of some sport with these superb fish are over for the Lancashire angler.

The Cheshire Dane

The Dane is one of the most picturesque and beautiful rivers in northern England. It rises in the southern Pennines and for perhaps the first third of its length it could be described as a mountain stream. The lower two-thirds, which are barbel country, meander over the Cheshire Plain, flowing west and emptying into the River Weaver at Northwich. The river in this section alternates between fast shallows and deep pools, some of which reach 20 feet in depth. Some areas are full of ranunculus weed. It is a small river of immense character, full of chub and some good roach and dace. The barbel are now well established in most of the middle and lower river.

The Dane has not always supported barbel, as they are not an indigenous species to the western side of the Pennines. Barbel were first introduced about 1970 with fish brought from the River Severn. These first stockings amounted to about 150 fish, from 5lb to over 9lb. They were introduced at Swettenham into a club length. Predictably, they disappeared, but around 1980 they started to show up in numbers at various points along the river. From that initial stocking fish into double figures have now been taken, and a very good average of about

A good example of an undercut far bank swim on the River Dane.

4lb. The river has received several more stockings in recent years at the lower end near Davenham. A club with water at the lower end of the river obtained 262 from the Severn Water Authority, some of which were reported as being fish of 10lb+. In September of 1984, 96 fish, mostly larger specimens, some of 8–10lb, were introduced and two days later a further 166 smaller fish in the 1–3lb class were also introduced by the same club. These are not the only stockings, as several other clubs with water have introduced fish into the river on an individual basis in recent years. These fish are also spreading along the river, with individual fish to 10lb 10oz being taken. The barbel has found the Dane to its liking and very small fish from 4 to 6 inches are reported as being caught from all areas, thus showing successful spawning.

The barbel is now definitely at home in almost any snaggy area below Holmes Chapel. But if you try for it be prepared – these fish are tough and can reach snags in an instant. The tackle required to land these barbel would make the average Dane angler wide-eyed in disbelief. Line of 8–10lb is not enough in some areas, even for the average-sized specimen. This, together with the fact that a lot of fish are hooked and lost by the average angler, makes the Dane barbel very shy in the more heavily fished areas. Therefore the use of stepped-up rods and lines to 15lb BS make the hair rig a must to enable bites to develop at all. But, because these lively barbel live adjacent to or actually in the snags, the heavy gear is needed to have any chance of extracting them. These snags can be very formidable – a full tree across the

river is not uncommon. Large build-ups of tree roots and drifting debris accumulate with regularity in the small confines of this river. The barbel knowingly live in the worst areas and will take full advantage when hooked. The spot to look for amongst the snags is where the pace of the flow increases past the snag. This clears the bottom down to the gravel and creates a potential feeding area. In the evening, barbel tend to leave the cover of the daytime lies and move upstream into the usually adjacent faster runs, where sport can be brisk during the first few hours of dusk and darkness.

Fish of 10lb+ are showing in various areas and fish of the 7–8lb bracket can be expected to turn up anywhere from Somerford downstream. In such a small river, it must be asked whether the water can sustain such large individual fish or, indeed, the large numbers of smaller brethren. The barbel in the river are very healthy fish and appear to suit the water. If you try for the Dane's stock, please use appropriate gear in this very snaggy river – too many fish have hooks and line left in their mouths by anglers who have underestimated their strength. Keepnets are out for barbel, so return your fish immediately and make sure that he has recovered enough to hold his own in the current. If you require a photograph, please look to the welfare of the barbel. Don't keep him out of water long. Remember, you can set up all your photographic and weighing equipment whilst the fish is retained in the landing net, so keep the fish in the water until the last possible second. The barbel is a tough old fish but out of water he still cannot breathe and is tired after the fight. Dry hands will damage the fish, so wet yours before handling any fish you are lucky enough to catch. Damage caused from bad handling can result in fungal growths, which can spread to other fish and be responsible for the loss of good fish.

The future of the river's stock depends greatly on maintaining this healthy stock so that we can enjoy many future years of exceptional fishing in this delightful little river.

The Wye

The River Wye has never been officially stocked with barbel, but as the river now holds a large head of them it must be assumed that they were transferred illegally. Judging by the first reports of barbel captures this must have taken place some time in the late 1960s or early 1970s, probably at Ross and further upstream near Hereford. I would like to state here and now that although the Barbel Catchers Club encourages the stocking of barbel into new rivers this must be done with the river authorities' blessing – unofficial stockings are completely irresponsible. That said, barbel are now present throughout the middle section of the river. They have been reported above Hay-on-Wye and as far downstream as Monmouth.

The barbel have obviously found the part of the river around Bredwardine above Hereford to their liking and have spawned successfully as there are now many small fish in 1–3lb range. These small fish are caught regularly from the shallow, streamier areas of the river. They first started to show in the early 1980s, which indicates they are second-,

possibly third-generation descendants of the original stocking. Below Hereford, similar-sized fish are starting to appear in reasonable numbers at Mordiford, Holme Lacy and Brockhampton. There are many rumours of much larger double-figure fish being taken by salmon anglers. Like most fishing tales, these should be taken with a pinch of salt, but I feel certain that there is more than a grain of truth in most of them. Three years ago in the Wye championships a match angler fishing near Moccas weighed in three barbel which are reported to have tipped the scales at 27lb – a fantastic catch by any standards. I feel it is fair to say that double-figure fish do exist in the Wye, possibly in larger numbers than any of us think. The major problem for anybody trying to get to grips with them is access, as in the main the river is closed to the coarse fisherman throughout the salmon season – that is, from the middle of January to the end of September. Even outside these dates there are miles and miles of river that have never seen a coarse fisherman and in many cases never will.

The Wye is a big river in every respect. It has the potential to produce huge barbel of record-breaking proportions. The challenge of these big fish to the dedicated barbel angler is enormous and truly exciting, but I fear it will remain an enigma for a few more years to come yet.

The River Lugg is a tributary which joins the Wye at Mordiford, just below Hereford, and this lovely little river holds a good head of barbel. There are numbers of smaller fish in the 1–3lb range and quite a few larger ones. The biggest I know of weighed 9lb and many fish up to 7lb have been caught. The barbel appear to have spread throughout the lower half of the river fairly evenly and, which is often the case, seem to be moving further upstream every year.

Stillwater Barbel

PETER RAYMENT

Despite the vast amount that has been written, even the most recent authors give the impression that barbel are only to be found in rivers. While this is generally true, it should be realised that barbel can also be caught in lakes, reservoirs and ponds – where they have either been stocked or have entered the water by more natural means. While barbel are found in the odd canal – such as the Worcester and the Kennet and Avon – for the purpose of this contribution I shall be discussing only waters that can be described as landlocked.

Reports of barbel caught from still water date back at least a hundred years – perhaps earlier still if one counts the reported 12lb fish taken from the Serpentine, although there is a conflict of opinion about whether it was actually hooked or found dead. With this knowledge, it is curious that the barbel should still be widely recognised as a river-only species. My own investigation is based on a period of seven years spent studying and fishing for barbel in still waters. My carefully recorded trips show a total of more than 1,500 barbel captured from still waters, so this contribution is based on research and experience rather than theory.

The barbel is a hardy and adaptable species that can be successfully transferred to new waters. Such successful removals of barbel from one river to another are of course common knowledge, and for this we must thank some of the river authorities which have proved to be forward-thinking, such as Thames and Severn-Trent. What is not so widely known is that barbel have also been successfully moved from rivers to lakes and pools and even from still waters back to rivers as well as to other lakes and pools. As with transfers between one river to another, success is not certain. One failure was in a gravel pit in the Warwickshire Avon catchment, from which the barbel completely disappeared. It is believed that they escaped through a ditch.

Some 500 barbel were taken from Trimpley Reservoir, tagged and restocked in four selected stretches of the River Alne, a small 'ripple and pool' type Warwickshire river. Some time later stretches were electro-fished to check on the progress of the introduced stock, and the results were analysed in conjunction with angling returns. The majority of barbel had remained within two miles of the place of introduction, movement being equally divided between upstream and downstream. One fish, however, captured nine months after stocking, had moved 23½ miles and had increased in weight by

14½oz. It would be reasonable to assume, therefore, that transferring barbel from rivers to still waters, or from still waters to rivers, or indeed other lakes and ponds, can be successful. However, no angler, angling club or association should stock waters with any 'alien' species without first obtaining professional advice and the permission of the local water authority. Many angling clubs may fear stocking with a new species because of the possibility of that species overbreeding, which may be detrimental to the stock of fish already in the water. Barbel seem to offer a great advantage in this respect, for there is little evidence that they will breed in still water. It is therefore a species which can be controlled – which is rare amongst coarse fish.

At present there is just a theory that barbel may be able to breed in gravel-bottomed waters which receive a slow feeding of water from subsurface streams. One glimmer of evidence on this came to my attention when I was informed that one of the club members at Ham Pool (Gloucestershire) claimed to have trapped two tiny barbel in a minnow trap. This small gravel pit is believed to be fed by underwater springs owing to the fact that the water level remains constant, and is 3 feet higher than that of the neighbouring pits. It is doubtful, however, whether the water temperature from springs in the majority of waters can ever be high enough to stimulate the barbel to spawn. Even if they did spawn, whether the spawn would survive is questionable.

However, another interesting case was brought to my attention by Dr Bruno Broughton and later by Neville Fickling – both respected in the world of fishery biology. Bruno told me of a 3-acre gravel pit run by a small syndicate in which nine barbel of between 1 and 3lb were stocked. Just before the first of these was caught on rod and line some eighteen months later, a 3-inch baby barbel was taken in a small hand-net along with gudgeon fry. This small barbel was witnessed by two Severn-Trent fisheries inspectors, who took photographs of their exciting discovery. Neville is almost convinced that the barbel had been bred in the pit.

From discussions with Bruno and Neville, it came to light that the pit is just 500 yards from a river which contains barbel and is prone to flooding – although this is believed not to have happened for two years before the stocking. There is also a 6-inch-diameter pipe which runs from the pit to the river, although the river end is above river level. Later I will mention how barbel will move from a river into a still water, so bringing about 'natural' stocking. I believe that much more conclusive evidence is needed before we can say for certain that barbel will breed in still water, and my research so far suggests that the chances of them doing so are on a par with rainbow trout doing the same.

It is difficult to define what types of water are most suitable for the stocking of barbel. What is known is that barbel have been stocked in still waters of great variance – reservoirs, lakes, pools, and almost farmyard-sized ponds. They appear to survive well in the waters they are introduced to, but the growth rate of the fish does of course depend on many factors. There is some indication that waters with soft bottoms – mud and silt – are slightly better suited to barbel, but no hard-and-fast rule should be made from this.

Because the species is so popular, barbel are difficult to obtain for stocking. In 1985 one inquiry to the only fish farm that could supply the species at the time revealed that they were also expensive to buy – a minimum order of 100lb cost £4.60 per pound, including delivery. However, getting friendly with your local river authority may just get you the fish you want.

Stillwater Distribution

Very little is known of the actual distribution of stillwater barbel in England, so I shall list a fairly widespread selection of waters, and include points of interest on each. (Trimpley Reservoir in Worcestershire is dealt with in much greater detail later.)

A lagoon situated alongside Trimpley is 8 acres in size, varies in depth between 4 and 18 feet, and has a bottom of mud and silt. Also nearby is a small pond of ½ acre which is badly silted up and very shallow. In both these waters the barbel are of a higher average weight than those in the reservoir and, apart from the type of bottom, these waters have a higher pH level. Both the lagoon and the pond were stocked with barbel taken from the reservoir.

Still in Worcestershire and near to Droitwich lie the Ombersley gravel pits, which were stocked with barbel by the Severn-Trent Water Authority. The growth rate of these fish can be likened to that of barbel from the River Severn. On the outskirts of Worcester is the 1-acre Grove Farm pool. The depths range from 6 to 15 feet, the bottom is very muddy and the water is often badly coloured. The barbel average 2lb in weight, with the best fish – a 7-pounder – taken in 1981.

The Lydney Boating Lake in Gloucestershire is a gravel pit with a number of barbel stocked by the Severn-Trent Water Authority. Five acres in size, it has depths of 3–5 feet and the barbel are mostly found around the inlet of the small feeder stream. The best fish is believed to be one of 5lb 3oz. At South Cerney is the 2-acre Ham Pool, with depths going down to 20 feet. Thirty-six barbel taken from the River Loddon – a tributary of the Thames – were stocked by the Thames Water Authority in 1978. The weights ranged from 1 to 1½lb, and after only two years a fish of 2½lb was taken.

At Stoneacres Lake in Oxfordshire the Thames Water Authority tried to breed barbel taken from the River Windrush by placing them in a large container in the lake. Their efforts failed and the fish – from 1 to 4lb – were released and are often caught around the inflow to the lake, which is at present an any-method trout fishery.

In Hertfordshire, the St Albans pool has a small concentration of barbel, while the nearby Centre Lagoon has provided excellent barbel fishing from the east bank, with fish in the 5–6lb range. Stockley Road Carp Lakes in Middlesex were stocked with 20 barbel from the Thames and these proved to have an excellent growth rate, with a definite 9-pounder taken and reports of the odd double-figure fish. An interesting point with this 5-acre water is that the barbel have occasionally fallen to fly-fishing lures.

Near Wigan in Lancashire is Worth-

180

ington Lake, where fish were first stocked in 1976 and catches up to nine barbel in a session have been taken in the past. Yorkshire can boast of its Elvington Lake near Wheldrake, 3 acres in size and up to 35 feet deep, and containing barbel up to 9lb. Northingales Fish Ponds at Cawood are adjacent to the River Ouse and subject to natural restocking, and the odd barbel has started to turn up in catches here. Barbel have also been reported at Sugden End Reservoir at Keighley, where they have taken a liking to baits based on cat food. In Cheshire, Lymm Vale provides barbel to 5½lb amongst its excellent fishing.

The experience of all these waters demonstrates that barbel stocked into still waters not only survive well but can also show signs of maintaining a good growth rate after being transferred from another water. However, let us now look at the growth rates of

barbel in Trimpley Reservoir, because here we have a different situation – it is the only water I know for certain where the barbel are not stocked, but enter the water in a natural manner.

Trimpley Reservoir

Trimpley Reservoir is situated alongside the River Severn in Worcestershire. The reservoir is roughly oval in shape, covers an area of 29 acres and has a maximum depth of 36 feet. The sides and the bottom are constructed entirely from concrete, with the sides sloping at an angle of 40 degrees to the bottom. The scenery around the reservoir is of great beauty, with the forests and hills offering the reservoir shelter from high winds.

Water for treatment is pumped from the Severn via a moving band screen, and it is through this screen that barbel and other fry move into the reservoir,

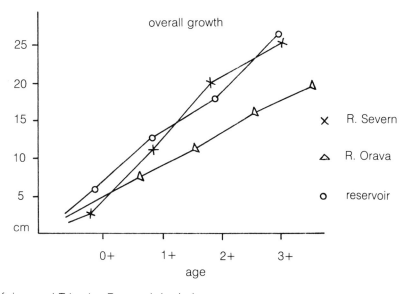

Comparison of river and Trimpley Reservoir barbel.

181

with small fish of up to about 3½ inches possibly being able to bypass the screen. This can't help but raise a very interesting point: if barbel are not suited to living in still water, why would they naturally move into it?

A study of the growth characteristics of barbel in the reservoir was carried out by Mr C.V.M. Davies, B.Sc., of the Severn-Trent Water Authority. Because of its size and depth, electro-fishing and seining were not possible as a means of obtaining fish. Therefore a system of using four plastic-netting traps was used. The traps were usually baited with stale bread. Other baits used – including potatoes, eggshells and dog biscuits – did not meet with very good results.

In eighteen months well over a thousand barbel taken were weighed to the nearest gram and measured to the nearest millimetre. A sample of scales for use in age determination was taken from each fish, from above the lateral line and directly below the dorsal fin. The barbel were then tagged before being used to restock a number of habitats for further study.

To demonstrate the seasonal pattern of growth in still water, scales of all fish caught were examined and the pattern determined. It was clear that the scales of barbel in Trimpley began to check in the autumn and that in most cases this was completed by the end of November. Rapid growth of fish and scales commenced again in the spring and continued until the following autumn. In some cases a summer check was formed. The percentage of fish of all sizes which had a check at or near the edge of the scale was calculated.

The formation of the check on the scales coincided with the cessation of rapid growth of the fish and scales and with the cooler weather of autumn. This causes some complication in designating the age class of the barbel because most cyprinids form their check at about the time of spawning or at the onset of rapid growth immediately afterwards. As the spawning of barbel in the River Severn appears to occur during late May or early June in most years, it was decided to take 14 June as the 'birthday' of the fish. The first check was formed at 0+ years then at 1+ years and so on. The mean weights and lengths of each sample

Peter Rayment fishing the hotspot at Trimpley Reservoir.

182

barbel for each age group were calculated and plotted against time to show the seasonal cycle of growth.

The growth rates determined proved that the barbel in Trimpley were similar to the barbel in the Severn. In fact barbel between 14 and 27cm actually grew faster in the reservoir. What is very interesting, in my opinion, is that barbel taken from Trimpley Reservoir and restocked into the River Orava showed a *decline* in growth rate.

Various samples of barbel were examined for parasites; 60 per cent harboured between 1 and 10 *Pomphoryncus laevis* parasites, mainly in the upper intestines, yet none of the parasites were mature. Chub from the reservoir were examined and manifested the same percentage of infested fish, but in the chub many of the parasites were mature. Although the parasite *Ligula intestinalis* was found to be present in the reservoir's gudgeon, roach, dace, chub and rainbow trout, none were found in barbel. The brown trout showed no parasites present – no wonder they grow big.

The small pool adjacent to Trimpley mentioned above was included in the survey and its barbel were of a better growth rate than those in the reservoir. Although the picture is far from complete, it seems that the size of the water that barbel are stocked in makes no difference whatsoever. Rather, it is in still waters with soft bottoms of mud and silt that barbel appear to grow

Peter's son in action netting a barbel from Trimpley Reservoir.

much better. However, until more details of the growth rate of stillwater barbel are at hand, it would be dangerous to be dogmatic about this.

It was interesting to study the monthly trappings of barbel at Trimpley. I must confess to being rather surprised to find that the months where barbel are normally regarded as inactive – and less likely to be caught by anglers – were the most productive for obtaining fish samples. Over a period of one year the figures were: September, 20; October, 26; November, 245; February, 432; March, 57; June, 23; and August 54. No figures were available for the missing months.

The study of the feeding habits of stillwater barbel is far from complete. At Trimpley there is no macroflora in the reservoir and the list of food organisms is unimpressive in its diversity. For the scientific record, the following invertebrates were included in the fauna, which is severely hit each year by sudden drops in water level below the rocks around the margins: *Valvata piscinalis*, *Pisidium*, *H. jenkinsi*, *Physa fontinalis*, Tubifex, *Asellus aquaticus*, *Gammarus pulex* and *Chironomis*.

However, I have on the odd occasion examined the stomach contents of its barbel, and found that they eat large quantities of bloodworms and snails – in fact one fish had eaten no less than 52 snails, each roughly $\frac{3}{16}$-inch in diameter. Caddis and various nymphs were also present, along with the remains of one worm. It was, however, the discovery of the snails that proved to be important to me.

When I first fished Trimpley I was under the impression that the water did not contain many barbel. This was based on the fact that an individual catch might contain only one or two barbel, and that many anglers on the day did not have any at all. However, with the discovery of the snails – which I believed were the type that clung to stone – I began to wonder just where the biggest concentrations would be. In the end, I decided to fish baits right up tight against the base of one or other of the two valve towers. I have since discovered that the snails are found on big stones lying on the bottom – with large concentrations of them in a few very small areas.

It appeared that I had made the right choice: catches of around a dozen barbel became common and the more I fished the higher my average catch became. Whether this success was due entirely to the discovery of the snail 'hot areas' is uncertain, and has to be considered along with another factor. Stillwater barbel appear to prefer the deeper water in waters that are open or contain little or no weed, because the light penetration is not so great. In shallow waters, fishing directly under weedbeds, under overhanging trees, or near trailing roots is always worth a try. An unromantic example is at Stockley Road Carp Lakes, where a sunken car is a favourite haunt for the barbel.

While the shoals of average-size barbel tend to stay put for some time in one area, the larger and often solitary fish behave differently. At Trimpley, I have spent hours lying on my stomach during the close season watching the odd fish in the 6–8lb range patrolling the margins and quite clearly feeding on roach fry. The fact that every now and again a trout angler will hook one on his fly tackle seems to bear this out.

Naturally, when the coarse season opens these large fish are rarely seen.

Records kept over a seven-year period indicate that the best time for catching the barbel is late morning and early evening. First light, or (surprisingly) the last hour before dark have on average proved to be poor periods. Providing the bait is lying in deep water, 12 feet or more, the barbel have always fed well in bright sunshine. However, as you will see later, there will always be an exception to the rule.

Successful baits are really no different from those used for barbel in rivers. On many waters, cubes of luncheon meat have proved to be one of the top baits. The list of baits that I have caught stillwater barbel on include luncheon meat, worms, maggots, casters, bread flake, crust, catfood paste, sweetcorn, dog food, fish paste and cheese. There is one bait I have not yet succeeded with and that's a deadbait. I undertook a heavy prebaiting with sections of sprats but they were not successful. The big problem at Trimpley is trying *not* to catch roach, bream, chub and various other species. This often leads me to use exceptionally large baits – and certainly the barbel have not objected to this. I can tell you, though, that rainbow trout are extremely fond of sweetcorn.

Considering the depths of water I have fished, it is not surprising to find that legering has been my most successful method. To get large quantities of maggots hard on the bottom, the swimfeeder has proved excellent. A feeder packed with sweetcorn can be very successful and it does not matter if the corn cannot get out of the feeder; the smell, I think, is the attraction.

For small baits I usually fish with the bale arm of the reel in the closed position, using a form of 'butt' indicator. When using quite large baits – for example a 1-inch cube of luncheon meat – I tend to leave the reel's bale arm in the open position, allowing the barbel to run for a short distance before closing the bale arm and giving a tug.

In dull weather the barbel may be caught in water less than 12 feet deep by float fishing with the bait lying hard on the bottom. It is of course possible to float-fish in the deeper water with a slider float – which is a favourite method of my son Steven.

Stillwater barbel do nothing to help solve what to me is one of the biggest mysteries in barbel fishing: why do they for no apparent reason or logic, start feeding on or near the surface? At Trimpley I must have caught about 200 fish just under the surface and over a depth of 30 feet or more of water. While I have caught the accidental surface fish from the Severn, the Trent and the Hampshire Avon, at Trimpley I have deliberately set out for and caught without difficulty surface feeders on the very few occasions each season when they behave this way. These barbel have often been fish of under 1lb in weight. We now know that barbel fry spend the first three weeks of their life feeding on the surface, despite very bright light. Could it be that barbel of under 1lb feed more on the surface than we realise? However, the mystery remains why even on heavily fished waters like the Royalty at Christchurch it is rare to catch a barbel under a couple of pounds. For the record my Trimpley surface fish were taken with either a float set shallow or a feeder with the lead strip taken off, allowing the bait to sink slowly.

However, the best catches were made by fishing hard on the bottom, or – on occasions when bites were rare – by inching the bait slowly along the bottom at intervals. One particular occasion illustrates just how small an area barbel will feed in. The boat was firmly anchored in 34 feet of water directly over what was believed to be the hotspot. Throughout the session we switched between straight leger, swimfeeder and slider-float, and simply lowered the baits over the side. Fishing in this way, Steven and I had our best ever catch of sixty barbel between us, all of those fish came from an area no larger than five feet square. No amount of feed or time fishing outside that area resulted in a single barbel being caught.

Finally, the answer to the question I get asked most often. Yes, stillwater barbel do fight as long and hard as the river fish. But why not find out for yourself?

The Future of Barbel

PETE TILLOTSON

Looking ahead, the future of barbel looks assured for many years to come. During the past thirty years barbel have been stocked into rivers that have never previously held them, and this is a trend that I hope will continue. Some rivers that already hold barbel have also been stocked in areas which did not hold them. The Hampshire Avon is one example that springs to mind.

Barbel are also appearing in rivers that have never been stocked at all and the Wye and the Ribble are notable examples. It can only be assumed that these fish have been placed in these rivers illegally. Both rivers are renowned salmon waters and barbel are treated as vermin by some game fishermen. It would be true to say that the appearance of barbel in these rivers is viewed with dismay both by the water authorities and the salmon anglers themselves. Indeed, the North West Water Authority is very loath to admit their existence in the Ribble! In my opinion, the Wye offers great potential. It is ideally suited for the species and in the future I am sure some very big barbel will come from this river.

Most barbel carry a parasite which is inhibiting the spread of the fish. Water authorities with rivers that are devoid of barbel are very reluctant to stock with infected fish from other areas. This is proving to be a considerable barrier to increasing the spread of the species. There has been a successful attempt at breeding barbel, and should these fish turn out to be parasite-free it is possible that this could remove the main objections of the water authorities. However, these are early days yet and maybe in a few years these artificially bred barbel will be accepted for stocking purposes.

There is no doubt that barbel are now far more widespread than they were years ago. I have mentioned the stocking – both legal and illegal – of barbel, but there is strong evidence that they are also spreading by themselves. There are definite signs that in some rivers barbel are moving out of the main river and into the tributaries. Indeed, they are even venturing into tributaries of tributaries. The Thames and the Severn are examples. More and more barbel are appearing in more and more tributaries. There is evidence that they are spawning in these tributaries and are very much established in some areas.

I'm sure this is another trend that will continue in the foreseeable future, providing even more opportunities for the barbel angler.

The stocking of the River Severn in the mid-1950s proved highly successful, though some match men might not agree. Nevertheless, it is a fact that barbel quickly established themselves in the Severn and in many areas they became the predominant species. However, although numbers were high the quality was not so good, and originally the average weight of middle-Severn barbel was very low indeed. There are now signs that the barbel are thinning out a little and there is a corresponding increase in their average weight. The River Trent, once a prime barbel river, is now showing signs of recovery after almost being denuded of the species. Like the Severn, the fish are of a small average size and it is a reasonable assumption that in the future the Trent will follow the same pattern. The warm water pumped into the river by numerous power stations dotted along its banks may well affect the growth rate of its barbel.

The question of the potential size of barbel is far less clear-cut; it has long been – and doubtless will continue to be – the subject of discussion. At present there are two record fish lists in the country, so consequently there are currently two 'record' barbel. The BRFC lists a 13lb 12oz Avon fish as the record whilst the NASA lists a 14lb 6oz barbel, again from the Avon, as its record. I personally regard Aylmer Tryon's 14lb 6oz fish (the NASA record barbel) as the record, but that is neither really here nor there.

The real question is, can the record be beaten? This has been discussed at great length by the Barbel Catchers. Historically the signs are not good. Aylmer Tryon's 14lb 6oz fish has stood unchallenged for over fifty years and the only authentic barbel to approach it are Greg Buxton's 14lb 1oz fish from the Dorset Stour, in the 1984–5 season and, more recently, Pete Reading's 14lb 2oz fish from a Wessex river in 1987–8. Whilst the records of species like carp, tench and bream have all been surpassed the barbel record has stood firm, despite considerable efforts by many experienced and competent barbel anglers. The barbel record has proved to be a very elusive target, and anybody managing to beat it would certainly have achieved something to be proud of.

However, looking at the question from an optimistic point of view there are some good signs. In the 1950s the late Richard Walker, Fred Taylor and friends spotted what they estimated to be barbel of at least 20lb in the middle Avon. They are most emphatic about these sightings and there is really no reason to question these very respected anglers. It should be mentioned, though, that they all failed to hook any of these monster fish.

Other barbel reported over the record include several found dead on the banks of the Avon at the Royalty, the barbel foul-hooked by salmon anglers during the close season, including one oft-mentioned 16lb 1oz fish taken from Ibsley, again on the Hampshire Avon. Over the years a kind of folklore has built up over some enormous barbel caught in several rivers, including the Thames, the Lee, the Kennet and the Hampshire Avon, but almost all these 'legends' can be dismissed.

One could speculate endlessly about the maximum size of barbel. On balance I think the record will remain unbeaten, but I would be delighted to be proved wrong. I would concede, though, there is a definite possibility that a few fish over the record do exist. Where – in the thousands of miles of barbel-holding water – are they most likely to be?

Well, the Hampshire Avon regularly produces barbel of over 13lb and one cannot discount the possibility of a new record coming from this river. In the 1960s it was considered likely that if a record-breaking barbel were caught from the Avon it would come from the Royalty at Christchurch, but nowadays I very much doubt it. There is strong evidence that in recent years the average weight of Royalty barbel has declined and these days very few barbel over 12lb are caught. I believe that one must look further upstream for these possible record breakers. Areas above Fordingbridge and Ibsley are what I consider the likely holding areas. The Dorset Stour is another likely candidate for a record barbel. Again, I would look upstream. I would discount Throop and look at areas around Longham and above. There is no doubt that some of the barbel in the middle reaches of the Dorset Stour are very large and this river could definitely provide a possible record breaker. A short stretch of the river Wensum has in recent years produced several very large barbel, including fish of over 13lb, and it is conceivable that a record fish could come from this river. However, there are plans to divert a lot of the water away from this stretch, which would have a very detrimental effect on the river here. Other rivers less likely to hold record fish include the Kennet, the Great Ouse, the Severn, and – a rank outsider for the future – the Wye. However, if I were going all out to catch a barbel over 14lb 6oz I would at present fish the Dorset Stour and Hampshire Avon.

Catching these supposed record breakers is another matter. Over the years not one barbel over 14lb 6oz has been caught by conventional methods. The only rod-caught barbel over this weight reported are those taken by salmon anglers during the close season. So who knows? Perhaps a plug or live-bait fished during the early part of the season may do the trick. It would certainly be a brave angler who would use these methods exclusively in an attempt to catch a record barbel. However, I do think you could increase your chances a little by carefully selecting when you fish. The early season (when barbel could still be carrying spawn) and the autumn months of September, October and November are all promising periods for catching bigger barbel, but in my opinion the best of all is the last few weeks of the season. When the cold weather of the winter relents, and it gets warmer, it invariably rains. The warmer water, and the high, coloured rivers seem to induce the biggest barbel to feed. There is strong evidence to support this claim and, providing the weather does actually warm up, the back end of the season can provide the fish of a lifetime and, who knows, even a record breaker.

So, to sum up the future. The signs

Terrible dorsal fin damage caused by the fish being placed in a keepnet. These barbel also show clear evidence of eye fluke.

are good for the overall spread of barbel. They are appearing in more and more rivers and I expect this trend to continue. The question of the size of barbel is much less clear; barbel between 13 and 14lb are caught in most seasons, but the possibility of a bigger one is much less certain.

Finally, one cannot write of the future without mentioning the handling of barbel. The use of keepnets is to be discouraged. A barbel's large dorsal fin is prone to getting caught up in even the smallest mesh. It is not uncommon to see barbel hanging by this fin during the weigh-ins of matches. I personally never use a keepnet. Barbel also fight very hard indeed and by the time you have netted them they are very often exhausted. So never put them straight back into the river or they may turn belly up and float off downstream. When returning barbel to the river, hold them carefully in the water until you feel that they are strong enough to swim off on an even keel.

Both these points and others are covered by the following fish-handling code, which has been devised by the Barbel Catchers Club.

Fish-handling Code – Barbel

1   Use the strongest tackle you can get away with; this enables you to land fish as quickly as possible.

2   Use a knotless landing net and lay landed fish on a wet polythene sheet or a patch of damp grass, not on gravel, concrete or dry earth.

3   When unhooking be confident and take charge of the fish; use artery forceps or a Drennan-type disgorger. Steady gentle pressure should see the hook safely out. Sometimes it may be better to thread the hook through and cut the line above the hook.

4   If the fish is not required for a photograph, return it immediately after weighing. Hold it facing upstream, which allows a free passage of water through the gills. Do not let the barbel kick out of your grasp until it can maintain its balance.

5   For weighing, use a dampened sling or a strong poly bag.

6   If an exceptional fish is to be retained, it should be for the shortest time possible. Keepnets should not be used; if they must, it should be a *large knotless* keepnet staked out with the entrance facing downstream. Carp sacks are much better but should still be used with care.

7   Fish in heavily fished waters will be caught several times each season and dozens of times over a period of years. Think about your fish and invest in the future quality of your sport by returning the fish you catch in the same condition as you caught them in.

Monsters

Barbel Catchers Club All-Time Top Fifty

	lb oz	Captor	Location	Season
1	14 02	Pete Reading	A Wessex River	1987–8
2	14 01	Greg Buxton	Dorset Stour	1984–5
3	13 07	Andy Orme	Hants Avon	1982–3
4	13 06	Kevin Hodges	Dorset Stour	1985–6
	13 06	Dave Plummer	Wensum	1983–4
6	13 02	Dave Plummer	Wensum	1983–4
7	12 14	Greg Buxton	Dorset Stour	1985–6
8	12 13	Kevin Hodges	Dorset Stour	1985–6
9	12 12	Trefor West	Wensum	1983–4
10	12 06	Trefor West	Wensum	1985–6
11	12 04	Mike Lamb	Hants Avon	1985–6
	12 04	Trefor West	Wensum	1985–6
	12 04	Phil White	Dorset Stour	1983–4
14	12 02	Dave Plummer	Wensum	1982–3
	12 02	Roger Baker	Great Ouse	1979–80
16	12 01	Tony Hart	Hants Avon	1981–2
	12 01	Kevin Hodges	Dorset Stour	1985–6
18	11 14	Dave Burden	Hants Avon	1979–80
	11 14	Phil White	Dorset Stour	1981–2
	11 14	Trefor West	Wensum	1985–6
21	11 12	Dave Plummer	Wensum	1982–3
22	11 11	John Kelly	Hants Avon	1983–4
	11 11	Greg Buxton	Hants Avon	1984–5
24	11 10	Trefor West	Wensum	1986–7
25	11 09	Greg Buxton	Dorset Stour	1985–6
	11 09	Phil White	Dorset Stour	1983–4
27	11 08	Tony Hart	Hants Avon	1983–4
28	11 06	Tony Hart	Hants Avon	1983–4
	11 06	Tony Hart	Hants Avon	1980–1
	11 06	Roger Baker	Great Ouse	1978–9
31	11 05	Dave Plummer	Wensum	1983–4
32	11 04	Jon Wolfe	Swale	1985–6
	11 04	Jon Wolfe	Hants Avon	1985–6
	11 04	Mike Lamb	Hants Avon	1986–7
35	11 03	Roger Baker	Great Ouse	1979–80
	11 03	Pete McMurray	Hants Avon	1982–3

	lb oz	Captor	Location	Season
	11 03	Greg Buxton	Hants Avon	1985–6
	11 03	Trefor West	Wensum	1985–6
39	11 02	Mike Lamb	Hants Avon	1985–6
	11 02	Steve Smith	Hants Avon	1985–6
	11 02	Tony Hart	Hants Avon	1982–3
	11 02	Roger Baker	Hants Avon	1982–3
	11 02	Dave Plummer	Wensum	1983–4
44	11 01	Greg Buxton	Dorset Stour	1983–4
	11 01	Pete Tillotson	Hants Avon	1984–5
	11 01	Greg Buxton	Hants Avon	1984–5
	11 01	Kevin Mayhen	Hants Avon	1982–3
	11 01	Tony Hart	Hants Avon	1982–3
	11 01	Pete Reading	Hants Avon	1985–6
	11 01	Trefor West	Wensum	1985–6

Barbel Catchers Club River Records

River	Captor	Season	lb oz
Avon, Bristol	K. Parsons	1978–9	10 02
Avon, Hants	A. Orme	1982–3	13 07
Avon, Warks	P. McMurray	1983–4	9 01
Cherwell	T. West	1980–1	6 06
Colne Brook	S. Williams	1981–2	6 12
Dane	J. Winterbottom	1984–5	8 08
Derwent, Derbys	Open		
Derwent, Yorks	J. Wolfe	1986–7	10 15
Dove, Derbys	R. Nash	1977–8	8 02
Kennet	P. Tillotson	1978–9	10 12
Lee	R. Bates	1985–6	10 00
Loddon	P. Tillotson	1983–4	7 04
Medway	I. Beadle	1985–6	10 06
Nidd	N. Milbourne	1982–3	7 11
Ouse, Great	R. Baker	1979–80	12 02
Ouse, Yorks	D. Mason	1979–80	9 14
	B. Pinning	1981–2	9 14
Ribble	J. Wolfe	1986–7	6 15
St Patrick's Stream	P. Tillotson	1982–3	7 04
Severn	P. McMurray	1984–5	9 07
Stour, Dorset	G. Buxton	1984–5	14 01
Stour, Warks	A. Bayliss		4 04
Swale	J. Wolfe	1985–6	11 04
Teme	P. McMurray	1980–1	7 03
Thames	M. Brown	1983–4	10 01
	J. Kelly	1986–7	10 01
Trent	R. Singleton	1986–7	7 04
Ure	P. Duston		7 04
Wensum	D. Plummer	1983–4	13 06
Wey	M. Newland	1983–4	9 01
Wharfe	Open		
Windrush	J. Everard	1980–1	9 06

11lb 4oz Swale Barbel

Although this short piece is devoted entirely to the capture of just one fish, I feel that without an explanation of the events leading up to that day the tale is only half told.

I start my account of the capture with a brief description of a barbel's movements; for anybody wishing to get to grips with his own river's large barbel, an understanding of these movements will be of help, especially if the fishing is to be practised in a blind fashion.

The theory of resident and travelling fish was first formulated during scientific experiments on the River Severn by Doctor Peter Hunt. It points to there being two groups or types of barbel. The first group are the residents. These fish live in a small area of river maybe three or four hundred yards long. This area may contain a number of swims; some of them will be unoccupied most of the time, but nevertheless they are still barbel swims. Probably one of them will be a favourite swim. The barbel may leave this favourite swim from time to time because of excessive angling pressure, or because rising levels force them to seek out slacker water, but, whatever reason they move for, it won't be far.

The second group are the travellers. These fish have no permanent home and are forever on the move. They may tag on to a group of residents for a short time but their nomadic instincts keep them moving on. I have been told that both groups contain big fish but that the travelling group contains a higher percentage of big ones.

Whether this theory of resident and travelling fish applied to all barbel rivers I didn't know, but by the autumn of 1985 I was beginning to doubt whether it was applicable to the River Swale. My tactics until then had been to concentrate on just one stretch at a time, hopefully catching most of the resident fish and also picking off any travellers which tagged on to the resident shoals. These tactics had accounted for two different nine-pounders; one of them I had caught three times and the other one I witnessed being caught from a nearby swim nine months after I caught it. I classed both these fish as residents, along with virtually all my other big fish from this river. In fact I caught only one 8lb+ fish which might have been a traveller; all the others over this weight were recaptured by myself or a friend at later dates, suggesting to me that they were resident fish. It can now be seen why I was beginning to doubt that my immobile tactics would ever produce the hoped-for double. If these very rare fish were of the resident type, then it made the task so much harder – rather like searching for the proverbial needle in the haystack.

The first sign of things to come was in late October of the same year. During a very productive afternoon session I landed four fish, one of which was a new Yorkshire personal best weighing 9lb 12oz. Although I was well pleased with this fish, a nagging thought in the back of my mind just wouldn't go away. Two out of the four barbel were recognisable as residents, but the 9lb 12oz fish and the other one were both 'new' fish. If these two were part of a group of travellers, then they might still be occupying the same area. More

A massive Swale barbel of 11lb 4oz, caught by Jon Wolfe in 1985.

important, the 9lb 12oz fish might not be the largest in the group. There was only one way to find out.

Two days later after finishing my day shifts I loaded the car up and set off on the fifty-mile journey, arriving in darkness. It was still dark as I tackled up the next morning. Four droppers of particles were placed in the 3-foot-deep swim and I sat back unprepared for what was about to happen. It wasn't long before the rod crashed round and I found myself attached to a powerful fish. The Swale is not a pleasant river in which to play a hard-fighting fish even on 8lb line. The bottom is littered with snags and at any time during the fight your line can fall slack as the barbel finds sanctuary in an underwater jungle of willow tree roots.

The first run of the fish carried him ten or fifteen yards downriver. I could have stopped it going so far if needed, but it was running into snag-free water so I let it go. Holding the rod high so as to clear a couple of willow bushes, I stumbled after it, slowly taking in line to keep a good bend in the rod. The fish was only seen a couple of times during the fight and even then it was a quick glimpse as it lashed the surface with its large tail. For the greater part of its struggle for freedom it sulked around on the bottom as only a big fish knows how. With steady pressure I found I could gently steer it around in front of me, gradually tiring it. If I gained too much line by bending into it, it quickly took it back, and a bit more as well. I stayed calm and my patience was rewarded when I carefully enveloped it in my large net.

I always believed that if I was ever to crack the ten-pound barrier it would be by ounces, so I am therefore not over-stating the fact that I was dumbfounded by the 11lb 4oz reading on the Avon scales. The fish was as fat as a pig, and, measured later from a photograph, only 28½ inches long. It goes without saying that this was a 'new' fish to me, as was the 9lb 1oz specimen caught later that day.

The next trip I recaptured the 9lb 12oz fish at a lighter weight. A day after that they were gone. To the best of my knowledge they haven't been seen in the area since. Travelling fish – here today, gone tomorrow!

Jon Wolfe

13lb 7oz Hampshire Avon Barbel

At the beginning of the 1982–3 fishing season I had but one aim in mind – I wanted a barbel over 12lb and I reckoned that the middle reaches of the Hampshire Avon would provide it for me.

During previous seasons I had developed a strategy for catching middle-Avon barbel based upon being in the right place at the time. Quite simply I waited for torrential rain to flood the river and then fished swims that provided the fish with shelter. These tactics worked throughout the year but in winter they worked especially well.

I reasoned that all I needed to do was put my approach to work on a stretch where I knew huge fish lived and they would end up in my net. Such optimism is rewarded by dedication of approach. Whenever the conditions were right I leapt into my car and sped down to the river.

Between 16 June and 31 December 1982 I managed fifteen trips in perfect conditions and landed twenty-four barbel. None was particularly big but I did manage five 9-pounders, the best of which was two ounces under ten pounds.

1983 arrived with perfect barbel weather – warm westerly winds bearing lots of lovely rain to swell the river. Even at night the air temperature was 50°F and that is like a heat-wave in January.

At 3.30 p.m. on 4 January I had a bait in a favourite swim at Ibsley. To say that I felt confident was an understatement because the river temperature was 49°F and the water was a lovely dark brown and flooding over the banks. Two hours later a fine barbel of 9lb 3oz was in the net and I grinned to myself because I knew the fish were feeding.

I caught no more fish that session but retired to my car, where I spent the night trying to sleep. The following dawn I emerged red-eyed and absolutely shattered because torrential rain had lashed against the car roof, making kip impossible. In a daze I drove to Ibsley Bridge and looked at the river. I can remember thinking, 'Shall I bother' – but some force compelled me to drag myself down to the bank.

Like an automaton I threaded the line through the rings on my Mark IV Avon, fixed up a simple link-leger rig, lobbed several chunks of chopped ham with pork into my swim and cast out. Still the gale lashed the Avon Valley but I was quite snug under my brolly and the slack in which I was fishing looked absolutely perfect.

During the next hour and a half something had given a few very fast, snatchy bites which I had not hit. Thinking that my size 4 hook to 6lb line was perhaps a bit crude, I replaced it with a size 12 to 3lb BS nylon. Almost immediately after flicking this lighter rig into the slack I had a confident take and a fish was on.

The fish was slow and powerful and hugged the bottom, which meant that it was almost certainly a barbel. Without my being able to do anything about it the beast swam slowly and doggedly out into the full force of the Avon current. Gentle pressure from me produced no result and so I piled on as much as I dared on the flimsy set-up. Very, very slowly I gained a few feet of line but then the rod was wrenched down ferociously and I had no option but to backwind as fast as I could as the fish set off downstream. Again and again I retrieved line by straining the tackle to the limit but always the response was an awesome retaliatory surge of power.

For ten minutes the as yet unseen adversary stubbornly resisted my efforts to defeat it but then very gradually I began to gain line and suddenly the fish left the sanctuary of the river bed and began to swim up and down the slack in midwater. Rather rashly I heaved it to the surface just to get a glimpse of what I was fighting, and was treated to the sight of a huge tail cleaving the water. The water boiled and effortlessly the barbel regained station on the bottom. However, it was most definitely tiring.

Soon after seeing my quarry for the first time I had the fish sliding towards the outstretched arms of my landing net and it was with an almost desperate sigh of relief that I engulfed it in the mesh.

A quick heave had my prize on the bank and from the mesh of the net a truly wonderful barbel stared out – a perfect, huge deep-bodied fish that simply took my breath away. After many years of barbelling I had at last landed the fish of my dreams and tears of emotion filled my eyes. 13lb 7oz – if I said that figure to myself once that day I must have said it a hundred times.

Watching that lovely creature regain her strength and then swim powerfully back into the depths of the Avon was without any shadow of doubt the best moment of my 28-year angling career.

Andy Orme

13lb 6oz Wensum Barbel

John Bailey: Dave, do you now think that your previous all-round barbel experience was of great help when you tackled the Wensum?
Dave Plummer: Undoubtedly. I

had experience of Yorkshire barbel dating from the mid-1960s, culminating in a best ever 10lb 4oz Derwent fish in 1975. I fished all the Yorkshire rivers very hard in that period until I found selected stretches which held big fish, or at least fish much bigger than the average. For example, on the Swale and the Nidd the average is only 2½–3½lb, but after two years I began to single out far better specimens. The variety of Yorkshire rivers also helped me. The Ure, for example, is shallow and clear and you can watch fish there. The Ouse, by contrast, is deep, slower and featureless. By the time I left Yorkshire I had barbel knowledge of most river types.

JB: And other non-Yorkshire rivers?

DP: Certainly. I moved on to the Severn, the Hampshire Avon and even experienced a trip to the Danube between Yorkshire and a move to the Wensum in the early 1980s. I looked at the river with practical eyes, you could say! At that time, nearly all the barbel were between Costessey and Hellesdon Mills – a mere three miles. Location was not a problem for I was used to far worse complications. The Wensum

Dave Plummer's record Wensum barbel of 13lb 6oz.

also reminded me of the Ure, so I could bring my low, clear water stalking tactics into play.

JB: Location was obviously your first step towards these big fish.

DP: Yes, crucial. The first year made me realise there was not a great number of barbel at all. They would hang at the top end the first one or two months of the season until angling pressure forced them to disperse. Then they could move 1, 1½ or 2, even 2½ miles downriver to deeper, slower, safer water. You're looking at the key here!

JB: Did you find any special swims lower down towards Hellesdon?

DP: Yes – the difficult ones! They involved a lot of hard work. The bed would be littered with streamer and blanket weed and I dragged swims with my three-pronged rake. What I wanted was a little patch of gravel cleared next to overhanging trees where I could present a bait. This took two seasons – to pinpoint fish and then get them feeding.

JB: Was catching barbel a problem then?

DP: Small ones, no. It was the big ones that presented the challenge. I soon realised that the shoal fish, up to 9lb, were easy. Often a group of ten such fish hung with one big one. To isolate these big fish needed a different approach.

JB: Which was?

DP: What I began to do was to prebait two areas within one swim. Heavy prebaiting in the top area would draw barbel and chub in big numbers. At the same time I would lightly feed the downstream area and there the biggest fish would sneak in and feed undisturbed. I had to avoid the temptation of the 7–10lb barbel and concentrate on the 11–13lb fish below. This isolation procedure was very important.

JB: And the next hurdle?

DP: To get big fish to take the bait in clear water on an 8lb, line which so obviously spooked them! I began to use a longer hooklength than normal and ally that to a hair rig. Sweetcorn, meat, casters and maggots were all devastating baits. Now, all I had to do was to put the bait in without causing disturbance. I waited for the big fish to leave the area to chew their pickings. Then I placed the bait to await them on their return and bang!

JB: It sounds easy!

DP: In the end, yes. At the start, no. But I stuck at it because there were so many big fish. There were in excess of nine doubles, which is phenomenal for a small river.

JB: Did you see the thirteen in this period?

DP: No – I had fish to over 12lb in the summer, but for the huge one I had to wait. I had barbelled in Yorkshire in winter, but the rivers were so unpredictable that a seventy-mile journey could easily be wasted. The Wensum was easier. Here I could judge conditions, watch the river come up and recede to just within its banks, and be down there at once. Living on the spot was so vital. This is very much the approach of Andy Orme – it was Andy who had actually badgered me into forsaking my winter piking to concentrate on Wensum barbel when the conditions were right.

These hit first at Christmas. On the way back from Yorkshire I stopped off for Neville Fickling and travelled back on the Boxing Day. First look at the

199

river and I saw that it was bank-high but dropping. I went straight to a deep hole under the bank and pre-baited with meat. That first session was encouraging with chub and barbel to over 6lb. The next afternoon I was back in the same swim to find it even more perfect. Within forty minutes I had the 13lb 2oz fish – perfect proof of the system!

JB: And then you were to catch it again . . .

DP: Yes. I had to wait till the end of the season till the river looked right again. There were a lot of anglers on the stretch and I couldn't get the swim I originally wanted. I was with my partner Derrick Amies and we gambled on a move to the very lightly fished shallows. We sat for two hours for one small chub, but at 8.30 p.m. a 7lb 12oz barbel came along. It was the first Derrick had ever seen, and after a great deal of admiration, it was quickly returned.

The temperatures dropped as the south-westerlies disappeared. It was close on freezing when the rod tip went around but I was playing the 13lb 6oz barbel. It was the same fish, but in fantastic condition. I couldn't have wished for a better looking fish – fat as butter and fighting fit.

The Contributors

Archie Braddock

Born in 1938, Archie has lived at Long Eaton on the Trent for most of his life. He started fishing at the age of 13, and according to him he has never stopped since. Having spent a decade in the 1960s as a fanatic carp angler, Archie switched to barbel around 1970 and fished hard for them for the next ten years.

Archie once did a full year's baiting up on the Derbyshire Dove, using hundreds of pounds of luncheon meat. He then marked every barbel caught with a blue dye, proving that most fish are caught time after time on the same bait.

Nowadays, Archie fishes for nearly every species in its season, although the barbel is still a special favourite. Archie prefers to think of himself as an 'advanced pleasure angler', trying to catch the best fish from his nearby waters rather than chasing around the country notching up known fish. His favourite river is the Trent.

Archie has written extensively over the years for all the leading monthly and weekly fishing journals, and has contributed to a number of multi–contributor angling books. He has also produced his own booklet on fishing the Trent.

Stuart Hamilton

Stuart was a founder member of the Barbel Catchers Club and its chairman from its inception until 1986. He caught his first barbel at Throop in August 1972 and has fished for them ever since. His captures include barbel of over 8lb from the Thames, the Kennet, the Hampshire Avon, the Severn and the Dorset Stour. His best specimen weighed 9lb 9oz.

Stuart is an all-round angler and has caught pike to 32lb, roach to 2lb 15oz, bream to 9lb, eels to 4lb 14oz, rudd to 2lb 12oz and perch to 2lb 11oz. Nowadays he tends to fish locally, but this is no hardship as the lower Severn contains many good barbel.

Stuart hopes to see barbel become more widespread in the future. His other wish is that rivers may be less polluted and interfered with.

Tony Hart

Tony Hart began fishing at the age of 16, mainly for carp in the lakes and ponds around his East London home. In 1973 he moved to Basingstoke to concentrate on the barbel of the River Kennet and in 1977 became a founder member of the re-formed Barbel Catchers Club. By this time he was fishing exclusively for barbel, even through the depths of winter, in an attempt to prove that winter barbelling is a serious pastime.

Since 1980 he has put more time in on the Hampshire Avon, and in three and a half seasons caught five barbel over 10lb, five over 11lb and one of 12lb 1oz. His proudest achievement was taking both the Barbel Catchers' big fish trophy and the NASA barbel trophy in 1980–81 and 1981–82, followed in 1982–83 with the Barbel Catchers' trophy for the best season of all its members. He has two main ambitions – one is a Kennet double, which has always eluded him, despite concentrating solidly on that river for the last three seasons. The other is a thirteen from anywhere, but even Tony admits that that may be asking a bit much!

Alan Hayes

Having lived in North London all his life, Alan Hayes has had since childhood many expeditions to the Lee in search of different species. He caught his first Lee barbel in the early 1970s, and promptly decided to make barbel his main quarry. He set out to find what other parts of the Lee were still able to hold them, and over the years he has enjoyed moderate success in areas where many anglers gave up trying to catch barbel years ago, simply because they said it didn't look right.

When the Barbel Catchers' Club re-formed in 1977, Alan was appointed Regional Organiser for the Southern (London) Region. His personal best from the Lee stands at 8lb 6oz, and he has caught many 7lb+ fish from the

river. His first fish from the Royalty on the Avon weighed in at 10lb.

Married, with a young daughter, Alan thinks he has the best years yet ahead of him. As far as the Lee is concerned, he is optimistic that the river can only improve.

Pete McMurray

Aged 35 and married with one son, Pete has been fishing since he was 7. He has a deep love of barbel and barbel fishing, though he is an all-round specimen hunter whose personal bests include bream of 13lb, barbel of 11lb 3oz, carp of 25lb, pike of 32lb 12oz and rudd of 3lb 4oz.

He enjoys catching any barbel regardless of size, but would love to catch a double from both his local rivers, the Severn and Warwickshire Avon. He has come close to realising this ambition with fish of 9lb from both rivers.

David Mason

Nearly all Dave's fishing has been confined to his native county of Yorkshire, where his time is spent in search of the rivers' specimen barbel and chub. He has taken chub of over 5lb, topped by a 5lb 6oz Swale specimen, with fish of 4lb coming from six different rivers.

Dave's main interest is barbel fishing, and he has recorded captures from the Yorkshire Ouse, the Swale, the Nidd, the Wharfe and the Derwent. Rare excursions to more southerly rivers have produced barbel from the Hampshire Avon and the Middle Severn.

Personal best specimens include fish of 10lb from the Yorkshire Derwent, the first Yorkshire double to be reported by a Barbel Catchers Club member; 9lb 14oz from the Yorkshire Ouse; 8lb 6oz from the Swale; and 9lb 15oz from the Hampshire Avon.

Andy Orme

Dr Andy Orme caught his first barbel when he was 12 years old while dangling his legs over a bridge on the River Kennet. He is now 34 and has spent 22 years after Old Whiskers.

A trained freshwater biologist, Andy has used his knowledge to capture over a thousand barbel from rivers such as the Thames, the Kennet, the Severn, the Dorset Stour and the Hampshire Avon. Many have been over the magical 10lb mark, but Andy is pleased to catch any barbel, whatever its size. He has pioneered winter barbelling, culminating in the capture of a 13lb 7oz specimen from the Hampshire Avon in January – one of the largest from the river in recent years.

Andy dislikes the aggressive competitiveness that has crept into specimen barbel hunting and is very concerned that all barbel should be handled properly after capture.

Dave Plummer

Aged 38, Dave is married to Linda and they have an angling fanatic son aged 18 years. Most of his adult life was spent as a British Rail train driver, until a move from Yorkshire to Norfolk saw him enter the tackle trade. Now he owns The Norwich Angling Centre along with his partner, big-pike man Derrick Amies.

Dave has proved himself one of

Britain's most successful all-round big-fish anglers. He has not only big barbel to his credit, but also exceptional roach, rudd, bream, tench, carp, pike and chub.

Peter Rayment

Peter is well known as an all-round angler who, in his 47 years of fishing, has fished for and caught some sixty-eight different species, including many specimens. Although he admits to be happy fishing 'for just about anything', those who know him find that he talks most about fishing for roach, barbel and river pike during the summer.

As an author Peter has contributed to several books and virtually every angling magazine and newspaper for over twenty-five years, including reporting on many of the top match-angling events for the *Angler's Mail* and the *Sunday Mercury*. Although the last thing he will call himself is a photographer, he has had almost 400 angling photographs published. He has also on a few occasions managed the feat of catching fish to order for the television cameras.

Peter's barbel fishing has seen him catch the species from nine different rivers, and includes a couple of doubles from his beloved Hampshire Avon. However, it is with catching barbel from still waters that he is often quoted as being more expert than any other angler. To date, his total stands in excess of 1,500. He once shared a catch of 60 barbel with his son Steven in a seven-hour session with their baits only a foot apart. This is possibly one of the best catches of stillwater barbel ever recorded.

203

Pete Reading

Pete started fishing for barbel on the Dorset Stour and the Hampshire Avon in 1970 and now has thirteen doubles to his name, eight of them over 11lb, with best fish of 11lb 12oz and 14lb 2oz from the Wessex rivers. However, for Pete barbel fishing is now much more than just hunting doubles and in recent years he has spent more time seeking out new fish in new swims on both his favourite rivers.

Pete considers an 8lb fish big by any standards, and finds fishing actively for barbel you can see particularly exciting. While sitting and waiting for unseen fish has its place, stalking barbel – or coaxing a shoal into a feeding mood – can be particularly rewarding. He especially enjoys the opportunity to pick out a big fish from a shoal.

Peter hates float fishing for barbel and much prefers to lie back and wait for them to pull the rod in. He notes that particle baits, high protein, the hair rig and the bolt rig are all the inventions of barbel fishermen.

Bill Rushmer

Bill Rushmer is the regional organiser for the London Region of the National Association of Specialist Anglers and has nearly thirty years angling experience on many southern rivers. He has landed double-figure barbel from four different rivers, the Thames, the Kennet, the Wey and the Hampshire Avon, the best an 11lb 2oz fish from the Avon. Although Bill is predominantly a float angler, he has used and mastered other techniques in his efforts for all-round

success. His personal bests include: tench, 9lb 10oz; carp 25lb 1oz; roach, 2lb 10oz; perch, 3lb 5oz; pike, 33lb 6oz; chub, 5lb 6oz; bream, 9lb 5oz; brown trout (on fly) 6lb 12oz, rainbow trout (on fly) 10lb 10oz, grey mullet, 5lb 2oz; grayling 2lb 2oz; dace, 14½oz; and crucian, 2lb 10½oz.

Apart from specimen hunting, Bill takes an active interest in punt fishing and his local stretch of the Thames at Twickenham. He still fishes punt matches with the local Francis Francis Angling Club. This club is thought to be the last remaining punt-fishing club in the country that still moors in the traditional manner.

Mal Storey

Mal is one of the best-known match anglers in the country, renowned for his successes especially on the River Severn, where for the last ten years he has had countless big barbel catches up to 70lb and caught several barbel of more than 8lb. He also has to his name the capture of a specimen chub of 5lb 3oz.

His exploits on the River Trent include a best-ever match catch of 96lb of chub taken at Holme Marsh. He has caught carp over 12lb at the same venue.

Of late Mal has been noted for his development of several items of fishing tackle, including the renowned Severn Trent carbonfeeder rod.

Pete Tillotson

Peter has fished for barbel for over twenty years. He started his barbel fishing on the River Lee and his heaviest fish from that river weighed 9lb 1oz. After a few years – in the hope of catching more of the bigger fish – he started to fish the River Kennet, and was eventually rewarded with doubles from the river, the best weighing 10lb 12oz. He also fishes the Hampshire Avon, where he has taken several doubles to 11lb 1oz. Other rivers to receive his attention include the Yorkshire Derwent, the Severn, the Bristol Avon, the Dorset Stour, the Great Ouse and the Thames.

Pete was a founder member of the Barbel Catchers Club and is its current chairman. He is also the editor of the club's magazine, *Barbus*, as he has been for seven of the last nine years.

Ray Walton

Ray had not caught a barbel before the 1970s. He was introduced to the Royalty at this time by the Eade family – to whom he will be for ever grateful – and has since caught many barbel.

During the 1970s Ray fished the Royalty about four times a year and was lucky if he caught one fish a day. He expanded his knowledge by fishing more locally at King's Weir on the River Lee and also on little-known parts of the Kennet.

On joining the Barbel Catchers Club in 1983, Ray set about making barbel catching part of his life, his intention being to help improve the general understanding of the species.

Paul Woodings

Paul first fished for barbel at the age of 15 – fifteen years ago. His first fish, from the Dorset Stour, weighed 7lb. After he witnessed the capture of a barbel some time before his first fish, the species became nothing short of an obsession. Even though he has fished for and caught all the 'regular' species, both before and since then, barbel have remained the only 'real' fish as far as he is concerned – the bull terrier of the fish world!

Over the years he has fished the majority of barbel rivers in the country taking fish from a total of seven. His biggest fish to date is a fish of 10lb 1oz from the Hampshire Avon. He particularly likes fishing the upper Thames and enjoys barbel fishing best when using a float and centrepin reel. He considers float fishing to be not only a very effective and enjoyable method, but also one very much neglected by present-day barbel fishermen and specialist anglers generally.

He joined the Barbel Catchers Club in 1980 and resigned in 1986.

Among his outside interests he likes drawing, painting and photography. Among his passions, apart from barbel fishing, he lists a really good pint of ale and – surprise, surprise, bull terriers!

Other fishing titles available from The Crowood Press

COARSE

Bream – Tales and Tactics   *John Baily and Roger Miller*   1 85223 097 5
Carp – The Quest for the Queen   *John Bailey and Martyn Page*   0 946284 19 9
Carp Fishing   *Tim Paisley*   1 85223 119 X
Hooked on Bass   *Mike Ladle and Alan Vaughan*   1 85223 082 7
In Visible Waters   *John Bailey*   0 946284 80 6
Pike – The Predator becomes the Prey   *John Bailey and Martyn Page*   0 946284 47 4
Reflections from the Water's Edge   *John Bailey*   1 85223 080 0
River Fishing   *Len Head*   0 946284 71 7
Roach – The Gentle Giants   *John Bailey*   1 85223 035 5
Stillwater Coarse Fishing   *Melvyn Russ*   0 946284 83 0
Tench   *Len Head*   0 946284 72 5

GAME

Bob Church's Guide to Trout Flies   0 946284 49 0
Fly Fishing for Salmon and Sea Trout   *Arthur Oglesby*   0 946284 87 3
Imitations of the Trout's World   *Bob Church and Peter Gathercole*   1 85223 017 7
My Way with Trout   *Arthur Cove*   0 946284 24 5
Reservoir Trout Fishing   *Alan Pearson*   0 946284 60 1
Travels with a Two Piece   *John Bailey*   0 946284 27 X

SEA

The Beach Fisherman's Tackle Guide   *John Holden*   0 946284 25 3
Beach Fishing   *John Holden*   1 85223 005 3
Boat Fishing   *Mike Millman, Richard Stapley and John Holden*   0 946284 91 1
The Complete Boat Angler   *Bob Gledhill*   1 85223 118 1
Long Distance Casting   *John Holden*   0 946284 00 8

GENERAL

Fisherman's Year   *John Holden*   1 85223 095 9
Rods and Rod Building   *Len Head*   0 946284 65 2